SEP   2011

W 9/1,
W 12/14
W 9/17

INSIDERS' GUIDE® TO
DES MOINES

HELP US KEEP THIS GUIDE UP TO DATE

We would love to hear from you concerning your experiences with this guide and how you feel it could be improved and kept up to date. Please send your comments and suggestions to:

editorial@GlobePequot.com

Thanks for your input, and happy travels!

INSIDERS' GUIDE® TO

DES MOINES

FIRST EDITION

MICHAEL REAM

INSIDERS' GUIDE

GUILFORD, CONNECTICUT
AN IMPRINT OF GLOBE PEQUOT PRESS

All the information in this guidebook is subject to change. We recommend that you call ahead to obtain current information before traveling.

INSIDERS' GUIDE ®

Editor: Kevin Sirois
Project Editor: Heather Santiago
Layout: Kevin Mak
Text Design: Sheryl Kober
Maps: Sue Murray © Morris Book Publishing, LLC

ISBN 978-0-7627-6470-9

Printed in the United States of America
10 9 8 7 6 5 4 3 2 1

CONTENTS

CONTENTS

Directory of Maps

ABOUT THE AUTHOR

Michael Ream is a travel writer who has filed stories from three continents and throughout the United States but always finds his way home to the Midwest. He is the author of *Best Easy Day Hikes Lincoln and Omaha* and *Best Easy Day Hikes Des Moines,* both available from Globe Pequot Press, and has contributed to publications including *Midwest Traveler, Southern Traveler, Saveur* and *South American Explorer,* as well as guidebooks covering the Smoky Mountains, the Arkansas and Missouri Ozarks, Tennessee, Mississippi and Texas. A native of Chicago, he earned a master's degree in journalism from the Medill School of Journalism at Northwestern University. He lives in Des Moines with his family.

ACKNOWLEDGMENTS

Thanks are due to the many helpful people who provided insight on the numerous interesting things to see and do in Des Moines and central Iowa. All were generous with their time and resources in giving me a complete picture of the vibrant and colorful tapestry to be found both in Des Moines' neighborhoods and among its residents.

I am indebted to the staff of the Greater Des Moines Convention and Visitors Bureau, and especially to Tiffany Tauscheck, who pointed me in the right direction to discover the many gems the city has to offer. Lauren Burt and the Greater Des Moines Partnership gave me a look behind the scenes of the evolution of Des Moines into a diverse and dynamic urban area, while MD Isley and Susan Hatten gave me a heads-up on some of the hidden treasures to be found in the city and surrounding area. Zachary Mannheimer was a wealth of tips and insights related to the growth of the arts in Des Moines and Christopher Diebel provided a close-up view of the city's restaurant and hotel scene.

I must also acknowledge the wisdom and foresight of civic and business leaders who laid the foundation for the many amenities available throughout the Des Moines area. Their efforts have made Des Moines one of the most liveable cities around, full of delightful surprises to the casual visitor and longtime resident alike. My many friends and colleagues in Des Moines and surrounding communities were always happy to recommend another spot for me to check out, leading me to find some great places off the beaten path.

My editor, Kevin Sirois, and project editor, Heather Santiago, provided invaluable advice and guidance from the inception of the book. I am grateful to them for giving me the opportunity to write about my hometown. Finally, thanks are due to my wife Judy and daughter Sofia, who tolerated my many nights away researching and typing. It is truly a pleasure to have them as companions to explore our great city!

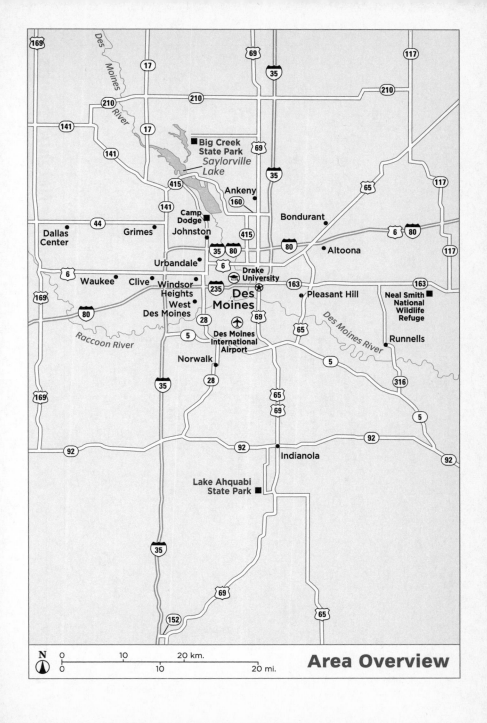

Area Overview

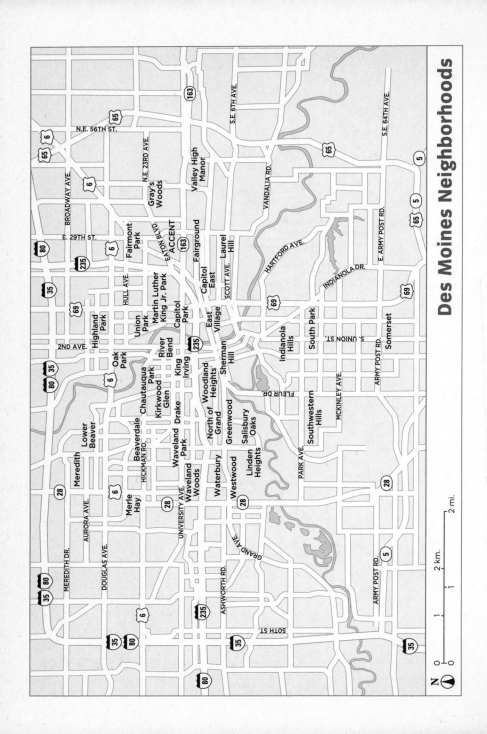

Des Moines Neighborhoods

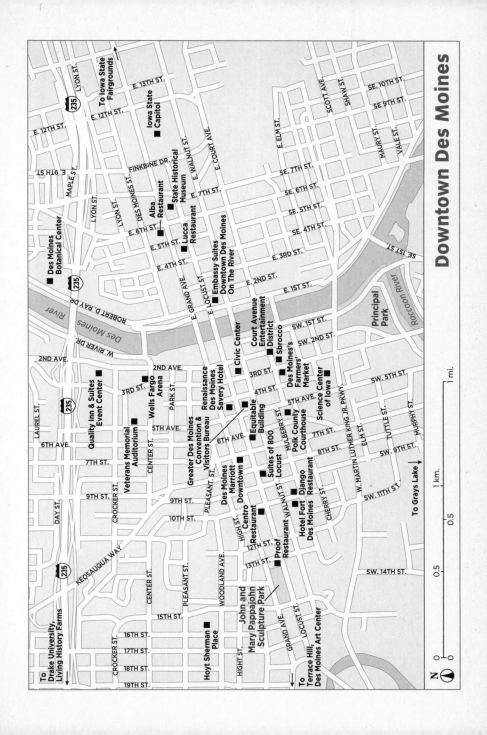

Downtown Des Moines

To Iowa State Fairgrounds
LYON ST.
E. 13TH ST.
E. 12TH ST.
E. 12TH ST.
SE. 10TH ST.
SE. 9TH ST.
SCOTT AVE.
SHAW ST.

Iowa State Capitol

E. 9TH ST.
MAPLE ST.
LYON ST.
LYON ST.
DES MOINES ST.
FINKBINE DR.
SE. 7TH ST.
SE. 6TH ST.
SE. 5TH ST.
SE. 4TH ST.
E. ELM ST.
MAURY ST.
VALE ST.

State Historical Museum
E. WALNUT ST.
E. 7TH ST.
E. COURT AVE.

Alba Restaurant
E. 6TH ST.
E. 5TH ST.
Lucca Restaurant
E. 4TH ST.
E. 3RD ST.
SE. 1ST ST.

Des Moines Botanical Center

235

Embassy Suites Downtown Des Moines On The River
E. GRAND AVE.
E. LOCUST ST.
E. 2ND ST.
E. 1ST ST.

River
Des Moines River
W. RIVER DR.
ROBERT D. RAY DR.

Raccoon River

Principal Park

Court Avenue Entertainment District
Civic Center
Sbrocco
SW. 1ST ST.
SW. 2ND ST.

2ND AVE.
2ND AVE.
Wells Fargo Arena
PARK ST.
Renaissance Des Moines Savery Hotel
Des Moines's Farmers' Market
3RD ST.
4TH ST.

Quality Inn & Suites Event Center
3RD ST.
Science Center of Iowa
SW. 5TH ST.

LAUREL ST.
235
Veterans Memorial Auditorium
CENTER ST.
5TH AVE.
Greater Des Moines Convention & Visitors Bureau
Equitable Building
5TH AVE.
Polk County Courthouse
MULBERRY ST.
7TH ST.
8TH ST.
ELM ST.
TUTTLE ST.
SW. 9TH ST.
MURPHY ST.

6TH AVE.
7TH ST.
CROCKER ST.
6TH AVE.
Suites of 800 Locust
W. MARTIN LUTHER KING JR. PKWY.

9TH ST.
9TH ST.
Des Moines Marriott Downtown
PLEASANT ST.
SW. 11TH ST.

DAY ST.
10TH ST.
HIGH ST.
Centro Restaurant
12TH ST.
Django Restaurant
Hotel Fort Des Moines
WALNUT ST.
Restaurant WALNUT ST.
Proof
CHERRY ST.
To Grays Lake

235
KEOSAUQUA WAY
CENTER ST.
PLEASANT ST.
13TH ST.
SW. 14TH ST.

15TH ST.
John and Mary Pappajohn Sculpture Park
WOODLAND AVE.
GRAND AVE.
LOCUST ST.

CROCKER ST.
16TH ST.
Hoyt Sherman Place
17TH ST.
18TH ST.
19TH ST.
HIGHT ST.
To Terrace Hill, Des Moines Art Center

To Drake University, Living History Farms

N

0   0.5   1 km.
0   0.5   1 mi.

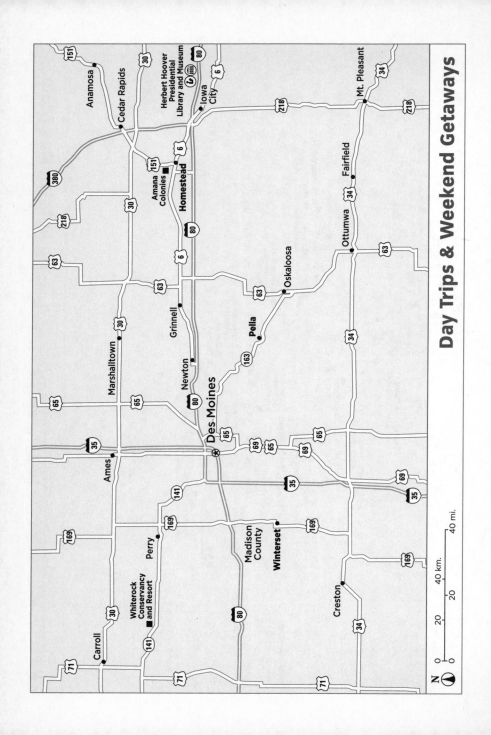

Day Trips & Weekend Getaways

INTRODUCTION

At the turn of the 21st century, Des Moines was still thought of by many as a dull, provincial town—a boring little midwestern burg upon the plains of America. Yet the city has acquired some cosmopolitan flair, due to both visionary local leaders who have spearheaded efforts to revive it, and a strong economy that has lured newcomers from all over as well as retained young natives, many of whom have found hidden treasures in this midsize, underappreciated city.

As the capital of the state perhaps most identified with agriculture (some 90 percent of Iowa's land is under cultivation), Des Moines's roots, metaphorically and literally, are in the cornfields, whose golden stalks stretch endlessly to the horizon as you drive into town. Companies such as Pioneer Hi-Bred still work on developing seed for farmers and there's a large John Deere works nearby, but the city doesn't feel like a cow town: Des Moines, which was ranked number one on *Forbes* magazine's 2010 list of the Best Places for Businesses and Careers, is America's second-largest insurance center, after Hartford, Connecticut, with thousands of white-collar workers heading to jobs in downtown steel-and-glass office buildings. Also downtown is publisher Meredith Inc., whose flagship publication, *Better Homes and Gardens,* is supplemented by such titles as *Midwest Living* and *Successful Farming,* as well as *Ready Made,* a hipper look at domestic life. On the east bank of the Des Moines River, at the foot of the State Capitol, is the East Village, a trendy little neighborhood where funky restaurants and shops have popped up along the main drags and side streets. Some 5,000 students hit the books at Drake University, an urban campus tucked into 150 acres just west of downtown. The west side is also home to neighborhoods like Beaverdale, known for its brick houses, and Ingersoll Avenue, which has a long row of shops and restaurants as well as Terrace Hill, the Iowa governor's mansion. Just over the city limits in the suburb of West Des Moines is Valley Junction, where many locals go for unique shopping.

All those state government and insurance company employees don't make for a staid, buttoned-down town: Des Moines has a vibrant cultural scene, with a first-rate symphony, good selections in theater, and an art museum designed by three world-class architects and hidden away in a residential neighborhood. The city's art festival every June draws artists from around the country, who take over downtown streets to display their creations. The well-regarded Des Moines Metro Opera, founded in 1974, takes to the stage every summer at Simpson College in nearby Indianola. Des Moines's science and history museums are good places to take kids, while Living History Farms in the western suburbs provides an in-depth look at the history of farming with exhibits and demonstrations.

Locals cheer on the Iowa Cubs, an affiliate of the Chicago team, at Principal Park south of downtown, where the golden dome of the Capitol looms over center field. Nearby is the Court Avenue Entertainment District, a former warehouse area reborn as a nightlife mecca, with several blocks of bars and music clubs as well as some of Des Moines's better restaurants.

Court Avenue is also home to the city's wildly popular farmers' market, held every Saturday from spring through fall. But the crown jewel of Des Moines's (and Iowa's) agricultural heritage comes every August at the Iowa State Fair, when one million visitors (in a metro area of 600,000) descend on the fairgrounds on the east side of the city. This is one time and place where Des Moines lives squarely up to its image: The food and carnival midways feel like a timeless dose of Americana, while the show barns positively overflow with farm boys and girls tending to their livestock, judges awarding prizes to the largest boar and bull, among other categories. Don't forget the butter sculptures on display: Past creations have included Harry Potter, Elvis Presley, Iowa native John Wayne, and iconic Iowa artwork *American Gothic* as well as the fair's butter cow mainstay, which celebrates its 100th anniversary at the fair in 2011.

Since the 1970s, Des Moines has welcomed a stream of refugees from such distant points of the globe as Southeast Asia, Somalia, and Bosnia, bringing welcome diversity as well as greater choices in restaurants. There are still plenty of steakhouses serving up Iowa's signature hunks of beef, but Des Moines's dining scene has matured, with many restaurants, including quite a few in the downtown area, offering fresh ingredients and innovative preparations. (You may still have to eat a pork tenderloin sandwich or pick up some sweet corn from a farmstand, just to prove you've been to Iowa.)

Yes, it's cold in winter. And there's a *lot* of snow. But Des Moines residents deal with it in some innovative ways: first of all, by moving above streets in the center of the city on the downtown skywalk, whose 3 miles of glass-walled elevated passageways connect offices, shops, and dining spots. Second, by embracing it: Winter sports are popular here, including ice-skating at an outdoor rink downtown, sledding at whatever hills residents can find amid the flat landscape, and cross-country skiing on the many trails that wind through the city and into the countryside. But the trails really come alive in the spring, when people hop onto their bikes and take advantage of the endless flat spaces to pedal for miles and miles. There are also designated bike lanes on several streets in the center of the city. Des Moines hosts an annual marathon and triathlon, each of which attracts more than 1,000 competitors, while every April Drake Stadium hosts the Drake Relays, a top track-and-field meet with athletes including Olympic contenders and medalists.

Presidential hopefuls and the national media descend on Iowa every four years for the state's first-in-the-nation caucuses, putting Des Moines in the national spotlight. Many candidates make the city their Iowa headquarters, and it's easy to find locals who have encountered them, or at least their entourages. Otherwise, Des Moines enjoys a fairly low-key, laid-back style and attitude: People are friendly here, and more than willing to let you know the best place to eat or shop. Bragging isn't really Des Moines residents' forte, but they have plenty to be proud of, including a school system consistently near the top of national rankings, highly affordable housing, and a relaxed, 20-minute average commute time.

So don't think you'll be bored in Des Moines. On the contrary—there is so much to see and do, you won't have time to fit it all in on one visit! The city is alive, engaging, and fun. Everything is easy to get to, with friendly locals to help guide you there. You'll always find something else to check out—the options here are as limitless as the horizon that stretches out into the cornfields, giving a sense of endless possibilities.

HOW TO USE THIS BOOK

This book is divided into detailed chapters about Des Moines. Des Moines has plenty to see and do, especially in the center of the city.

The book's maps give you a sense of how the city is laid out—as a compact city with a grid street system and many attractions concentrated in downtown and a handful of neighborhoods, Des Moines is fairly easy to navigate. Throughout the book are **Insiders' Tips** (indicated by an ![i]), which give you some tidbits gleaned from locals on things you might not otherwise find, as well as sidebars, which condense practical information and basic facts into an easy-to-read list. **Close-ups** go into more depth about particular aspects of Des Moines.

The **Getting Here, Getting Around** chapter shows you the best ways to find your way from place to place, everything from making it from the airport to downtown to exploring Des Moines by car, bicycle or foot, and all other transportation options. The **Accommodations** chapter is divided geographically and shows price codes, so you can decide how much you'd like to spend and where you'd like to stay. **Restaurants** are listed by cuisine and have price codes as well. **Nightlife** covers a wide spectrum of options, while **The Arts** takes in offerings on the stage and otherwise. The **Shopping** chapter will lead to the rich variety of stores found in Des Moines, while **Attractions** is a wide-encompassing chapter that has information on everything from historic sites to museums and hidden neighborhood spots and everything in between.

Des Moines's many kid-friendly attractions get their own chapter in **Kidstuff,** while **Spectator Sports** showcases the surprising number of minor league and college athletic teams you can watch play. **Recreation** is organized by activity and contains a plethora of them, including golf, tennis, and cycling, as well as family-friendly activities. The **Annual Events** chapter is a valuable guide to Des Moines's well-stocked schedule of gatherings and celebrations—just bear in mind that many event dates often change, and thus the dates listed here are estimates and include only the month of the event. **Day Trips & Weekend Getaways** introduces you to some of the rich possibilities found throughout central Iowa, which has treasures ranging from the Herbert Hoover Presidential Library and Museum to the Amana Colonies, many of which are at most a few hours from Des Moines and are easily accessible from major highways.

Many chapters can easily be cross-referenced with other chapters—the Recreation chapter, for example, takes note of parks that can then be checked out in the **Parks** chapter, and many of the listings in the Attractions chapter make for good destinations for kids, along with those in the Kidstuff chapter. Don't try to do everything in this book—curb your appetite for seeing as much as you possibly can, and take some time to just wander around different areas and see what you can find off the beaten path. Des Moines has lots to discover, and you're sure to have a satisfying visit if you're open to the city and all it has to offer. Remember, too, that restaurants close, attractions shorten their hours seasonally, and traffic or weather may prohibit visiting some places—it's a good idea to call ahead just to make sure.

You'll also find listings accompanied by the ✳ symbol—these are our top picks for attractions, restaurants, accommodations, and everything in between that you shouldn't miss while you're in the area. You want the best this region has to offer? Go with our **Insiders' Choice.**

Finally, if you're moving to the Des Moines area or already live here, be sure to check out the blue-tabbed pages at the back of the book. There you will find the **Living Here** appendix that offers sections on relocation, child care, education, health care, and retirement.

AREA OVERVIEW

With a population of roughly 200,000 in the city proper and 600,000 in a five-county metropolitan area, Des Moines is a midsize city and feels like it. The wide-open farm fields surrounding the city make some distances seem farther than they really are—it usually takes 20 minutes at most to reach any given location in the city, slightly longer if you're heading to the suburbs or outlying areas.

Interstate highways lead to the midwestern metropolises of Chicago and Minneapolis, with which Des Moines shares a similar culture—in the middle of Iowa and the middle of the country, Des Moines is midwestern at heart. Nearly one million people, about 30 percent of Iowa's population, live within a one-hour drive of Des Moines, and it's definitely the state's nerve center for commerce, government, and culture.

Des Moines is laid out east–west, with the majestic Iowa State Capitol standing sentry on a hill overlooking the downtown business district. Contrary to popular belief, the terrain here is not all flat—the city has several (yes, several) notable hills, but the more prominent topographic features in Des Moines are the rivers: The Des Moines River splits downtown into east and west halves before joining the Raccoon River at the southeast edge of downtown, and then flows southeast across Iowa to join the Mississippi on the Iowa-Illinois-Missouri border. This confluence roughly divides the city into the west, east, and south sides (there's a small north side as well), while along the rivers lie parkland and woods striped with trails used by cyclists and walkers. Also along the rivers are lakes that are enjoyed in warmer months for swimming and boating, including Gray's Lake near downtown, Blue Heron Lake at Raccoon River Park, and Saylorville Lake, a large, dammed lake north of the city.

Much of Des Moines is residential, with attractions concentrated mainly in and near downtown and sprinkled throughout the city and suburbs. The Getting Here, Getting Around section has more details about finding your way around Des Moines, which is fairly easy to do. Listed below are some notes on different parts of the city and metro area as well as information on the weather.

DOWNTOWN

Bounded to the north by I-235, the east by the State Capitol, and the west by M. L. King Jr. Parkway, which also curves and forms the southern border of downtown—for now. Although development is beginning to creep in among the old warehouses to the south, closer to the Raccoon River, downtown is essentially split into two halves. To the east of the Des Moines River, the gold-domed Iowa State Capitol stands on a hill overlooking Locust Street. Surrounding the Capitol is the East Village, a city neighborhood transformed into a funky little slice of hip shops and restaurants. Just to the west of the river is the Court Avenue Entertainment District, a compact strip of bars, restaurants, and live music halls, while the core of the downtown business district is on the main east–west streets Mulberry, Walnut, Locust, and Grand. To the west along Grand and Locust lies Western Gateway, until recently a run-down area, but reborn with nice restaurants, new office buildings, and a delightful outdoor sculpture park. On the northwest edge of downtown, Sherman Hill is an old residential neighborhood, slowly being reclaimed by homeowners moving into its fine Victorian houses.

spaces that gradually turn to farmland. Yet the south side is also a treasure trove of old residential neighborhoods. Many families have been here for generations, and it's not uncommon to find multiple-family households living in the same neighborhood. Just over the confluence of the Des Moines and Raccoon Rivers from downtown are restaurants that are reminders of Des Moines's old "Little Italy," when large numbers of Italian immigrants settled in the city. Today the south side, like the rest of the city, is home to newcomers from even more distant lands. Easter Lake County Park, a popular spot for boating, fishing, and swimming, is here as well.

WEST SIDE

Extending from M. L. King Jr. Parkway to 63rd Street along both sides of I-235, the west side includes many—although certainly not all—of Des Moines's attractions, including the city's art museum and Drake University, which is centered at University Avenue and 25th Street. Farther west on University and a little bit north is Beaverdale, a middle-class neighborhood with modest houses on quiet streets. To the south of I-235, Ingersoll Avenue is a bustling commercial area with lots of small shops and restaurants. Farther south is South of Grand, where large, elegant homes stand on winding streets; this is also the location of the Iowa governor's mansion.

SOUTH SIDE

The most prominent landmark here is Des Moines International Airport, which is located on Fleur Drive, just 5 miles from the center of downtown. The south side is roughly bounded by the Raccoon and Des Moines Rivers, while to the south are wide-open

Visitor Centers

Greater Des Moines Convention & Visitors Bureau
400 Locust St., Suite 265
(515) 286-4960

Des Moines International Airport
5800 Fleur Dr.
(515) 256-5575
www.seedesmoines.com
The downtown office of the Convention & Visitors Bureau is located on the mezzanine level of the Capital Square building, just west of Nollen Plaza, and is accessible via the downtown skywalk. Stop in for brochures and helpful information about Des Moines and the surrounding area. They also have free booklets of coupons and discounts. The airport location is between the ticket and rental car counters and has a full selection of tourist literature.

Vital Statistics

Mayor/governor: Frank Cownie/Terry Branstad

Population (2009 estimate): City: 198,460; metro area: 562,906; Iowa: 3,007,856

Area: City: 77.2 square miles; Iowa: 56,272 square miles

Average temperatures: July: 76.6 F; January: 19.4 F

Average rainfall: 34.72 inches; June is the rainiest month, with 4.8 inches

Average snowfall: 33.3 inches; January is the snowiest month, with 8.3 inches

Founded: 1843 (as Fort Des Moines)

Major colleges and universities: Drake University, Grand View University, Des Moines University, Simpson College, Des Moines Area Community College

Major employers: Principal Financial, Wells Fargo, Nationwide Insurance, Iowa Health Systems, Mercy Health, Des Moines Public Schools, Hy-Vee food stores

Famous Sons & Daughter of Des Moines:
Bill Bryson, Author
Shawn Johnson, Olympic Gymnast and Reality Television Star
Lolo Jones, Track & Field Athlete
Cloris Leachman, Actress
Kyle Orton, NFL Quarterback
Ronald Reagan, US President (Worked as a radio announcer in Des Moines after growing up in Illinois)
Slipknot, Heavy Metal Band

EAST & NORTH SIDES

Also largely residential, with plenty of nice homes along tree-lined streets, the east side is bounded by the Des Moines River to the west and I-35/80 to the north, with its eastern edge marked by the communities of Altoona and Pleasant Hill. The most important thing to know about the east side is it's the home of the State Fairgrounds, which are a mile or so east of I-235 on E. University Avenue—this stretch of road fills up every August on fair days. The north side is carved out of the east side, pressed in by I-35/80, the Des Moines River, and I-235 as

it curves from southwest to northeast. Here you'll find some parks along the river along with the campus of Grand View University and smaller neighborhood business districts.

WEST DES MOINES

Primarily a bedroom community with a smattering of office buildings along three interstate highways, West Des Moines, which is a separate city from Des Moines, also has the hidden gem of Valley Junction, an old railroad neighborhood reborn as a shopping mecca, with lots of neat little stores. It also boasts Des Moines's newest and largest shopping mall, the Jordan Creek Town Center, and mile after mile of big-box stores, which spread out on the west side of town past West Glen, a shopping and nightlife area. On the southern fringe of West Des Moines is Raccoon River Park, which has a lake with a beach popular for swimming.

SUBURBAN AREAS

Numerous rural towns have exploded in population in response to Des Moines's growing prosperity, with new housing tracts rising among the cornfields. Clive, Grimes, Johnston, and Urbandale have all seen their populations mushroom, as has Waukee, out past West Des Moines. These towns enjoy plenty of green space and access to the Des Moines area's vast network of trails for cycling and walking. To the east, Altoona, Bondurant, and Pleasant Hill are all located near Adventureland Amusement Park and Prairie Meadows Racetrack and Casino. Ankeny, to the north, has seen perhaps the most dramatic growth of all, owing in part to its location halfway between Des Moines and Ames, home of Iowa State University.

SEASONS & WEATHER

There are four distinct seasons in Des Moines. Springtime can be a paradise: In May, once the downtown farmers' market gets going and residents retrieve their bicycles from the basement or garage, temperatures are mild, with breezes blowing into the city from the surrounding flat countryside. The mild weather continues through much of the summer, although there's a fair amount of rain. While July and August can be hot, with air-conditioning definitely needed, you shouldn't experience too many blistering, murderously hot days. The warmth may linger well after Labor Day, making for a pleasant Indian summer. Leaf colors are at their best in October, when the many greenbelts around Des Moines are positively bursting with the yellows, oranges, and reds of autumn. Come November, temperatures begin to drop, a foreboding of what's coming.

First impressions notwithstanding, especially if you arrive anytime from December through March, winter in Des Moines is no worse than in other parts of the Midwest (for what that's worth). Snow may fall as early as mid-November, and drifts can easily top a few feet, if not more, by the end of December. There may be as many as half a dozen "snow days," which shut down area schools. Bitterly cold temperatures usually arrive in January, when the mercury rarely rises above freezing, and winds, with little to stop them from roaring across the plains, can be absolutely brutal. Things pick up, albeit very slowly, from then, though there may be frozen creeks and lakes and snow on the ground until the end of March, and snowstorms are not unheard of in April.

GETTING HERE, GETTING AROUND

A classic midwestern city, Des Moines is laid out on an orderly grid. It is a fairly compact city with highway access and numerous wide, east–west avenues, making it easy to get to destinations all over town . Residents enjoy an average 20-minute commute, and convenient highway interchanges and extensive arterial roads make it easy to get around.

First the basics: North–south streets are numbered, with numbers running higher as you move east or west from downtown. West-side streets have no directional (e.g., 1st Street), while east-side streets include a directional (e.g., E. 1st Street or NE 14th Street).

I-235 cuts east–west across the center of Des Moines, past the State Capitol and just north of downtown's cluster of office towers, before running west toward Drake University and nearby Ingersoll Avenue, home to some of Des Moines's hidden treasures in dining and shopping. Nearby are the older residential neighborhoods of Beaverdale, with its rows of brick houses, and South of Grand, which has blocks of elegant, tasteful homes. Back closer to downtown is Sherman Hill, a neighborhood that has rebounded with new townhouses, condominiums, and funky office spaces.

On- and off-ramps for I-235 run onto downtown streets that alternate running one-way north or south—stay alert as you approach downtown on the highway. Also pay attention if you are leaving downtown and heading north on 6th Street to merge onto I-235—it is a four-lane street that fills up with traffic, which can make it difficult to reach the entrance ramp if you are all the way on the other side of the street.

Just west of downtown on I-235 is the exit to M. L. King Jr. Parkway and Fleur Drive, where the road runs south before splitting into two roads: Fleur continues south, heading toward Gray's Lake and Water Works Park, the latter of which includes an arboretum, and the airport and zoo, while M. L. King splits off and heads east, running along the south edge of downtown and passing near the Court Avenue Entertainment District, a former warehouse district turned dining and barhopping mecca, and Principal Park, home of the Iowa Cubs baseball team. Court Avenue can get crowded with traffic before and after games, and is closed completely to traffic on Saturday mornings from spring through fall for Des Moines's popular farmers' market.

OVERVIEW

Majòr streets in downtown run east–west and include Grand Avenue, which is a one-way street running west, and Locust Street, which is a one-way street running east. You can spot the Iowa State Capitol from downtown just by looking east along Locust Street: It stands at the far end of the East Village, a trendy shopping and dining neighborhood. A section of Walnut Street, 1 block south of Locust, is closed to cars during the workday. The extensive downtown skywalk blankets downtown, its passages providing a welcome relief during Des Moines's bitter winters and a convenience the rest of the year. The second story–level passageways crisscross downtown's streets, with easy access to hotels, parking garages, and shopping areas.

For a full map of the skywalk, go to http://arcgis.dmgov.org/extmapcenter /maps/skywalk.pdf. Directories are also located along the passageways.

Overall, downtown Des Moines, as well as the rest of the city, is refreshingly easy to get around by car: At rush hour the traffic still rushes, and traffic overall moves fairly smoothly and quickly along.

It's easy to get around Des Moines by bicycle as well: Recently installed bike lanes on Ingersoll Avenue complement the plethora of trails that wind through downtown and out to the outer reaches of the city and surrounding countryside.

BY CAR

Located in the middle of Iowa at the intersection of two major interstates—**I-35** and **I-80**—Des Moines is easily accessible from several major cities: Chicago is a 5- to 6-hour drive east along I-80, which also runs west to

Omaha, about 2 hours away. Kansas City and Minneapolis are 3 hours to the south and 4 hours to the north, respectively, on I-35. Arriving in Des Moines, it's an easy merge from both highways onto **I-235** into the center of the city.

Parking in downtown is fairly easy, with numerous meters and garages available. Parking meters generally cost $1.25 for an hour. Parking meters take coins, and some also take SmartCards, which can be purchased at three locations: the garages at **3rd and Court** and **9th and Locust,** and **City Hall,** on the east side of the Des Moines River at 400 Robert D. Ray Dr. Parking limits differ depending on the meter and include limits of 2, 3, 4 and 10 hours. Downtown has numerous garages open for public parking, which are a good value at $1.50 for the first hour and either $1 or $1.25 for additional hours, depending on the garage. Rates drop at night, again depending on the garage, and parking is free at both garages and meters on weekends, beginning Saturday mornings. Meters are also free weekday evenings after 6 p.m.

For more on parking, check out the parking info page of the City of Des Moines website: **www.dmgov.org/departments /engineering/pages/parking.aspx.** Also check the engineering pages for information on plowing in the winter, which can affect parking, as well as info on road closings. Information on highway construction and road conditions can be found on the **Iowa Department of Transportation** website: **www.iowadot.gov.**

BY PLANE

An easy 10- to 15-minute drive from downtown along tree-lined Fleur Drive, **Des Moines International Airport (DSM)** has flights on AirTran/SkyWest, Allegiant, American/American Eagle, Branson AirExpress, Delta, Continental Express, Midwest/Frontier, United, and US Airways, with direct, nonstop flights to Atlanta, Branson, Chicago, Dallas, Denver, Detroit, Houston, Las Vegas, Los Angeles, Memphis, Milwaukee, Minneapolis, New York, Orlando, Phoenix, Tampa–St. Petersburg, and Washington, D.C. The single terminal has 12 gates along 2 concourses, with numerous souvenir shops and dining options, including a food court and Capital City Brew Pub. Nine rental car agencies serve the airport, with desks located in the baggage claim area on the ground-floor level, and a pickup lot conveniently located right next door (return lots are just a short walk or shuttle bus ride).

Short- and long-term parking is available in two garages and three surface lots, two of which are a short walk from the terminal with a third across the street from the airport in a shuttle bus lot. Shuttle buses operate 24 hours a day. A "cell phone lot" in one of the closer surface lots is set aside for those who are picking up incoming passengers—you must stay with your car in this lot.

Taxis stop in front of the terminal at a designated taxi stand. Des Moines Area Regional Transit (DART) bus #8 (SW 14th Havens, NOT South Union route) stops along Fleur Drive on selected routes, but does not go to the terminal, and doesn't even run on weekends, so it's inconvenient at best.

Plane charters are available from **Elliott Aviation** (515-285-6551; www.elliottaviation.com), with service around the Midwest, or **Signature Flight Support** (515-256-5330; www.signatureflightsupport.com), with service nationwide. A nearby small airport is **Ankeny Regional Airport,** a short drive north of Des Moines, which has two runways, charter services, and flight instruction.

TAXIS, LIMOUSINES & CAR RENTALS

Taxis & Limos

Taxis run about $2 per mile, and there is a $2 fee when you get in the cab (it goes up to $4 after 10 p.m.). A taxi from the airport to downtown or West Des Moines (where many hotels are located) generally runs $15–$20. Taxis stop at a designated taxi stand right outside the airport baggage claim.

Capitol Cab and **Yellow Cab** are actually both operated by the same company, and provide good service. Call (515) 282-8111 or (515) 243-1111; www.transiowa.com.

Limo rental companies include:
- **Albee's Old Market Limo Co.,** (515) 727-4868.
- **C & C Limo Services,** (515) 780-7452.
- **Gene's Transportation,** (515) 249-1127.
- **Majestic Limousine,** (515) 986-0305.

Car Rentals

All major car rental companies operate at the Des Moines airport. Some have offices elsewhere in the city as well.
- **Advantage,** (515) 256-5842.
- **Alamo,** (515) 256-5353 or (888) 426-3299.
- **Avis,** (515) 256-5623 or (800) 831-2847.
- **Budget,** (515) 287-2612 or (800) 527-0700.
- **Dollar,** (515) 256-5852 or (800) 800-4000.
- **Enterprise,** (515) 256-5665 or (800) 736-8222.
- **Hertz,** (515) 285-9650 or (800) 654-3131.
- **National,** (515) 256-5353 or (800) 227-7368.
- **Thrifty,** (515) 256-5850 or (800) 847-4389.

BY BUS OR TRAIN

Intercity Buses

The city's bus station is located at **1107 Keosauqua Way** (usually shortened to Keo Way, including on highway signs; 515-243-1773). Buses from all the lines listed below stop at the station, which is just off I-235 northwest of downtown. It is just over a mile east of Drake University, and is generally safe.

BURLINGTON TRAILWAYS

(515) 243-5283 or (800) 992-4618
www.burlingtontrailways.com
Burlington Trailways connects Des Moines with Chicago, Indianapolis, St. Louis, Denver, and smaller cities and towns across the Midwest and Rocky Mountains. They may have special "walk-up" fares that must be purchased at the station rather than online.

GREYHOUND BUSES

(515) 243-1773 or (800) 231-2222
www.greyhound.com
Greyhound Buses links Des Moines with its nationwide network, usually through connections in Chicago, Minneapolis, Omaha, Denver, Kansas City, and St. Louis (there's also a daily bus that departs for New York). They also offer service to numerous cities in Iowa.

JEFFERSON LINES

(515) 283-0074 or (800) 451-5333
Jefferson Lines, based out of Minneapolis, runs to destinations across the middle of the United States, from Montana and the Dakotas down to Texas.

MEGABUS

(877) 462-8362
www.megabus.com

MegaBus has service from Des Moines to Chicago and Iowa City. You can sometimes get great low fares, but it helps to book further in advance.

Trains

Des Moines has no regular train service, although there is a push to get high-speed rail to Chicago. **Amtrak's California Zephyr line** stops daily in Osceola, roughly 40 miles south of Des Moines on I-35. The station has very limited services and does not sell tickets. Call (800) 872-7245 or go to **www.amtrak.com.**

Des Moines Area Regional Transit (DART)

There are regular bus routes that cover all sides of the city, with some routes split into subroutes that take slightly different streets in between major intersections. Service is adequate, although not as effective outside of peak commuting times. Some bus routes do not operate on weekends.

Fare for city buses is $1.50, while express buses, which run to the suburbs, cost $1.75. You must have the exact fare—drivers do not give change.

DART buses are equipped with racks on the front that allow you to store your bike while on the bus (children's bikes fit on the racks as well, although tandem and recumbent bikes do not).

Free downtown shuttles run Mon through Fri from early morning to early evening. The D Line runs east–west, circling from the Capitol to Western Gateway along Grand and Locust, while the Link runs north–south along several streets.

BY BICYCLE

With hundreds of miles of bicycle trails throughout the city and surrounding area, Des Moines is a bike-friendly town. Trails are usually paved, although not always well marked. From downtown the **Meredith Trail** winds southwest, past Principal Park baseball stadium to Gray's Lake and Water Works parks, or east across the Des Moines River, where it hooks up with the **John Pat Dorrian Trail** as it runs along the riverfront. On the west side of Des Moines, the **M. L. King Trail** runs concurrent with the Meredith Trail to the east, while to the west it leads to Ingersoll Avenue, which has dedicated bicycle lanes. Further information on bicycling can be found in the Recreation chapter.

The city's **B-Cycle** program gives residents and visitors the opportunity to rent a bicycle to pedal around downtown. After purchasing a 24-hour pass, you may pick up a bike at any of the B-cycle stations: at 13th and Grand, 7th and Grand, outside Principal Park, or at Brenton Skating Plaza, just east of the Des Moines River on Grand. After riding you return the bike to any station (additional fees are charged for rides of more than an hour).

HISTORY

The history of Des Moines is closely intertwined with westward expansion and the settling of the frontier. The Native American tribes who lived throughout what is now Iowa were displaced to make room for settlers who tamed the prairie, established farms and towns, and created a new nation.

Prehistoric settlements dating back at least 3,000 years have been found in Iowa. Mound Builder culture flourished, with earthworks and stone mounds the legacy of five distinct civilizations. The Woodland were the most prolific, with their stone mounds found in practically every county in Iowa, including effigy mounds in the shapes of various creatures. They also left behind a plethora of chipped flint instruments and pottery objects. The Hopewellian civilization was concentrated along the banks of the Mississippi River, the Oneota and Mill Creek in northwestern Iowa, and the Glenwood in southwestern Iowa.

The Mound Builders were the ancestors of the Indian tribes who lived in Iowa at the time of European exploration and conquest. The Sauk (or Sac) and Fox were perhaps the most numerous, spread out over Illinois, Wisconsin, and Iowa, hunting and growing pumpkins, corn, beans, potatoes, and melons. The Sioux also used the area as a hunting ground, moving their tepees across the northern part of present-day Iowa. Other tribes included the Winnebago, Pottawatomie, and Mascoutin, as well as the Ioway people, who gave the state its name.

The first Europeans in Iowa were Father Jacques Marquette and Louis Joliet, whose 1673 expedition down the Mississippi landed on the west bank of the river and made note of the soaring bluffs. With the Louisiana Purchase in 1803, the vast sweep of prairie and rivers became part of the United States. Lead mining drew a wave of settlement to the Dubuque area along the Mississippi, while British and French fur trappers stalked farther and farther west.

Meriwether Lewis and William Clark passed by the western edge of present-day Iowa as they moved up the Missouri River. The 1805–06 Zebulon Pike expedition led to the establishment in 1809 of Fort Madison, the first US military installation in Iowa, located on the Mississippi between Keokuk and Burlington. The Sauk and Fox viewed the fort as a violation of an earlier treaty and, led by their chief, Black Hawk, who had allied his warriors with the British in the War of 1812, attacked the fort in 1813. American troops burned the fort as they retreated.

BLACK HAWK WAR & WHITE SETTLEMENT

The stage was set for even greater conflict between the natives and newcomers. The Sauk were pushed west of the Mississippi and out of their traditional farming areas around the village of Saukenuk (present-day Rock Island, Illinois). Tensions rose in 1831 when settlers invaded Indian villages, tearing down dwellings and destroying cornfields. Black Hawk himself was beaten by settlers. Breaking with Sauk chief Keokuk, who voluntarily moved west with many Sauk and Fox, Black Hawk rallied 1,000 braves, women, and children in April 1832 and crossed the Mississippi into Illinois, where he hoped to form an alliance with the Winnebago. Failing to do so, Black Hawk sent a surrender party to meet with federal troops. In the confusion, a Sauk warrior was killed, and Black Hawk retaliated with a large war party, killing 11 federals. Exaggerated claims of the size and threat presented by Black Hawk's group spread terror through the region, and the simmering conflict exploded into full-blown war.

i There is no single definitive history of Des Moines, but a good detailed account of the city's early days and eventual growth is *Des Moines: Capital City,* published in 1978 by Orin Dahl.

Skirmishes broke out over the next few months, as Black Hawk and his band moved slowly to the north, up the Rock River and past present-day Madison, Wisconsin. The battle of Wisconsin Heights, near present-day Sauk City, was Black Hawk's last great stand. Over 70 Sauk died as they held off federal troops while crossing the Wisconsin

River. The Sauk could not outrun the federals forever: Ten days later, as Black Hawk waved the white flag of surrender at the Battle of Bad Axe, troops massacred the Sauk as they crossed the Bad Axe River, including women and children, as did Sioux who allied themselves with the US forces. Black Hawk himself was imprisoned before returning to Iowa, where he died in 1838, the same year Iowa became a US territory.

With the decisive victory of US forces in the Black Hawk War, native tribes ceded more and more land to settlers, and within 20 years the tribes had given up all of the Iowa country. Settlers began moving into Iowa, and small farms dotted the vast prairie, although a massive land grab was thwarted by the daunting crossing of the Mississippi, which was still a wild and raging river, not to mention the brutal winters, which, then as now, tested residents' resolve, with one writing of a "storm that lasted about three days before the gale lessened" (Dahl, 19). There was also a brief boom in coal mining nearby in southern Iowa, although most of the mines were played out within a few decades.

BEGINNINGS OF A CITY

The first Fort Des Moines, one of three military posts to use the name, was established in 1834 near Keokuk, on the Mississippi River, as a way station for units moving farther west into Indian Territory. The following year, Stephen Kearney led a military expedition through Wisconsin and Iowa (during this time Iowa was part of the territory of Wisconsin). The scouting party included Albert Lea, who noted the advantages for development in central Iowa, especially the excellent soil and possibilities for water traffic along the Des Moines and Raccoon Rivers. Further surveys of the area followed, and a second

Fort Des Moines was established just north of the confluence of the two rivers, on the west bank of the Des Moines River in 1843.

Fort Des Moines No. 2, which eventually became the capital city, is commemorated with a log cabin placed at the north end of the Principal Park baseball stadium parking lots, just west of the Des Moines River and SW 1st Street. However, the cabin is almost swallowed up by the widening of M. L. King Jr. Parkway and a bridge across the river.

Captain James Allen, commander of the fort, originally proposed naming it Fort Raccoon, a suggestion that was met with some derision, to say the least. Fort Des Moines No. 2 was, like its namesake, a temporary stopover for patrols moving through Indian Territory.

At the stroke of midnight on October 11, 1845, after the Sauk and Fox had relinquished their rights to the land, a shot sounded out from the fort, and settlers rushed into the Des Moines River valley, claiming land for themselves and burning down abandoned wigwams. Iowa statehood came in 1846, with slavery prohibited, as it had been in the Iowa Territory under the terms of the 1820 Missouri Compromise. The state capital stayed at Iowa City, which had been arbitrarily selected as the territorial capital and also became the site of the state university. The military garrison of Fort Des Moines was closed in 1846, and the town of Fort Des Moines was surveyed, with the population standing at 127, before being incorporated 5 years later.

Throughout the 1840s, the new city saw many migrations pass through, from Mormons making their long trek under Brigham Young, to "forty-niners" off to seek their fortune in the California gold fields, to endless covered wagons heading for a hopeful better life on the western frontier. Ferry operators on the Des Moines River, outfitters, and other businesses prospered, and Des Moines's population reached 500 by 1850.

CREATION OF A CAPITAL

Political machinations to move the capital to Des Moines had been going on since statehood, and it was declared the capital in 1857, the same year its name was changed from Fort Des Moines to Des Moines. Even then, there was wheeling and dealing over the site of the Capitol building, with dueling factions from the east and west sides of the Des Moines River. The east side won out, bringing to the table 10 acres of land and a building that cost more than $35,000—to be leased to the state for $1 a year. East–west differences only intensified with the establishment of four wards west of the river and three to the east.

The actual *moving* of the Capitol was even more dramatic: Four heavy safes full of records, among furniture and other items, had to be lugged over 100 miles from Iowa City, across rugged prairie and over streams and creeks without bridges. The project actually had to wait until winter, when teams of oxen hauled bobsleds into the city. The first State Capitol was a 3-story brick structure.

i Abolitionist John Brown made his headquarters in Iowa for three years, bringing in escaping slaves to several active stations on the Underground Railroad.

Des Moines continued to grow and prosper as steamboats plied the waterways and dropped anchor near the confluence of the Des Moines and Raccoon Rivers.

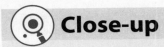

Close-up

What Does "Des Moines" Mean, Anyway?

Despite the best efforts of many, it's far from clear what the meaning is of the name of Iowa's capital city. Native Americans called the main river in the area *Moingona, Moingonis,* or *Moingounas,* which all seem to mean "River of the Mounds." But they could also mean the name of any of several tribes who lived in the area. The French explorers and trappers who came to the area in the wake of the Joliet and Marquette expedition dubbed the same river *La Riviere des Moines,* which may refer to the monks who for a time lived in huts along the water—or it may be a corruption of the French *De Moyen,* meaning "The Middle." With a slight twist, this could also be construed to mean "the less" or "the smaller" in reference to yet another tribe who lived near the river. Confusing the issue further are the variety of phonetic spellings the French bestowed upon it: *De Moin* and *Demoine,* plus of course *Des Moines.* Ultimately, of course, it's better to quibble over the name Des Moines than to be stuck with Fort Raccoon, which is what the military commander of the fort that became the city wanted to call it!

Struggles developed between river and railroad interests, but the city soon had a much bigger issue on its hands.

THE CIVIL WAR

When news of Fort Sumter reached Des Moines, passions were aroused on both sides, with at least one newspaper editor attacking Lincoln's policies, and Southern sympathizers moving to take control of the Democratic Party in Iowa. Union units were almost immediately organized, with a recruiting station set up by the Capitol. Iowa regiments invaded Missouri in June 1861, and troops from Des Moines fought at Fort Donelson, Pea Ridge, Shiloh, and Corinth. In total, 75,000 men, or nearly one-third of Iowa's population, served in the war. Funerals of casualties attracted thousands in Des Moines. At news of Robert E. Lee's surrender, cannons and guns were fired in celebration across the city.

The outbreak of war also dovetailed with the decline of steamboat traffic: by 1862, navigation on the Des Moines River had virtually ended, and the railroads soon became dominant in the area's transportation infrastructure. The Keokuk and Des Moines Valley Railroad, running from the Mississippi along the Des Moines River, pulled into Des Moines in 1866. At the same time, the frontier to the west was closing, with the last stagecoach leaving Des Moines in 1870.

A MODERN CITY EMERGES

Following the war, Des Moines continued to grow and develop, with the population shooting up to 12,000 by 1870. The Equitable Life Insurance Company was founded in 1867, setting the stage for Des Moines as a major insurance center, while Younkers Department Store, familiar today to shoppers all over the Midwest, began in Des Moines in 1874 as the branch of a Keokuk-based dry-goods store founded by Polish immigrants. Drake University was founded in 1881, and a new Capitol was completed in 1886, with five domes, including the 275-foot-high central dome covered in 23-karat gold leaf, rising at the east end of downtown. The year before, a permanent site on the city's east side was selected for the Iowa State Fair, which would arguably do as much as the Capitol to put Des Moines on the map.

Reach for the Sky

At 19 stories, the **Equitable Building,** located at 604 Locust St. downtown, was the tallest building in Iowa from 1924 until 1973, when the **Financial Center** and then the **Ruan Center** opened. Eventually the spire-topped building at 801 Grand, also known as **Principal Tower,** bypassed them all, standing head and shoulders above every other building on the downtown skyline.

There was also an effort to pretty up the city a bit. Following rapid urban growth in the 1850s, during which "there was, literally, not a shade tree in Des Moines" (Dahl, 43), the Des Moines Horticultural Society staged a major exhibition in 1862 that displayed a wide variety of flowers, trees, shrubs, and other ornamental plants. By the turn of the 20th century, Greenwood Park had opened as the city's first public park. Around the beginning of the 20th century Des Moines began a City Beautiful project, part of the Beaux Arts movement, which

put ornamental, elegant fountains along the river and created some of downtown's more striking buildings, such as City Hall and the old central library building, both of which still stand on the riverfront, with the library being remodeled to serve as home of the World Food Prize.

A slight jolt in the steady march of commerce and development came in April 1894, when "Kelly's Army" descended on Des Moines. This ragtag group of some 1,000 unemployed men, including sympathetic allies like the author Jack London, were moving east to Washington to press their grievances on the federal government. After failing to obtain transportation onward from Omaha, they marched across Iowa on foot and stopped in Des Moines, taking shelter from a rainstorm. Local residents, determined not to anger the "army," provided meals and ultimately coughed up the money to build 150 rafts, which the group, rechristened "Kelly's Navy," proceeded to ride down the river toward Keokuk.

THE 20TH CENTURY: CHANGES & CHALLENGES

With the population of Des Moines at 62,000 in 1900, the city continued to go about its business. With some of the less attractive parts of downtown cleaned up, a major building boom now commenced, with numerous office and commercial buildings rising from the cornfields, and attendant development in roads and utilities. There was also an echo of the city's past as a frontier fort: In 1903 Fort Des Moines No. 3 was opened as a cavalry post on the city's south side. Although it was later abandoned, it served as a training ground for African-American officers during World War I, when

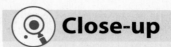 **Close-up**

Norman Borlaug & the World Food Prize

A pioneering plant geneticist who spent a career working on projects that benefited untold numbers of people worldwide, **Norman Borlaug** is perhaps the most unknown yet influential Iowa native. He dedicated his career to ending world hunger by finding ways to improve how food is grown around the world, and is known as "the father of the Green Revolution" for his efforts to bring more effective farming techniques to poor countries.

Born on an Iowa farm in 1914 to Norwegian immigrants, Borlaug was a standout wrestler in high school and college who earned a PhD in plant pathology and genetics from the University of Minnesota in 1942. After working on military projects during World War II, Borlaug turned his attention to boosting wheat production in Mexico. Among his innovations were increasing the resistance of wheat plants to disease as well as "dwarfing," a process that allows a thicker stalk of wheat to support more grains, thus increasing the plant's yield. His work with wheat would consume some 35 years and would take him around the world, notably to India and Pakistan, where his work was credited with doubling wheat yields and easing famine that raged through South Asia.

Later Borlaug taught and conducted seminars around the world. In 1986 he created the **World Food Prize,** which recognizes efforts worldwide to improve the food supply and end world hunger. He received numerous awards, including the Nobel Peace Prize and the Presidential Medal of Freedom. Borlaug died in 2009.

The World Food Prize is awarded every October in Des Moines, as part of a symposium set up to discuss issues raised by Borlaug's work and the continuing challenges of solving world hunger. The World Food Prize Foundation plans to move into a new headquarters at the old Des Moines Public Library at 100 Locust St., on the corner of 2nd Avenue, right next to the west bank of the Des Moines River. The salmon-colored Beaux Arts structure of Minnesota sandstone was built in 1900 as part of the City Beautiful movement in Des Moines, and closed when the new downtown library opened in 2006. A scaled-down model of the Library of Congress, it is undergoing a massive $30 million renovation, which will give the building skylights and a view of the river. The new World Food Prize Hall of Laureates will feature a museum with displays on Borlaug's work as well as information on recipients of the prize.

Des Moines also saw 100,000 soldiers train at Camp Dodge, just northwest of the city.

The first Drake Relays were held in 1910, with barely 100 spectators turning out for the races at the university, giving no sign as to the hugely significant international track and field event it would become. Population passed 100,000 by 1920 and business continued to grow. The Meredith Publishing Company, later to become Meredith Corporation and doing business in Des Moines since 1892, brought out perhaps its best-known title, *Better Homes and Gardens* (changed from its original name of *Fruit Garden and Home*) in 1924.

The city continued building, adding a municipal airport, later to become Des Moines International Airport, on the south side. Fort Des Moines was pressed into service again, this time to train the female soldiers who would become the army's first female officers as part of the Women's Army Auxiliary Corps, later renamed the Women's Army Corps (WAC).

ℹ️ **Ronald Reagan served with a cavalry unit at Fort Des Moines while he was living in Des Moines during his early radio career, getting in some early riding experience after enlisting in the army reserves in 1937.**

Following World War II, Des Moines saw the opening of the city's art museum in Greenwood Park on the city's west side. Several years later Veterans Auditorium opened, and for decades was the city's showcase venue for big-time entertainment. New residential and shopping options began cropping up on the outskirts of the city, with Clive and Pleasant Hill both incorporating in 1956, and Merle Hay Mall opening in 1959. That same year, Nikita Khrushchev addressed a business group in Des Moines as part of the Soviet leader's tour of the United States, in which he also visited an Iowa corn farm. As the decade came to a close, the population of the city passed 200,000.

The city zoo, which eventually grew into Blank Park Zoo, began near the site of Fort Des Moines in 1964, while the following year brought construction of the Saylorville Dam and Reservoir, which transformed central Iowa's water supply and brought abundant recreation opportunities to the area. Yet even with all the building and development, parts of the city slowly began to decline, just as suburban areas began growth of their own (the city lost population between 1960 and 2000, while the overall metro area

grew). Even as new skyscrapers joined the skyline in the 1970s, parts of downtown became known for vacant lots and a general run-down atmosphere, dovetailing with the end of regular passenger rail service to Des Moines in 1970. Fortunately, that same year the city saw the opening of a science museum in Greenwood Park on the west side, preceding the present-day Science Center of Iowa downtown as well as Living History Farms in the northwest corner

---

Downtown Redevelopment

Des Moines's downtown has been transformed in recent years, particularly the area dubbed **Western Gateway,** which centers on the copper-skinned new central library building on Locust Street between 10th and 12th Streets, and features a nice plaza with a slow-moving fountain unfolding in front of the building. Nearby rise new steel and glass office towers for health-care and insurance companies, as well as a plethora of new shops and restaurants. On the corner of 10th and Locust Streets stands a former Masonic Temple saved from the wrecking ball and reborn as a performing arts center, with trendy restaurants occupying the ground floor. A few blocks south on 10th Street, the Hotel Fort Des Moines, an old, elegant hotel that has hosted statesmen and celebrities for more than a century, is undergoing a yearlong facelift in 2011 before it too joins the new and improved downtown.

of the metro area. In 1972 the forerunner of Des Moines University, a school offering numerous medical degrees, moved to Grand Avenue on the city's west side.

Fortunately, even as decline persisted in some parts of downtown, local business leaders John Ruan and David Kruidenier spearheaded a downtown turnaround, which led to the downtown skywalk, new office buildings, a revitalized riverfront, and trendy restaurants and entertainment spots sprinkled on both the east and west banks of the river. The city took a setback in 1993, when massive floods overflowed the banks of the Des Moines and Raccoon Rivers, shutting down the city's water treatment plant and leaving residents without water for weeks, but it soon recovered and shored up its defenses should such floods strike again.

As the 21st century unfolded, longtimers and new residents alike were grateful for an economic and cultural renaissance in Des Moines—as much as they were glad they didn't live in Fort Raccoon.

ACCOMMODATIONS

As a midsize city, Des Moines does not have as great a selection of accommodations as bigger metropolitan areas, but there are still plenty of choices, including luxury hotels, cheaper chain lodgings, and bed-and-breakfasts, some of which are located in rural areas and provide a wonderful, peaceful setting to recharge for a weekend.

Most Des Moines area hotels and motels are grouped near major attractions and/or shopping areas, including Adventureland Amusement Park and Prairie Meadows Racetrack and Casino to the northeast of the city, Living History Farms to the northwest, and West Glen Town Center nightlife district to the southwest. There are several hotels near the Des Moines airport, a short cab or shuttle ride south of downtown (make sure the shuttle operates at a time convenient for you to make your flight).

Downtown hotels are clustered near the core of the downtown business district on the west side of the Des Moines River, a bit of a walk (or short drive or cab ride) from the East Village and State Capitol to the east or the Court Street Entertainment District and Saturday farmers' market to the south. Parking is ample downtown in city garages or at street meters.

Most outlying accommodations are conveniently located near highway interchanges, no more than a 10- or 15-minute drive from downtown, and near chain restaurants and shopping.

Unless indicated otherwise, all listed hotels accept credit cards. Since 2008 smoking in Iowa hotels has been severely restricted, although some hotels still offer smoking rooms—unless indicated otherwise, all listed hotels are smoke-free.

Price Code

The following price codes are based on a one-night stay in a regular room with double occupancy and reflect basic room rates ("rack rates") during the peak season. Prices here do not include local sales and room taxes, tips, service charge, or other additional fees.

$ . . . . Less than $100
$$ . . . . $100 to $150
$$$ . . . . $150 to $200
$$$$ . . . . More than $200

BED-AND-BREAKFASTS

✱BUTLER HOUSE ON GRAND　　$$
4507 Grand Ave.
(515) 255-4096 or (866) 455-4096
www.butlerhouseongrand.com
Located across the street from the Des Moines Art Center, this half-timbered 3-story house in one of Des Moines's more elegant neighborhoods boasts 7 unique guest rooms, with decor in each room created by a local artist or designer. All rooms have a private bath, television with cable and wireless Internet, as well as in-room telephones. Complimentary snacks, sodas, and bottled water are available for guests.

Each room is equipped with a comfortable, queen-size bed, and guests rave about how comfortable the beds are—some have a featherbed mattress. Some of the rooms include a bathtub, others just a shower. Views include the walled garden outside and the I. M. Pei, Eliel Saarinen, and Richard Meier-designed art museum.

No pets are permitted, and children are allowed only in the third-floor rooms. Rooms are not wheelchair accessible. They may be able to take you to the airport, depending on when your flight is leaving.

GARDEN AND GALLEY BED & BREAKFAST　　$$
1321 Jefferson Way, Indianola
(515) 961-7749
www.gardenandgalley.com

Four rooms in a Frank Lloyd Wright–style home on a 9-acre hillside property about 20 minutes south of Des Moines. Each room has its own theme, including a retro 1950s room and a room dedicated to Simpson College, which is just a few minutes' drive from the house. While all rooms have a private bath, the bath for the Harvest Room is across the hallway. Rooms have satellite television and Wi-Fi access. The 900-square-foot Garden Suite has its own patio and provides an extra layer of privacy.

The full breakfast includes such unique delights as pesto shirred eggs and chardonnay chive eggs, as well as a full selection of baked goods, fruit, and breakfast meats. Other meals are available, including romantic candlelit dinners, for which you must make arrangements well in advance.

DVD players and a selection of movies are available for guests. Numerous walking paths wind around the property, which includes a pond, woods, pasture, and apple orchard, which provides fresh fruit for many yummy items at the dining table.

Dogs are allowed for a charge. Rooms are not wheelchair accessible. This is a good base to check out Madison County's covered bridges, which are just over 20 miles from here.

TIMBERPINE LODGE BED & BREAKFAST $$
23675 Sportsmans Club Lane, Adel
(515) 993-3386
www.timberpinelodge.com
Surrounded by woods, this B&B on a former Christmas tree farm is a great spot if you're looking for a relaxing, rural getaway. The house is rustic, with rough-hewn logs fitted together on notches, but inside the one roomy suite has a fireplace and Jacuzzi, while

the second guest room has a shower only. Both rooms have satellite television and a DVD player, as well as Wi-Fi (although the knotty pine walls remind you you're out in the country).

A loft adjoining the guest rooms has a refrigerator and microwave for guest use, and is stocked with drinks and snacks. Save room, though, for the big country breakfast, which emphasizes fresh ingredients and includes a selection of eggs, ham, fruit, and bread, as well as great coffee, which you may want to take outside to watch the birds in the trees.

Rooms are not wheelchair accessible and pets are not permitted. There's an additional charge of $35 for a third person to stay in each room.

VICTORIA'S VINEYARD BED & BREAKFAST $$$
5096 NE 62nd Ave., Altoona
(515) 967-1980
www.victoriasvineyardbnb.com
As with most other local bed-and-breakfasts, this one is located in the countryside—yet it's also just a short drive from Prairie Meadows Racetrack and Casino and Adventureland Amusement Park. The "vineyard" in the name is authentic—there is a working vineyard on-site, which produces grapes for Iowa's burgeoning wine industry. Nearby is a pond, and the property also has row crops of corn and soybeans, as well as several acres of forest popular for strolls.

The 2 rooms are spare but comfortable, with a queen bed in each. One room has a Jacuzzi, while the other has a DVD player. Both rooms have a television and Internet access, as well as private baths, with robes provided for guests.

A full breakfast is included, and for a special treat, one of the owners, who hails from Spain, can fix you paella or another classic Spanish dish—notify well in advance if you'd like to do this. The owners are also horse enthusiasts, and they offer a "horse motel" for $28.50 per night, which includes fresh water, hay and grain, and access to an outdoor corral.

HOTELS & MOTELS

Downtown

DES MOINES MARRIOTT DOWNTOWN   **$$$**
700 Grand Ave.
(515) 245-5500
www.marriott.com/dsmia
At 33 stories tall and with 417 rooms, this is the largest hotel in Iowa, standing high among downtown's modest skyscrapers. It's conveniently located just a few blocks from Wells Fargo Arena, Polk County Convention Complex, and Hy-Vee Hall, as well as the Iowa State Capitol, East Village shopping, and the Court Avenue Entertainment District. The inside is a little sterile, but there are great amenities, including a 24-hour fitness center and larger-than-average lap pool, which is open from 5 a.m. to 11 p.m. An on-site business center and hair salon make this a convenient stop for business travelers, as does a Starbucks Coffee with "grab and go" breakfast bags. Access to the downtown skywalk makes this a good choice if you're visiting Des Moines in the winter.

Rooms were completely renovated in 2009 and are comfortable if a little bland. They feature either 1 king bed and an ergonomic chair with an ottoman, or 2 double beds with only the chair. All rooms have flat-panel televisions. There's a charge for wired Internet in the rooms, although free wireless Internet is available in public spaces.

A breakfast buffet is available in the hotel's full-service restaurant, which is open for lunch and dinner as well. Room service is available from 6 a.m. to 11 p.m. Pets are allowed for a fee and valet parking is available. A free airport shuttle runs from 5 a.m. to midnight every day of the year.

EMBASSY SUITES DOWNTOWN DES MOINES ON THE RIVER   **$$**
101 E. Locust St.
(515) 244-1700
www.embassysuitesdesmoines.com
A somewhat more modestly priced downtown choice, this hotel has a great location on the banks of the Des Moines River, a short walk from East Village shopping and a quick walk across the river to downtown attractions. It's also right next door to the Simon Estes Amphitheater, which hosts a popular summer concert series. Fairly standard 2-room suites are roomy and have microwaves and refrigerators, as well as coffeemaker, hair dryer, clock radio, iron, and ironing board. The breakfast is a step above the typical hotel breakfast, and a daily afternoon reception includes complimentary cocktails. There's an on-site restaurant, indoor pool, and hot tub. A few smoking rooms are available. The free airport shuttle conveniently runs every 30 minutes. There's a charge for Internet service, and there's a convenient on-site business center. No pets.

HOTEL FORT DES MOINES   **$$**
1000 Walnut St.
(515) 243-1161 or (800) 532-1466
www.hotelfortdesmoines.com
This venerable lodging in Western Gateway has been a Des Moines landmark since

opening in 1919, hosting a long roster of famous figures, including movie stars, musicians, politicians and other entertainers and luminaries. Twelve US Presidents have made a visit to the hotel, as did Nikita Khrushchev during his landmark tour of America. The large brick edifice has a lobby that feels like the epicenter of its long and storied history. There are 240 rooms, which come with coffeemakers, hair dryers, iron and ironing board and free high-speed Internet access. Suites also have a mini-fridge, sofa and microwave. There's a pool, whirlpool, sauna and exercise room available for guests.

Several restaurants are nearby, including Django and Raccoon River on the same block and Centro just a short walk from the front entrance. The hotel is smoke-free and no pets are allowed. Note: There are plans for an extensive renovation beginning in the fall of 2011 that will close the hotel temporarily, so be sure to plan accordingly.

QUALITY INN & SUITES
EVENT CENTER $
929 3rd St.
(515) 282-5251
http://discovermidwesthotels.com
What this hotel may lack in charm, it more than makes up for in location and price, being just a short walk north of Nollen Plaza and the riverfront while costing far less than other downtown hotels. There are about 150 rooms, including suites with microwaves and refrigerators. All rooms have coffeemaker, hair dryer, clock radio, iron, and ironing board. There's a hot breakfast buffet, a large indoor pool, and a fitness center, as well as complimentary access to a downtown gym. Free wireless Internet. Pets are welcome with a small charge. Free parking is a nice touch for exploring downtown,

freeing up time you might have spent finding parking at downtown garages or meters. The airport shuttle must be reserved an hour in advance. Located in the shadow of Wells Fargo Arena, literally just off I-235 at the 3rd Street exit—make sure you're able to make the left turn into the hotel.

✳RENAISSANCE DES MOINES
SAVERY HOTEL $$–$$$
401 Locust St.
(515) 244-2151
www.renaissancehotels.com
This Marriott Hotel, which dates to 1919 and has 210 rooms, has plenty of history both inside and outside—the Georgian redbrick building is on the National Register of Historic Places, while numerous presidential candidates have occupied the hotel during Iowa's first-in-the-nation presidential caucuses. Several have stayed in the hotel's two huge penthouses, which together occupy the entire top floor of the 12-story structure.

Rooms are light and airy, with contemporary furniture and comfortable beds. Suites include a microwave and refrigerator. Some rooms have windows that look west at two of downtown's most interesting high-rises: the neo-gothic Equitable Building and the sleek, pointed spire of 801 Grand Ave. Downtown attractions are a short walk, including performances at the Civic Center, shopping in the East Village, and numerous restaurants. The hotel's 51 concierge rooms occupy 3 floors and include complimentary continental breakfast, evening snacks, and nonalcoholic beverages.

Valet parking is available and there's also a garage next door. Access to the downtown skywalk is on the second floor. There's no complimentary breakfast, although the hotel's restaurant offers a breakfast buffet as well as lunch and dinner. The first-floor lounge is a nice place to grab a drink before heading out for dinner. The hotel's basement is impressively equipped with a 24-hour fitness center, pool, sauna, steam room, and lockers.

The hotel's business center has a charge, although the staff will print out your boarding pass for free. Free Wi-Fi is available throughout the hotel. No pets are allowed. There's a free airport shuttle.

✳THE SUITES OF 800 LOCUST $$$$
800 Locust St.
(515) 288-5800
www.800Locust.com
Since undergoing an extensive renovation starting in 2001, this former downtown businessmen's club and Shrine Temple has emerged as a well-appointed, tasteful boutique hotel. Despite the name, not all rooms are 2-room suites—among the 51 units are some standard rooms, which are on the small side. Most standard rooms have a king bed, although a couple have 2 queen beds. Suites are either "fireplace suites," which have gas fireplaces, or "whirlpool suites," which include a fireplace as well.

Views from the rooms are nothing special, although the interiors help make up for it—especially the corner suites with vaulted ceilings. Some rooms have the building's original brick walls on the interior. The rooms away from Locust Street are noticeably quieter—request an interior room if you desire less street noise (the downside is that these rooms have much less natural light—their only exterior light source comes from the hotel's atrium). Two presidential suites each have a kitchen and full-size living room, as well as a glass shower and whirlpool tub.

Rooms include desk, refrigerator, coffeemaker, hair dryer, iron and ironing board, telephone, and complimentary Internet access and have an "honor bar" with beer and wine, soda, and snacks. The hotel has a spacious fitness center, including a sauna, steam room, and whirlpool, but no swimming pool. A 4,800-square-foot spa is also on-site.

No pets are allowed. Valet parking is available and there's also a garage across the street. Newspapers, including the *New York Times* and *Wall Street Journal,* are available for delivery to rooms. Use of the 24-hour business center is included in the rate, as is a cooked-to-order breakfast on the first floor, featuring eggs and waffles. It's served in the Cosmopolitan Lounge, which is a swank joint—if you've ever wanted to feel like you're on an episode of *Mad Men,* stroll up to the bar, order a stiff cocktail, and take in the old-school atmosphere (sometimes there's a piano player tickling the ivories in the corner). Other than breakfast, there is no restaurant in the hotel, but delivery is available from some of downtown's nicer restaurants, including Centro, Raccoon River Brewing Company, and 801 Chophouse.

East & North Sides

BAYMONT INN & SUITES
** DES MOINES $**
4685 NE 14th St.
(515) 265-4777 or (877) 229-6668
www.baymontinndesmoines.com
On the northeast edge of Des Moines, near the intersection of I-35/80, and I-235. The scenery outside is nothing special, but the rooms are clean and comfortable. This is a somewhat unique hotel, with suites like the "California King," which offers a bit more room than a typical suite, and 5 Jacuzzi suites, which include robes and candles (one even has a canopy bed). All rooms have minifridge and

microwave, as well as coffeemaker, hair dryer, iron, and ironing board. There's an indoor pool and whirlpool, free continental breakfast and newspaper, and free wireless Internet. No pets.

SLEEP INN & SUITES $$
5850 Morning Star Court, Pleasant Hill
(515) 299-9922 or (877) 424-6423
www.sleepinn.com
To the east of Des Moines and conveniently located for visits to both Adventureland Amusement Park and the Iowa State Fair, this hotel is a standard-issue budget hotel, but a decent value in the off-season (rates go up quite a bit during summertime, especially around the state fair). There are 77 rooms, all of which have microwave and refrigerator, coffeemaker, hair dryer, iron and ironing board, and telephones with voice mail. The hotel has several smoking rooms—take this into account if you're a nonsmoker. Free local calls and weekday newspaper are provided, and both wired and wireless Internet are free. The hotel has a free continental breakfast, fitness center, indoor pool, and guest laundry. The pet fee is very reasonable.

South Side

BEST WESTERN MARQUIS DES MOINES
AIRPORT HOTEL $$
1810 Army Post Rd.
(515) 287-6464 or (800) 780-7234
www.bestwestern.com
Right by the airport and near Blank Park Zoo, this hotel with 140 rooms has placed first in a readers' poll of Des Moines hotels. Rooms are clean and comfortable, with refrigerator and microwave, clock radio, coffeemaker, hair dryer, and iron and ironing board, plus desk and desk chair and nice touches like granite vanities in the bathrooms. Free wireless

Internet is available. The hotel has a business center with 2 computers. There's an indoor pool and whirlpool, as well as a fitness center, which even includes free use of the hotel's in-house personal trainer. Water fitness classes are offered as well. The hotel has both a complimentary hot breakfast and an in-house restaurant and bar, which stays open late on weekends. The shuttle runs 24 hours a day. Pets incur a fee.

HAMPTON INN DES MOINES
AIRPORT $$
5001 Fleur Dr.
(515) 287-7300 or (800) 426-7866
www.hamptoninndesmoinesairport.com
Across the street from the airport, this hotel boasts 121 comfortable rooms. (Barack Obama and his entourage took up some 90 rooms during a September 2010 visit to Des Moines and turned the place into a "mini White House," according to the staff.) There are no suites, just single rooms, some with a king bed and some with 2 queens All rooms have a 32-inch LCD television, clock radio, coffeemaker, hair dryer, iron and ironing board, telephones with private voice mail, and portable lap desk. Some rooms have a refrigerator and microwave and all offer free Wi-Fi. Smoking rooms are even available.

The hotel has a heated outdoor pool and a fitness center. There's a free business center, and dry-cleaning service is available. No pets are allowed. Even with the location, there's a free, 24-hour airport shuttle. An extensive hot breakfast buffet is available, as well as breakfast bags for those who don't have time to stop for breakfast. Meals can be ordered and delivered from nearby restaurants, including Baratta's, a longtime neighborhood Italian place and local favorite.

West Side

BEST WESTERN PLUS DES MOINES
WEST $
1450 NW 118th St., Clive
(515) 221-2345 or (866) 788-7013
www.bestwesternclive.com

Part of the cluster of hotels grouped around the intersection of I-235 and I-35/80, this 62-room hotel caters to business travelers but is a good value for leisure visitors to Des Moines as well. Rooms are simple but stylish, with either 1 king-size bed or 2 queens. Some rooms have microwave and refrigerator, and all rooms include hair dryer, alarm clock, coffeemaker, and iron and ironing board. Flat-panel televisions are gradually being added to all rooms. There's no extra charge for up to 2 additional guests.

A complimentary hot breakfast is served every morning, and the hotel is near several restaurants. Mon through Wed there's a reception in the late afternoon with free beer and snacks. The pool and spa are both saltwater and thus chlorine-free, part of a growing number of "green" pools that eschew chemicals. This hotel is very pet friendly: In addition to a very modest pet charge, there is a pet exercise area on the premises.

CHASE SUITES HOTEL $$
1428 Forest Ave., Clive
(515) 223-7700 or (888) 433-6140
www.chasehoteldesmoines.com

This 112-room all-suite hotel near the intersection of I-235 and I-35/80 maintains a cozy feel, with warm colors and mood lighting. Even the smaller "studio suites" have quite a bit of space, at 500 square feet, and like all other rooms have a refrigerator, microwave, and cooking range, as well as a pull-out sofa bed (there's no charge for an extra person in the room). Free high-speed Wi-Fi is available,

as are DVD player rentals, and there's a business center. Complimentary newspapers are provided to guests. The hotel has an outdoor pool and whirlpool, and a small fitness center, and guests also have free access to a nearby gym.

A complimentary breakfast buffet is served every morning, while a social hour offers free beer, wine, and snacks Mon through Thurs 5 to 6 p.m. Numerous franchise restaurants are located nearby.

The hotel shuttle runs to and from the airport as well as to destinations in a 5-mile radius, but it must be reserved 2 days in advance. Pets are allowed with a fee.

HAMPTON INN WEST DES MOINES $$
7060 Lake Dr., West Des Moines
(515) 223-4700 or (800) 426-7866
www.hamptoninn.com

Clustered along with several other hotels near the I-80/35 section in West Des Moines, this hotel is a good value, with clean rooms and comfortable beds, and near both Jordan Creek shopping center and Living History Farms. There are 135 rooms, including some larger rooms with whirlpools (no suites). Rooms include coffeemaker, hair dryer, iron and ironing board, and desk with chair. Smoking rooms are available. The hotel has free wireless Internet, as well as a business center. There's a buffet breakfast as well as a reception with complimentary beverages, and room service is available. An indoor pool and whirlpool are on-site, too. No pets.

HILTON GARDEN INN DES MOINES/
URBANDALE $$
8600 Northpark Dr., Johnston
(515) 270-8890 or (877) 782-9444
www.desmoinesurbandale
.gardeninn.com

A more upscale choice among suburban chain lodgings, this hotel is a good choice for business travelers, with rooms equipped with work desks, ergonomic chairs, and free high-speed Internet. It's also conveniently located near Living History Farms, just a few miles down I-35/80. The cool, airy interiors include an atrium lobby and slightly larger rooms. The 148 rooms come with a choice of 1 king bed or 2 queens. All rooms have refrigerator, microwave, coffeemaker, dual-line phones with voice mail, hair dryer, and iron and ironing board. The hotel restaurant serves breakfast, lunch, and dinner and has an attached lounge. Evening room service is available as well, as are a fitness room, indoor pool, sauna, and whirlpool. The free airport shuttle is nice for a hotel this far outside the city, but it requires 24-hour advance notification. No pets allowed.

HILTON GARDEN INN WEST DES MOINES $$
205 S. 64th St., West Des Moines
(515) 223-0571 or (877) 782-9444
www.hiltongardeninn.com

A reasonably priced option, open since 2006 out on the fast-growing fringe of Des Moines's biggest suburb. Conveniently located right by Jordan Creek Town Center, the Des Moines area's newest, biggest shopping center (you can walk to the mall from the hotel), as well as numerous franchise restaurants. Comfortable rooms include microwave and refrigerator, clock radio, hair dryer, iron, and ironing board, as well as desk and lounge chair. The on-site restaurant includes breakfast, which is cooked to order and includes pancakes, omelets, and waffles. Room service is available as well. The hotel has a few smoking rooms. There's no airport shuttle, but a shuttle is available that runs anywhere within 5 miles of the hotel. No pets.

HOLIDAY INN EXPRESS AT DRAKE $$
1140 24th St.
(515) 255-4000
www.hiexpress.com/dsm-drakeuniv

This small, spartan hotel is lacking in amenities but is very convenient and a good value if you are visiting Drake University, 1 block away. There are 52 rooms, all with 2 queen beds. Rooms are nothing special but are decent-sized and have a coffeemaker, iron and ironing board, hair dryer, and clock radio. There's no additional charge for an extra person in the room.

Free Wi-Fi is available throughout the hotel. A basic breakfast is included, and a complimentary USA Today newspaper is provided. There's no restaurant in the hotel, although the Drake Diner, which has plenty of cheap and tasty offerings on the menu, is right next door. There's no pool, no business center, and no airport shuttle. No pets are allowed.

MARRIOTT WEST DES MOINES $$
1250 Jordan Creek Pkwy., West Des Moines
(515) 267-1500 or (888) 236-2427
www.marriott.com

On the outskirts of West Des Moines, this full-service hotel has a friendly and helpful staff who can help you find your way to nearby restaurants and attractions. There are 219 rooms, which are large and comfortable and have either a king or 2 queen beds. Rooms include clock radio, coffeemaker, hair dryer, iron and ironing board, and desk with chair. There's a nice indoor pool. No complimentary breakfast, but a restaurant and bar are on-site. A shuttle runs 7 a.m. to 11 p.m. Pets incur a somewhat steep fee.

**RAMADA TROPICS RESORT
& CONFERENCE CENTER** $–$$
5000 Merle Hay Rd.
(515) 278-0271 or (800) 272-6232
www.ramada.com

A full-blown water resort with an 18,000-square-foot indoor waterpark that has 4 pools, two 150-foot tube slides, a poolside tiki bar, and over 400 parking spaces, this is more of a destination in and of itself. In fact, it's not the most attractive or convenient location, on a busy commercial strip just north of Merle Hay Mall way up in the northwest corner of Des Moines, but it's not a bad value, either, with waterpark passes included in the rate. Among the 166 rooms, regular rooms have a refrigerator and microwave, safe, coffeemaker, hair dryer, clock radio, and iron and ironing board. There's no charge for additional people in the room.

There's a business center, free Wi-Fi throughout the resort, guest laundry, and fitness room. No pets are allowed. An on-site bar and grill is one dining option—there are also several franchise restaurants nearby.

SHERATON WEST DES MOINES $$
1800 50th St., West Des Moines
(515) 223-1800
www.starwoodhotels.com

This large chain hotel rises up above the intersection of I-35/80 and I-235 on the western edge of the city, making it a good location to reach just about anywhere in the metro area quickly. There are 285 rooms, with desk, coffeemaker, radio, hair dryer, iron, and ironing board. Suites also have a refrigerator and microwave. Numerous chain restaurants and shopping centers are nearby. There's a fitness center and indoor pool but no whirlpool. The convenient airport shuttle runs hourly. Pets incur a refundable deposit.

STONEY CREEK INN $$
5291 Stoney Creek Court, Johnston
(515) 334-9000 or (800) 659-2220
www.stoneycreekinn.com

This outpost of a chain of Northwoods-themed hotels is located in a small cluster of suburban lodgings several miles from downtown Des Moines. With its fishing- and hunting-themed rooms, this hotel is popular for business conferences, but it's a nice option for families as well, with an indoor-outdoor "swim-through" pool and game room. They really do take the hunting-lodge theme to the limit—this place has touches like knotty-pine staircases and rocking chairs in front of the lobby fireplace. Still, rooms are clean and comfortable, with either 1 king bed or 2 doubles. Some rooms have microwave and refrigerator, and all have a desk, lounge chair, coffeemaker, hair dryer, and telephone with voice mail and free local calls.

The hotel serves a sumptuous breakfast every morning, with coffee available 24 hours a day. The on-site lounge is a nice spot to relax, and there are restaurants nearby. In addition to the pool, there's a whirlpool, sauna, and fitness center, as well as a guest laundry and business center. No pets are allowed. A free airport shuttle is a nice perk, since this hotel is some distance from the airport, but it requires 24-hour advance notification.

**TOWNE PLACE SUITES DES MOINES
URBANDALE** $$
8800 Northpark Dr., Johnston
(515) 727-4066 or (888) 236-2427

This extended-stay hotel is not a bad value for families visiting Des Moines, and it's conveniently located near the interstate that forms a beltway around the city. There are

116 rooms on 4 stories. Rooms are good-sized, if not overly large, and include a sitting area with sofa, as well as alarm clock, hair dryer, iron and ironing board, and desk with ergonomic chair. Fully equipped kitchens have stovetop and dishwasher as well as refrigerator and microwave. A complimentary continental breakfast is provided, as are "grab and go" breakfast bags. A variety of restaurants are nearby.

There's an indoor pool and guest laundry. Pets are welcome, but there's a rather steep fee to bring them in. The hotel is located on the same block as the Hilton Garden Inn, and you may be able to use the airport shuttle, but you'll have to reserve well in advance and won't be able to use it at all on weekends.

RESTAURANTS

Des Moines's dining scene has grown much more interesting in recent years thanks in large part to a number of innovative chefs who have introduced new flavors and fresh ingredients to restaurant menus. You may find yourself admiring the bounty of produce at the farmers' market on Saturday morning and then see some of the same items turn up on your plate that same evening. Chefs have also taken their skills to that Iowa staple, the pig, transforming slabs of Nieman Ranch pork into some truly delicious creations. Aficionados of old-school red-meat meals will easily find some good steakhouses and barbecue joints, as well as purveyors of Iowa's ubiquitous pork tenderloin sandwich.

Yet the city has offerings well beyond the stereotypical midwestern meat and potatoes: Des Moines now boasts numerous Asian restaurants, including good selections in Thai, Vietnamese, and Indian, and even a place offering the cuisine of Hawaii! Skilled sushi chefs are found in Des Moines as well, with sushi bars sprinkled around downtown and outlying areas.

Many of these restaurants, including the fancier ones, are located in strip shopping centers along main roads, which makes for easy parking. Even Des Moines's fancier restaurants are casual in terms of dress code. Hours vary, but you're more likely to find late-night bites at trendier spots in the East Village and Ingersoll Avenue neighborhoods.

OVERVIEW

This chapter is organized by cuisine type, but it is worth checking out all the categories, as menus at American restaurants vary widely and Italian restaurants may have good pizza, for example.

Local weeklies *Juice* and *Cityview* publish restaurant reviews in print and online, as does the *Des Moines Register* online and in its datebook section, which comes out on Thursday. The site Metromix Des Moines (http://desmoines.metromix.com) has an extensive compendium of restaurant listings.

Under the Iowa Smokefree Air Act, passed in 2008, all restaurants in Iowa are nonsmoking.

Price Code

The price code in this chapter is based on the average price of two dinner entrees, excluding cocktails, wine, appetizers, desserts, tax, and tip. Unless otherwise noted, restaurants accept major credit cards.

$ . . . . Less than $20
$$ . . . . $20 to $40
$$$ . . . . $40 to $60
$$$$ . . . . More than $60

Quick Index by Name

A Dong, Des Moines, Vietnamese, $, 57

Alba, Des Moines, American, $$$, 33

Alohana Hawaiian Grill, Clive, Hawaiian, $, 45

Bagni di Lucca, Des Moines, Pizza, $, 52

Baratta's, Des Moines, Italian, $$, 46

Baru 66, Windsor Heights, French, $$$$, 43

Bistro Montage, Des Moines, French, $$$, 43

Centro, Des Moines, Italian, $$$, 47

Chef's Kitchen, Des Moines, American, $$, 33

Christopher's, Des Moines, Pizza, $$, 52

Cindy's Corner Cafe, Urbandale, Breakfast Joints, $, 37

Coach's Pizza, West Des Moines, Pizza, $, 53

The Continental, Des Moines, Tapas, $$, 55

Cool Basil, Clive, Thai, $$, 56

Court Avenue Restaurant & Brewing Co., Des Moines, Brewpubs & Microbreweries, $$, 37

Django, Des Moines, French, $$$, 44

Dos Rios Cantina and Tequila Lounge, Des Moines, Mexican, $$, 51

Drake Diner, Des Moines, American, $$, 34

801 Chophouse, Des Moines, Steakhouses, $$$$, 54

Flying Mango, Des Moines, Barbecue, $$, 36

Gateway Market Cafe, Des Moines, American, $, 34

Happi Sushi, Des Moines, Japanese & Sushi, $, 49

Hoshi, Des Moines, Japanese & Sushi, $$, 50

India Star, Des Moines, Indian, $$, 45

Irina's Restaurant & Bar, Des Moines, Russian, $$, 53

Java Joe's, Des Moines, Coffeehouses, $, 40

Jesse's Embers, Des Moines, Steakhouses, $$, 54

Johnny's Italian Steakhouse, Des Moines, Steakhouses, $$$, 55

Kwong Tung Restaurant, Des Moines, Chinese, $-$$, 39

La Mie, Des Moines, French, $$, 44

Lucca, Des Moines, Italian, $$$, 47

Maccabee's Deli, Des Moines, Delis, $, 41

Machine Shed, Urbandale, American, $$, 34

Mars Cafe, Des Moines, Coffeehouses, $, 40

Maxie's, West Des Moines, American, $$, 34

Miyabi 9, Des Moines, Japanese & Sushi, $$, 50

Mojos on 86th, Johnston, Contemporary Fine Dining, $$$, 42

Namaste Indian Groceries and Kitchen, Clive, Indian, $$, 45

Noah's Ark Ristorante, Des Moines, Italian, $$, 47

Nut Pob, Des Moines, Thai, $$, 57

Olympic Flame, Des Moines, Greek, $, 44

Open Sesame, Des Moines, Middle Eastern, $$, 52

Palmer's Deli & Market, Des Moines, Delis, $, 41

Paradise Pizza Cafe, West Des Moines, Pizza, $$, 53

Proof, Des Moines, Mediterranean, $$, 50

Raccoon River Brewing Company, Des Moines, Brewpubs & Microbreweries, $$, 38

Red China Bistro, Des Moines, Chinese, $$, 39

Ritual Cafe, Des Moines, Coffeehouses, $, 40

Sam & Gabe's Italian Bistro, Urbandale, Italian, $$$, 48

Sbrocco Wine Bar & Wine Shop, Des Moines, Contemporary Fine Dining, $$$, 42

Skip's, Des Moines, American, $$, 35

Smokey Row Coffee House & Soda Fountain, Des Moines, Coffeehouses, $, 40

South Union Bread Cafe, Des Moines, Delis, $, 41

Star Bar, Des Moines, American, $$, 36

Ted's Coney Island, Des Moines, Fast Food, $, 42

Trostel's Dish, Clive, Tapas, $$, 56

Tumea and Sons, Des
Moines, Italian, $$, 48
Tursi's Latin King, Des
Moines, Italian, $$, 49
Uncle Wendell's BBQ, Des
Moines, Barbecue, $, 36

Waterfront Seafood Market,
West Des Moines, Seafood,
$$, 54
Waveland Cafe, Des Moines,
Breakfast Joints, $, 37

Woody's Smoke Shack, Des
Moines, Barbecue, $$, 36
Zanzibar's Coffee
Adventure, Des Moines,
Coffeehouses, $, 41

AMERICAN

✳ALBA   **$$$**
524 E. 6th St.
(515) 244-0261
www.albadsm.com
At first glance, this restaurant on the edge of
the East Village looks like a rather standard
dining room, with an open kitchen facing a
long, curving bar and tables filling the din-
ing room. In the kitchen, however, Alba has
an exciting take on new American cooking,
with dishes like pork loin with chorizo and
pickled apples alongside Yukon potatoes,
and enticing short ribs braised with Guin-
ness stout and served with mustard spaetzle,
Roma tomatoes, and carrots. Iowa native
Jason Simon has returned home to run this
restaurant in a converted auto showroom.
His preparations also include first courses
like venison and apple ragu with Peppadew
peppers and an intriguing cocoa parpadelle
and acorn squash gnocchi with apples,
pumpkin seed oil, and toasted pecans—the
light flavoring of the oil mixes with the nuts
to make a light and crispy combination. Per-
haps even better is the chive potato gnocchi,
served with either chicken or prawns and
crème fraîche—the cream and herbs make
a perfect topping. Good lighter options
include a rabbit stew with shiitake mush-
rooms, faro, leeks, and thyme and delectable
caramelized brussels sprouts, served with an
anchovy vinaigrette and pickled red onion.
Molten chocolate cake and homemade ice

cream are both fabulous finishes. Closed
Sunday and Monday.

i Des Moines restaurant week in
August offers a great value for
diners looking to sample the local din-
ing scene, with numerous restaurants
around town offering 3-course dinners
for one set price. Past participants have
included everything from fine French
bistros to local brewpubs and diners.
Contact the Convention and Visitors
Bureau for more information.

CHEF'S KITCHEN   **$$**
1903 Beaver Ave.
(515) 255-4411
http://order.letsorderonline.com
/display/menu/chefskitchen
This family-friendly place in a residential
section of Des Moines feels like you could
be in somebody's dining room—it's a nice,
low-key neighborhood spot with simple,
well-prepared food. The menu is pretty
much straightforward steaks and seafood,
and the steaks are quite good—they're skill-
fully broiled and don't overwhelm the palate
like they do in some steakhouses. Fish can
be hit-or-miss, but the baked salmon has
just the right hints of lemon and garlic. The
menu also has pasta and pizza, which aren't
bad either, especially the pizzas, which have
a crispy crust and a thick red sauce with just
the right amount of spiciness. Desserts are
good if unexciting, and there's a jar of free

RESTAURANTS

chocolate chip cookies on the bar as you head out.

DRAKE DINER $$
1111 25th St.
(515) 277-1111
www.thedrakediner.com
With a phone-book-size menu, black-and-white tile floor, and din of conversation filling the narrow dining room, this is an authentic diner through and through. Famous for their chili, they also do a mean burger, with Maytag blue cheese, sautéed onions or mushrooms, or any other number of toppings. Any diner worth its salt has to get breakfast right, and the Drake does not disappoint: All day it serves pancakes that are light and fluffy, and omelets that are perfect half-circles with a wide choice of fillings, like mushrooms, onions, and peppers. Dinners tend toward heavier entrees like meatloaf and fried chicken, but there's also a long list of dinner salads, including Cobb, spinach, and smoked salmon. Don't leave without trying the apple butter bread pudding or one of the extra-thick milk shakes. Just a block from the Drake campus, it fills up with students, professors, and neighborhood folks, particularly at lunchtime and on weekends.

GATEWAY MARKET CAFE $
2002 Woodland Ave.
(515) 422-5109
Sharing space with the namesake market just off M. L. King Jr. Parkway in the Western Gateway, this popular, unpretentious cafe serves up a short-order version of favorite items from around the world. Sandwiches are big and tasty, like the Cuban stuffed with hot roast pork and Nieman Ranch ham and slathered with mustard on ciabatta (all the bread comes from the nearby South Union

Bakery), or the spicy blackened tuna with crisp lettuce. Asian shrimp salad, fish and chips, fish tacos, and pad thai show up on the menu as well, adding to the international flavor. They do a yummy breakfast, with huevos rancheros, a wide selection of omelets, and a perfect bowl of oatmeal with maple syrup and brown sugar among the offerings. You may have to hunt for a spot in the parking lot during the lunch rush, but the efficient staff keeps things moving along.

MACHINE SHED $$
11151 Hickman Rd., Urbandale
(515) 270-6818
www.machineshed.com
Located adjacent to the Living History Farms attractions, this is a no-frills, old-fashioned country restaurant, dishing out big portions of down-home favorites like chicken-fried steak, meatloaf, potpie, and fried chicken. Don't expect gourmet cooking or subtle seasonings, merely hearty, meat-and-potatoes fare. A nod to Iowa comes with the 1-pound burger topped with Maytag blue cheese and numerous pork entrees, including chops, tenderloins, and a prime cut of pork served with a mushroom wine sauce and Parmesan butter crust. Known for their breakfasts as well, with the monster cinnamon rolls being especially notable.

MAXIE'S $$
1311 Grand Ave., West Des Moines
(515) 223-1463
www.mymaxies.com
The facade at this longtime West Des Moines family favorite is a windowless brick wall. Inside, however, it's a comfy, homelike atmosphere with an all-American menu of steaks, seafood, and pasta. The seafood selection is particularly extensive, with numerous

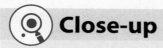 # Close-up

Pork Tenderloin Sandwiches

If there is one iconic Iowa food item, this is it: It seems like everywhere throughout the state, from Des Moines on down to the tiniest rural hamlet, has a place serving up these flat slabs of pork, which are pounded and tenderized before being breaded, deep-fried, and served on a plain white hamburger bun. At some places you can get sandwiches with a meat patty that measures nearly a foot across! (You may want to eschew side orders if you plan to eat the whole thing.)

Purists may be horrified if you order yours with cheese—the classic toppings are mustard, pickles, and raw onions. Locals tend to be fiercely loyal to their particular sandwich joint and will go to lengths to tell you why it's the best. Though you can find the sandwich at eateries ranging from roadside stands to fine dining establishments, it's a good bet that if you spot a no-frills building on which tenderloins are the main, if not only, item on the menu, they do a good piece of pork.

Three good choices for tenderloins in Des Moines are:

- **B&B Grocery, Meat & Deli.** 2001 SE 6th St.; (515) 243-7607; www.bbgrocerymeatdeli.com.

- **Mr. Bibb's.** 2705 Sixth Ave.; (515) 243-0929.

- **Smitty's.** 1401 SW Army Post Rd.; (515) 287-4742; www.smittystenderloins.com.

combinations of fish, including shrimp, clams, and scallops, as well as a few fillets. There are numerous lobster and crab leg dinners as well, with lots of side dishes to go with the seafood. The restaurant is especially proud of its prime aged top sirloin, broiled to perfection and laden with plenty of side dishes as well. Pasta choices include spaghetti and meatballs, lasagna, and fettuccine Alfredo. Kids' menu available. Closed Sunday.

SKIP'S   **$$**
4000 Fleur Dr.
(515) 287-1820
www.skipsdesmoines.com
Open for nearly 30 years, Skip's steadfastly refuses to be trendy—and its large crowd of regulars love that fact. Good, all-American food—and stiff drinks—are served up at this

old white frame house near the Des Moines airport, with a nice selection of steaks, seafood, and pasta. Pan-fried walleye and blackened salmon are both good fish choices, especially when accompanied by white cheddar scalloped potatoes. Their specialty is Des Moines's signature dish of Steak de Burgo, a filet cut into two medallions, sautéed in a garlic and herb butter sauce, and then topped with mushrooms. Pasta dishes can be just as rich, with cavatelli noodles topped with Italian sausage and melted mozzarella and blackened chicken pasta served with a Cajun cream sauce. Don't leave without trying one of the classic desserts, including dark chocolate cake, hot apple crisp, and bread pudding. Reservations not accepted. Closed Sunday.

STAR BAR $$
2811 Ingersoll Ave.
(515) 244-0790
www.starbardsm.com
The setting is deceptive: The redbrick exterior and a dim dining room with long, dark wood bar packed with a younger crowd make this look like a basic drinking den, but it's actually much more than your typical bar and grill. The extensive menu features both adventurous choices and all-American favorites. Small plates like pork dumplings and sesame crusted ahi tuna with ginger and wasabi are respectable Asian options, while the onion rings with chipotle sauce and garlic and Parmesan fries give a new twist to some old standbys. The several burgers on the menu are all good bets, from the southwest burger topped with Pepper Jack and avocado salsa, to the more standard one with bacon, grilled onions, and cheddar. Lots of other sandwiches on the menu, too, like a Cuban with roasted pork, ham and Swiss cheese, or a steak sandwich with caramelized onions, arugula, and aioli. Entrees are an eclectic selection of cuisines, bringing pan-fried chicken, blackened catfish tacos, and Cajun pasta with andouille sausage all under the same roof. Lighter fare includes a sesame-encrusted ahi tuna salad. Open into the wee hours.

BARBECUE

FLYING MANGO $$
4345 Hickman Rd.
(515) 255-4111
www.flyingmango.com
A southern-fried barbecue joint in a residential neighborhood, with elegant touches like tablecloths and the paintings of Mississippi Delta artist H. C. Porter on the warm orange walls. Fortunately, the subtlety doesn't extend to the 'cue: Ribs and brisket are big, thick, and meaty, with smoky goodness oozing out of the thick slabs. The chicken and pork aren't bad either. The menu has plenty of other southern touches, like Cajun shrimp with dirty rice, as well as a Latin strip steak with chimichurri sauce (similar to pesto). If you still have room for dessert, there are some tempting offerings. Parking is a challenge in the restaurant's tiny lot, but it's worth seeking out a space nearby to chow down on the smoked meats. (They also do carryout.) Closed Sunday and Monday.

UNCLE WENDELL'S BBQ $
2716 Ingersoll Ave.
(515) 288-3207
www.unclewendells.com
The flames painted on the walls and simple counter where you place your order let you know that you don't come here for the decor—or for fine dining. This is a no-apologies, unpretentious barbecue stand, where the staff focuses on dishing out big helpings of smoked meats that are then slathered with a selection of sauces (you pump your own from large plastic jugs). Pulled pork, beef, and brisket are good and tender, with plenty of smoky flavor and a nice crispy skin. Side dishes, including baked beans, cole slaw and potato salad, are an okay accompaniment to the meat, which is the star. Ribs turn up as a special item during the week. The jambalaya and barbecue chili are fairly tasty and come with corn bread to mop up the bottom of the bowl.

WOODY'S SMOKE SHACK $$
2511 Cottage Grove Ave.
(515) 277-0005
www.woodyssmokeshack.com
A line forms every day at lunchtime in this cramped room a few blocks from the Drake

campus, diners drawn in by the sweet, smoky smell wafting up from behind the low, brick building (dinnertime is a little less hectic). A good value is the "meal deal," with a choice of smoked brisket, ham, pulled pork, chicken, or ribs. The pulled pork is especially succulent and tender, and the ribs are fall-off-the-bone wonderful, with a rub that's not too spicy (you pick the sauce to squirt on the meat). Ribs are a limited item—they smoke only a certain amount each day, so get there early if you want to try them. A pan of free corn bread is set out for diners, and it's a crusty, filling delight. Side dishes aren't bad, with crispy coleslaw a particular standout. Woody's does daily specials like smoked salmon on Thurs. Yummy homemade pies are wonderful if you haven't already filled up on the 'cue. An outdoor patio provides a nice alfresco dining experience in warmer months. Closed Sunday.

BREAKFAST JOINTS

CINDY'S CORNER CAFE $
2731 100th St., Urbandale
(515) 868-0200
This warm, cozy room popular with locals is not too far from the hotels clustered near the intersection of I-35/80 and I-235. The menu is fairly standard, with the pancakes and waffles light and fluffy, and omelets offered with different fillings. Big breakfast offerings like steak and eggs and a hungry-man plate will fill up those who have a big appetite, and at a fairly low price. Good coffee, too. Also serves lunch, with several good sandwiches and salads. A kids' menu is available.

WAVELAND CAFE $
4708 University Ave.
(515) 279-4341

Grab a seat at the L-shaped counter or one of the vinyl booths in this cramped little neighborhood breakfast joint. All the standards are on the menu: egg dishes, pancakes (with fresh fruit or chocolate), French toast, and pigs-in-a-blanket. The eggs can be a little overcooked, but the hash browns are a perfect crispiness and the coffee is hot and good—regulars keep their mugs on hooks behind the counter. The Lumberman is a plateful of hash browns topped with 2 biscuits and a generous portion of white gravy that tastes of sausage, with a peppery kick. Lunch is served as well, but breakfast is the real draw: Lots of locals crowd the room, beginning when the door opens in the morning, including students from nearby Roosevelt High School.

BREWPUBS & MICROBREWERIES

COURT AVENUE RESTAURANT & BREWING CO. $$
309 Court Ave.
(515) 282-BREW
www.courtavebrew.com
An all-American brewpub serving all-American food: Big steaks and chops are featured here, including a 16-ounce prime rib, a delectable grilled rib eye with truffle creamed corn and roasted red potatoes, and bacon-wrapped pork tenderloin medallions with a black-currant wine sauce and white cheddar mashed potatoes and vegetables on the side. There are plenty of tasty lighter options, too, including pesto chicken pasta, a vegetarian burrito with falafel, black beans and Spanish rice served alongside mixed greens, fresh salsa, sour cream and southwest ranch dressing. Now, about the beer: It's good. Brewed on-site are such beers as a Belgian white, a nutty brown ale, a deep, dark stout, and an Indian Pale Ale known

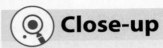 Close-up

Des Moines's Farmers' Markets & Sweet Corn Stands

Perhaps no place is better suited than Des Moines for Farmers' Markets. Farmers from around the state—not to mention other regions of the country—truck produce into town faithfully every weekend during growing and harvest season. The downtown farmers' market draws in throngs on Court Street, between the Polk County Courthouse and the Des Moines River, every Saturday starting at 7 a.m. from May 1 until the end of October, giving residents and visitors alike the chance to pick up some fresh fruits and vegetables, including ample cucumbers, ruby-red ripe tomatoes, crispy heads of lettuce, bushels of potatoes, and yellow gourds of squash.

Plenty of bakeries and restaurants set up shop along Court Street as well, and there are lots of free samples to be found, everything from cured beef sticks to fresh mozzarella and goat cheese and sweet baked goods. There's an international flair to the market, with crepes coming out of the pan down the street from a popular *pupusa* stand dishing up the unique Salvadoran snack, as well as Southeast Asian vendors offering lemongrass and other items used in the cooking of their homelands.

Outside of downtown there are also weekly markets around Drake University and Valley Junction in West Des Moines, as well as in surrounding communities—check local newspapers for dates and times.

Sweet corn stands are found on corners of major throughways in Des Moines throughout the summer—it's usually only a few bucks for several ears. Admittedly, it doesn't make sense if you're just visiting and staying in a hotel, but it's a nice little slice of Iowa, and a good place to take a photo commemorating your trip.

---

as Honest Lawyer. There's also a homemade root beer brewed with Iowa honey and a ginger beer with just the right amount of zip. Desserts are simple and satisfying, like a chocolate cheesecake and a bread pudding with caramel and whipped cream. The surroundings are dark wood and deep booths in a building that served as a saddlery in the 1880s. Take a look at the giant tanks used to brew the beer while you're there. Open 7 days a week.

**RACCOON RIVER
BREWING COMPANY**   **$$**
200 10th St.
(515) 362-5222
www.raccoonbrew.com

If you're hungry for a burger, this Western Gateway joint can set you up: The kitchen has found many ways to cook and serve up 8 ounces of beef, including toppings of onion rings and Gouda, Pepper Jack, and chipotle mayo. Other sandwiches are good for washing down with some of the house beers brewed in big copper tanks on display, including a beer-battered fish sandwich and a brisket sandwich with both barbecue and horseradish crème sauce on the side. Carnivore options are a good choice as well, such as the beef tips Gorgonzola with penne pasta, mushroom, and red onion. There are plenty of other choices on the extensive menu, including slow-smoked barbecued ribs with a beer-based sauce, linguine with hazelnut mushroom pesto, and panko-encrusted halibut with lemon butter sauce and garlic mashed potatoes. Pizzas include a Mediterranean variety with roasted red pepper, pine nuts, artichoke hearts, and sun-dried tomatoes and a pie with locally made Italian sausage. On the lighter side there's a good Thai Cobb salad. The house beers run the gamut from light to heavy, with an especially deep Stonecutter stout. Try a beer flight to sample three varieties of suds. The dining room has a clubby feel, with high booths and hardwood floors, but the casual menu and atmosphere also make it a nice place for families. Closed Sunday. The bar stays open late on weekends.

CHINESE

KWONG TUNG RESTAURANT $–$$
2721 Ingersoll Ave.
(515) 244-8813
The lengthy menu at this cozy Ingersoll Avenue spot has some tasty dishes, with especially good appetizers like barbecue riblets and spring rolls, but the real attraction here is dim sum, served Sun 10 a.m. to 2 p.m. While servers don't wheel the dim sum to the tables in carts, they do provide picture menus showing the extensive selections. The steamed barbecue pork buns are as fluffy and light as a pillow, with succulent meat inside. The many noodle dishes have plenty of good flavor and are fun to eat. More exotic choices include chicken feet in black bean sauce or curried squid. Lo Mai Gai is sticky rice and Chinese sausage wrapped in lotus leaves, and goes down well with hot mustard or chili sauce. Sweet items are yummy too, like sesame balls, sort of a Chinese doughnut filled with sweet red bean paste. Decor is classic Chinese restaurant,

with stylized dragons and country scenes on the walls and paper lanterns hanging from the ceiling. If you aren't there for the dim sum, try one of the family dinners, most of which include the excellent crab rangoon and a large selection of entrees like almond or cashew chicken, Szechwan shrimp, and several stir-fried choices, as well as old stand-bys like General Tso's Chicken. Only dim sum on Sun. Parking is a little tricky on busy Ingersoll Avenue.

RED CHINA BISTRO $$
2925 Ingersoll Ave.
(515) 274-0097
A relaxed, fun place with a sleek, modern design. The menu mixes things up a bit, with fusion choices like spinach chicken dumplings and South Asian beef stew, but reliable Chinese favorites are here as well, like cashew chicken, pot stickers, and orange chicken. The so-called small plates are ample enough for a meal, including some of the largest spring rolls you'll ever see, served with a tantalizing ginger dipping sauce, and good-size spicy chicken rolls. Curries are thick and creamy, and Mongolian beef manages to be a good blend of hearty and spicy. Many items come with a choice of beef or shrimp, and some entrees have whimsical names like Kung Pao Wow. Dishes include basil chicken, snow pea shrimp, pepper steak, Laos curry chicken, and some yummy lo mein noodles. Salads include vermicelli with a choice of spring rolls, curry beef, herb or spicy chicken or vegetable roll as well as pad thai and Asian chicken salads. Dashing bartenders whip up some inspired cocktail creations from behind the black lacquered bar. Stays open late Mon through Sat nights, and offers Sunday brunch.

COFFEEHOUSES

JAVA JOE'S $
214 4th St.
(515) 288-5282
www.javajoescoffeehouse.com
This high-ceilinged, hardwood-floored hangout is filled with the warm smell of fresh-roasted house blend and other, more exotic strains of coffee, thanks to the large roaster that sits in the front window. This is a great place for a pit stop if you hit the farmers' market on a Saturday morning. You may not find a table, but it's just as much fun to take your drink outside and people-watch. Or go at a less busy time and sink into one of the leather couches with a good book and a drink—they serve beer, wine, and nonalcoholic drinks as well as a full slate of coffees, espressos, cappuccinos, and lattes. The food menu is eclectic: It's virtually all vegetarian, with choices like ginger curry, potatoes, chickpeas, lentils, and red beans. The staff scoops up ice cream from a glass case in front of the counter.

MARS CAFE $
2318 University Ave.
(515) 369-6277
www.marscafe.net
Drake University students and neighborhood residents patronize this cafe for coffee and conversation, and it's also one of the city's better-kept secrets for Saturday or Sunday brunch. The menu is simple but fun and tasty: French toast is made with good, thick challah bread and comes with a selection of toppings, including berries, bananas, or chocolate. The ham and eggs have a twist: lavender Dijon (it's an acquired taste). Sandwiches and salads are also on the menu. The high-ceilinged, art-hung interior is also the perfect spot to grab a favorite

drink and take in the scene. In addition to coffee drinks, beer and wine are available, and the espresso shakes are thick, creamy, and delicious.

RITUAL CAFE $
1301 Locust St.
(515) 288-4872
www.ritualcafe.com
Looking for a hippie-ish coffee spot in Des Moines? This is the place, with the requisite Tibetan prayer flags and tie-dyed decor. It also whips up some tasty basic breakfasts, like oatmeal, eggs, bagels, and yogurt with hemp granola. There's also sandwiches like hummus with vegetables and a veggie po'boy with grilled peppers, onions, and marinated artichoke hearts. Hot drinks include the usual spread of mochas, cappuccinos, and other coffee options, as well as Cafe Cubano and Yerba Mate. Beer and wine, too, as well as smoothies packed with healthy stuff like protein powder and Vita Boost. Closed Sunday.

SMOKEY ROW COFFEE HOUSE
& SODA FOUNTAIN $
1910 Cottage Grove Ave.
(515) 244-2611
www.smokeyrow.com
Look for the old-fashioned blue neon sign outside this bustling joint just off I-235, straddling the dividing line between the Western Gateway and Ingersoll Avenue neighborhoods in the shadow of a redbrick church bell tower. Sunlight streams through the full-length plateglass windows and into the high-ceilinged rooms. In addition to a wide selection of coffee and tea drinks, there's a full menu of salads and sandwiches, including burgers and panini, as well as ice cream treats like sundaes, shakes, and phosphates.

Breakfast is served all day, with egg sandwiches, quiche, and giant cinnamon rolls among the offerings.

ZANZIBAR'S COFFEE ADVENTURE $
2723 Ingersoll Ave.
(515) 244-7694
www.zanzibarscoffee.com
A narrow little coffeehouse with some strong java. Their daily fresh blend might include coffee from New Guinea, Ethiopia, Hawaii, or points even farther. The selection of blended drinks has international touches as well, like a Mocha Mex with Mexican spiced hot chocolate, espresso, and steamed milk. There's a small breakfast menu with dishes like Eggs Expresso, which are steamed in the espresso machine and come out light and fluffy. With plants in the corners, stained glass in the windows, and a pressed-tin ceiling, there's a funky little vibe, and it's a nice spot to sit over coffee, even if tables are a little small.

DELIS

MACCABEE'S DELI $
1150 Polk Blvd.
(515) 277-1718
www.maccabeeskosherdeli.com
A corner of Brooklyn has landed in this cramped sandwich shop in a west-side residential neighborhood, on the first floor of a brick building housing the Iowa Lubavitch. Corned beef, pastrami, and other meats are piled high and hot on rye bread. For hungry eaters there are one-third-pound sandwiches, and for the truly decadent, try the Whole Megillah, with two-thirds of a pound of meat! Side dishes include good potato salad and coleslaw. Add a knish and a Dr. Brown's soda from the cooler, and you're all set.

PALMER'S DELI & MARKET $
2843 Ingersoll Ave.
(515) 274-4004
www.palmersdeliandmarket.com
A high-volume, bustling soup, sandwich, and salad joint that fills up with office workers at lunchtime and is a nice spot for a light dinner as well. Menu boards at several deli stations list what's on offer. A real highlight is the seemingly endless selection of sandwiches with fresh-cut meats and plenty of filling. The Reuben is piled high and hot with corned beef, pastrami, or turkey, while The Wave brings together albacore tuna, colby jack, and provolone grilled on sourdough bread. Meat lovers will enjoy JP's Favorite with ham, pastrami, and bacon, and there's also a vegetarian sandwich and some good salads, including a nice Cobb, a Caesar, and a Greek salad with the deli's own dressing. The chili is delicious and perfect for a good hot fix on a cold winter day. There are several other locations in the Des Moines metro area, including the Kaleidoscope Mall on the downtown skyway. Closed Sunday.

SOUTH UNION BREAD CAFE $
1007 Locust St.
(515) 248-1782
www.southuniontogo.com
A nice little lunch place, in the same building as Centro in Western Gateway. Meats and fillings spill out of the freshly baked bread of both hot and cold sandwiches, with specialties like Sarah's Revenge, with roast beef, bacon, horseradish sauce, and sautéed vegetables on focaccia. George's Special has ham, roast pork, and salami along with Swiss cheese and onions, while the Cajun tuna melt comes on focaccia and the Formaro Cheesesteak is made with roast beef and provolone. Daily specials during the week

include an Italian sausage grinder, an Italian beef with spicy peppers, and a chicken Parmesan sandwich. The potato Pepper Jack soup is a cheesy, tasty delight. You can also pick up a salad at the salad bar, or order a taco or Caesar salad, which includes chicken or bacon options. Closed Sat and Sun.

FAST FOOD

TED'S CONEY ISLAND $
3020 Ingersoll Ave.
(515) 243-8947
A nice spot if you want non-franchise fast food or are looking for a quick pit stop while shopping on Ingersoll Avenue, Ted's gyros have earned it a devoted local following. The meat is rolled up inside a soft pita and drizzled with a yogurt sauce that gets it right—not too tart and just creamy enough. Hot dogs and hamburgers are decent, and the French fries are okay but probably won't make anyone's all-time greatest list. They also have pork tenderloins with a selection of toppings including cheese and chili (purists will be happy to know you can get your breaded and fried slab of meat served plain). There are even some healthier options, like a Greek salad or a veggie wrap, but for the truly reckless there are chili cheese fries. Try the baklava for dessert. Ted's is as much a take-out place as a sit-down restaurant, and it's worth ordering your food at the drive-through window and taking it to a nearby park or picnic area. Closed Sunday. A second location is at 2667 NW 86th St. (515-276-2558).

CONTEMPORARY FINE DINING

MOJO'S ON 86TH $$$
6163 NW 86th St., Johnston
(515) 334-3699
www.mojoson86th.com

A hip, modern room in an upscale shopping center, with black lacquered chairs and cool tunes spilling out of the sound system. There are several interesting appetizers to start the meal, like a calamari with housemade andouille sausage, Parmesan reggiano and red pepper coulis, and smoked Iowa baby back ribs with whiskey grits, blackberry barbecue sauce and crispy leeks, as well as good soups, like an asparagus bisque and a chef's choice that changes regularly and may include a New England clam chowder. Large meat entrees with inventive sauces are a mainstay of the changing menu, including flavorful duck breast with smoked bacon and apple risotto and a cherry-basil compote, or Iowa pork medallions with chorizo and raisin bread pudding and a honey cream. Steaks are broiled to juicy perfection. There's usually at least one vegetarian entrée, like a grilled vegetable Napoleon with yellow squash, zucchini, onion, portobello mushroom, and a red pepper coulis, as well as pasta and a few salads, such as spinach and grilled Caesar. Desserts offer a variety of flavors, like a raspberry cheesecake or chai spice crème brûlée. Reservations recommended. Closed Sunday.

SBROCCO WINE BAR
& WINE SHOP $$$
208 Court Ave.
(515) 282-3663
http://sbroccowine.com
This hip spot presided over by noted Des Moines chef Andrew Meek is fine dining without the fuss: The long, narrow space is laid out with tables set against a painted brick wall facing the bar, behind which hang stained-glass fixtures salvaged from an old Des Moines church. The long list of small and large plates is a great way to sample a wide

variety of the chef's flavors: Try the grilled prawns, tuna tartare, or baba ghanoush, among many other offerings. The dinner menu frequently changes but has always featured inventive dishes with fresh, light ingredients, like Scottish salmon roasted and served with a Medjoul date, cucumber, and cashew salad, or linguine with homemade pork sausage, Galveston Bay shrimp, and fennel tomatoes. Really, you can't go wrong with the good selections of small plates, arranged around some of the great wine selections, like scallops on cauliflower puree with caramelized Maui onions, watercress, and apple cider syrup, or duck wings with a celery and blue cheese salad. The "smears" are gourmet spreads like whipped feta with cucumber and mint or white bean hummus with sirach, served with grilled bread and perfect with a bottle from the extensive wine list. Desserts tend to be on the heavy side, but still good. The wine selection has more than 40 wines by the glass and 200 by the bottle, as well as tastings and wine flights. Finally, tucked away by the restaurant's back alley entrance is a hidden drinking den known as Shorty's if you want a quiet cocktail. The restaurant is closed Sunday.

FRENCH

*BARU 66 $$$$
6587 University Ave., Windsor Heights
(515) 277-6627

In a restaurant-sparse neighborhood just past the western border of Des Moines sits this unassuming yet exceptional dining space, where globe-trotting chef David Baruthio brings the taste of his native France, yet in a simple bistro setting that helps set the mood for a relaxed and wonderful dining experience. The pâté de foie gras is as good as it gets and a good introduction to the

chef's style, with just the right combination of subtle and tantalizing flavors. The menu changes frequently but may include adventurous preparations with truffles, duck, and pheasant, such as a "Pheasant Supreme" dish with a rich flavor and delectable vegetable garnish, as well as bistro standbys like steak and frites. There's a nice French cheese plate and the staff can help you out with the best wine selection from the restaurant's extensive list. The thoroughly modern dining room has lots of black accents and a minimalist flair, allowing you to concentrate on the food. The macaroons that conclude many a meal are like tiny little jewel boxes filled with the most rich and subtle sweetness. Closed Sunday. Reservations recommended.

BISTRO MONTAGE $$$
2724 Ingersoll Ave.
(515) 557-1924
www.bistromontage.com

A cozy little neighborhood joint with a solid urban feel and a solid menu with lots of fresh ingredients and interesting preparations. The charcuterie plate is a good start, with pork terrine wrapped in bacon and accompanied by succulent duck pâté, which is also included with the cheese plate, a selection of good cheeses served with crostini. Intriguing meat, poultry, and fish dishes include some nice pork and lamb options, as well as a crispy and tasty chicken breast with risotto alongside, and a very nice duck with braised winter greens and turnips stuffed with fig compote. The kitchen shows inventiveness with side dishes as well, nicely preparing black and white truffles and vegetable offerings. There's even a good liver and onions with fava beans and potato rosti. Desserts include sumptuous dark chocolate cake, profiteroles, and palate-cleansing sorbet.

The two prix-fixe options have a good selection of appetizer, entree, and dessert. Closed Sunday and Monday. Reservations recommended, especially on weekends.

DJANGO $$$
210 10th St.
(515) 288-0268
www.djangodesmoines.com
The surroundings may scream "fancy restaurant," and while the menu is extensive at this brasserie on the first floor of the Hotel Fort Des Moines, there are also plenty of simple French favorites, prepared with fresh ingredients and innovative sauces. Start off with some duck frites, cooked in duck fat, and crispy and divine with béarnaise sauce and curry ketchup. Other good appetizers are spinach and goat cheese ravioli and sweetbreads sautéed with house-cured bacon, fresh peas, and veal demi-glace, and served with toasted brioche. Bouillabaisse is piping hot and nicely spiced, with a perfect mixture of scallops, mussels, halibut, and shrimp. Go with a standby like beef bourguignon or steak au poivre, or try something different like the Nieman ranch pork chops, grilled and served with Dijon cream and La Quercia prosciutto. The extensive and changing menu may have items like roasted duck breast with duck leg confit and demi-glace or Parmesan-encrusted chicken with béarnaise sauce served with Dauphinoise potatoes, as well as numerous pastas and sandwiches, including Le Bleu Burger and Le Royale with Cheese. At the center of the room sits a raw bar heaped with oysters, clams, mussels, and shrimp—it's a popular spot for the after-work crowd. The charcuterie plate is also an excellent choice if you aren't staying for a full meal. No corkage fee for wine. Lunch Mon through Fri only.

LA MIE $$
841 42nd St.
(515) 255-1625
www.lamiebakery.com
This nondescript storefront in a strip mall across from an elementary school is a nice neighborhood bistro-style place where the kitchen uses fresh ingredients to create simple, satisfying fare at reasonable prices. Fish is probably your best bet, with the Pacific tuna very flavorful and the prawns plump and tasty. Poached sea bass is exquisite, with a nice array of vegetables on the side. There are also some good pasta offerings, although the risotto can be a little too chewy. Salads are very fresh, with a good mix of greens and just the right amount of dressing. Bread comes from the in-house bakery and is often served as a complimentary appetizer with an eclectic spread like soft cheese with roasted pepper. Very reasonably priced wine list. Breakfast is also worth a visit: Croissants are as light and flaky as any you'll find in Paris, filled with rich chocolate or almond paste, and omelets are whipped up with gusto, with fillings like fresh asparagus, smoked salmon, and applewood bacon. Good coffee, too.

GREEK

OLYMPIC FLAME $
514 E. Grand Ave.
(515) 243-4361
A classic, no-frills Greek diner set amid the trendy shops and nightclubs of the East Village. The handful of tables in the slightly dusty, blue and white storefront fill up regularly with locals, and it's easy to see why: Gyros come piled high with meat on freshly baked pita bread, and the Greek salad has just the right mix of olive oil, vinegar, and feta cheese atop the lettuce and vegetables. The

burgers and fries are good, too, although the portions are on the small side. For dessert, another Greek standard bearer: sweet, crispy baklava. Parking can be a bit of a problem, but you shouldn't have to look for too long to find a spot on the street. Closed Sunday.

HAWAIIAN

ALOHANA HAWAIIAN GRILL   **$**
12931 University Ave., Clive
(515) 225-2279
Hawaiian food in Des Moines? Yes, this small fast-food-style shop, one of only four locations not in California, sits in a nondescript strip mall out near the western edge of the metro area, where it brings the flavors of a luau to the Iowa plains (for a surreal experience, eat there during a January blizzard). Grilled meats are the hallmark here, with plates of chicken, beef, and pork served up with sides of white rice and macaroni salad. The barbecued ribs are tangy and grilled just right. There are also some yummy fried chicken and shrimp options, and a few dishes made with Spam, including soup with grilled Spam and another item that looks like Spam sushi! The Loco Moco is marinated beef patties topped with a savory gravy and a fried egg. A seafood platter comes with fried shrimp and fish, and they also do some not-bad burgers, including barbecue beef and chicken options with nice french fries, and noodle dishes that are ramen-like, also with barbecued meats added. It's all Hawaiian comfort food, very cheap, and absolutely delicious. Fills up at lunchtime with hungry workers from nearby office parks. Pass your time waiting for your food watching the Hawaiian television shows on the monitors bolted to the ceiling. Closed Sunday.

INDIAN

INDIA STAR   **$$**
5514 Douglas Ave.
(515) 279-2118
It's a bit of a drive out to this restaurant, on a commercial strip near Merle Hay Mall, and the setting is institutional and uninspiring, but it's still worth the trip: This is good Indian food with pungent flavors that don't get too spicy. Appetizers are very modestly priced, giving you the opportunity to try several items, with the vegetable platter serving up an array of items, including samosas and crackling hot papadum. The tandoori chicken comes out sizzling and is juicy and tasty, with its red skin positively glowing. Lamb vindaloo, which is one of the hotter items on the menu, has just the right mixture of spices, and a nice ratio of lamb to potatoes in the greenish sauce. The curries are good as well, especially the chicken, which sits in an amber sauce, as is the chicken tikka masala. Other choices include chicken tikka and seafood options like *saag* shrimp, lobster masala, and karahi shrimp. Naan bread is puffy and hot-out-of-the-oven fresh. There are several vegetarian options, including *saag paneer, alu gobhi, malal kofta,* and mushroom *matar,* a vegan option of fresh peas with mushrooms. The rice pudding is a nice end-of-meal palate cleanser. Lunch buffet served on weekdays. Closed Sunday.

**NAMASTE INDIA GROCERIES
   AND KITCHEN**   **$$**
7500 University Ave., Clive
(515) 255-1698
Wedged into a narrow space next to an Indian grocery in a strip building packed among offices and warehouses just over the border from Des Moines, this slightly shabby room offers decent if not spectacular Indian

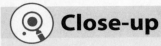 **Close-up**

Des Moines Area Wineries

Grapevines pop up occasionally among the cornfields at the growing number of central Iowa wineries, drawing on Iowa's status years ago as a large producer of grapes. Many vintners offer tastings and tours, as well as wine, cheese, and other items for sale. Listed below is a sampling of wineries in and near Des Moines.

Jasper Winery. 2400 George Flagg Pkwy.; (515) 282-9463; www.jasperwinery.com.
Rosey Acres Winery. 2477 SE 82nd St., Runnells; (515) 265-3432; www.roseyacres winery.com.
Summerset Winery. 15101 Fairfax St., Indianola; (515) 961-3545; www.summer setwine.com.

For more information on these and other wineries, check out **www.heartofiowa winetrail.com,** which includes a map you can use to plot a weekend driving tour of Des Moines–area wineries.

dishes. Many local Indians eat here, and the cuisine seems to reflect that: Dishes are a bit more authentic, with some spicy selections on the extensive menu of lamb, chicken, and vegetarian entrees. Chicken do Piaza, cooked with fresh ginger and green chiles, ratchets up the hot meter, while chicken *saag* is a little more manageable. The tandoori chicken is a good choice as well, with the meat tender and tasty. Pick out a selection from the list of dosa, a sort of Indian crepe made with rice flour and stuffed with all kinds of goodies, including some hot and spicy ones. Plenty of vegetarian options available as well, including *chana* masala (garbanzo beans), okra masala, or *navratan* korma, a combination of mixed vegetables cooked in a creamy sauce. A sweet *lassi*, or yogurt drink, may help cool down your mouth. Servers can be a bit inattentive. Lunch buffet served Tues through Sun. Closed Monday.

ITALIAN

BARATTA'S $$
2320 S. Union St.
(515) 243-4516
www.barattas.com

One of several neighborhood Italian places in Des Moines, Baratta's lies south of downtown, across the Des Moines River from Principal Park, smack in the middle of a residential block in the old "Little Italy" neighborhood. The menu ranges over everything from steaks and seafood to numerous old-school Italian-American specialties. Spinach-filled tortellini and veal piccata are among the highlights. Perhaps their best-known dish is chicken amaggio, which is marinated and rolled in bread crumbs, then charbroiled and served with roasted red peppers and mushrooms and an olive oil–based sauce with garlic, lemon juice, and white wine. The pizza is a good choice for families, with small and large pies and a large selection of toppings. Homemade cannoli is a good, reliable dessert. There's an extensive wine list, and ample parking is available. Cafe Baratta's, downtown in the state historical building, serves a more limited lunch menu every day but Sun.

✳CENTRO $$$
1011 Locust St.
(515) 248-1780
www.centrodining.com
A noisy, raucous, big-city-style Italian place on a street corner in Western Gateway, where portions are big and cocktails are poured strong. The menu is full of innovative items and old favorites: Pizzas come out of the coal-fired oven with a crispy, slightly charred crust and a rich, thick tomato sauce. Toppings include fresh herbs, and the mozzarella is divine. There are specialty pies like a Siciliana with capers and artichoke, a barbecue chicken, and a New Yorker with meatballs and roasted red pepper. New menu items are frequently added, as the kitchen takes full advantage of local and seasonal ingredients, like a Nieman Ranch pork chop, served with a Chianti sauce, or a butternut squash ravioli. The pasta list is extensive, and the gnocchi is in particular worth trying. Other pasta choices include cavatelli with Italian sausage, seafood fettuccine, and spicy rigatoni. Steaks are melt-in-your-mouth good and salads are a study in freshness, with crisp greens and tomatoes that explode with flavor. Specials are worth checking out, as they often have a very limited run, like soft-shell crab or gnocchi with stingy nettles and morels. Servers manage to be very attentive in the busy dining room.

✳LUCCA $$$
420 E. Locust St.
(515) 243-1115

The all-prix-fixe menu at this trendy East Village spot is like the decor: deceptively simple. In the narrow room with white walls, blond wood floors, and a small finishing kitchen hidden behind a central counter, the only list of offerings is a thin slip of paper with a few words written on it: the names of the dishes. A young, energetic server in black drops by your table and launches into descriptions of the most enticing sort, including pan-fried duck livers, gnocchi with sage, and lamb shoulder cooked with Moroccan spices. After a few descriptions it's tough to keep up, so you'll ask him or her to repeat the list—and still not be able to decide. When you do, however, the food is wonderful, exceptionally prepared, and with imaginative flavorings. Dinners, which frequently change, are served in 2 courses, a small plate followed by a large plate, which typically includes a number of selections including fish, chicken, and red-meat options. Small-plate mainstays include a fluffy risotto and nicely seasoned duck. The wine list is lengthy and varied and your server can recommend a good bottle.

NOAH'S ARK RISTORANTE $$
2400 Ingersoll Ave.
(515) 288-2246
Dark wood, dim lighting, and fireplaces give this space an old-fashioned, clubby feel and with good reason—it's been open since 1946. The cooking is old-school as well: Expect a blanket of red sauce on the al dente spaghettini, rigatoni, and ravioli, thick cream on the fettuccine, and liberal use of garlic and olive oil. You can also get pasta with chicken livers, as well as meatballs and stuffed green peppers. Starters are savory and delicious, especially the minestrone soup, and every table gets homemade rolls, soft and yeasty with a hint of garlic. Have a shrimp cocktail or fried

string cheese while waiting for your entree. The restaurant is known for Neapolitan-style pizza, which has only the classic toppings—no fancy stuff here. Steaks and chops come well-broiled and tasty. Other specials include Calabrese-style lasagna, veal alla mozzarella, and chicken Parmesan with spaghettini. The restaurant's nautical decor extends to a substantial seafood menu, including fried catfish, fresh Alaskan salmon with sauce meunière, and whole lobsters from a tank in the front room. Simple, sweet desserts like spumoni and cannoli provide a nice finish. Open until 11 p.m. during the week and past midnight on weekends. Closed Sunday.

SAM & GABE'S ITALIAN BISTRO $$$
8631 Hickman Rd., Urbandale
(515) 271-9200
www.samandgabes.com

Behind an anonymous facade just off a busy intersection is a cozy little restaurant that has very tasty food and exceptional service. The intimate, narrow space is decorated with stained-glass windows and prints of Italy under track lighting. The veal is a highlight of the menu, with the piccata-seasoned white wine and lemon-caper butter sauce and the marsala savory and tasty. Pastas go a little heavy on the spices, but they still have some decent sauces, including a nice basic lasagna and an intriguing penne alla Sophia with garlic, mushrooms, sun-dried tomatoes, and fresh basil in a light cream sauce. The prix fixe option includes choices like seafood cannelloni, broiled steak, beef tenderloin, and chicken piccata. Specials like grilled veal chop or Chilean sea bass are well-seasoned and well-prepared, too. Desserts are exceptional, like a French coconut tart and white chocolate bread pudding, as

well as a selection of gelato. Servers are friendly and professional and very knowledgeable of the wine list. The dimly lit bar is a popular spot to grab a drink after work, and serves tasty pizzas Tues through Thurs, like a Tuscan pollo pie with diced chicken, bacon, tomato, and red onion with a Parmesan ranch sauce and a *formaggio* with a thick red sauce and mozzarella, provolone, Asiago, provolone, and Romano. There's also a nice selection of appetizers if you don't want a full entree, including a nicely done grilled portobello mushroom served with caponata relish. Open for dinner only. Closed Sunday.

TUMEA AND SONS $$
1501 SE 1st St.
(515) 282-7964
www.tumeaandsons.com

Another family-owned Italian spot just south of downtown, with a strong neighborhood vibe and clientele—note the maps of Italy on the walls and straw-wrapped bottles of Chianti on the tables. The food is standard Italian-American, with lots of garlic, olive oil, and red sauce, and it's good and tasty, like comfort food should be. Veal Parmesan has a nice blend of Parmesan and mozzarella, while the numerous breaded meat dishes come out crispy and flavorful. Veal in general is a good choice: The veal saltimbocca is yummy in a savory Marsala sauce. The shrimp scampi is a worthwhile choice, too. Pasta is well-cooked, with a blanket of thick red sauce atop it, and the sausage is hand-made at a longtime Italian grocery a few blocks away. Desserts are hit-or-miss, but the cannolis are worth trying. In warmer months, step outside with a drink onto the bocce court tucked behind the restaurant, to roll a few balls yourself or just to watch.

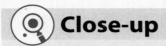 **Close-up**

Des Moines's "Little Italy"

Originally an independent town called **Sevastopol,** the area around S. Union Street just south of the confluence of the Raccoon and Des Moines Rivers attracted Italian immigrants beginning in the 1880s. At its height, the neighborhood boasted an Italian post of the American Legion and its own newspaper. Purveyors of Italian fruits and vegetables peddled their wares on the streets. **St. Anthony Catholic Church,** at 15 Indianola Ave., opened in 1906 and is one of the last links to that era, as is an Italian grocery opened in 1912 by Frank and Louis Graziano that still stands at 1601 S. Union St. Most of their business is wholesale now, but you can still stop in and pick up some freshly made hot Italian sausage. Nearby **Tumea and Sons,** a long fly ball from Principal Park, is one of a smattering of family-owned Italian restaurants on the south side. At the other end of the culinary spectrum, chef-about-town George Formaro, the son of Des Moines immigrants from Sicily and Calabria, is the man behind **Centro,** which turns out big plates of pasta and steak garnished with fresh ingredients. The city's annual **Italian-American festival,** which moved downtown in 2010 after some 30 years on the south side, offers a cornucopia of food and entertainment.

TURSI'S LATIN KING $$
2200 Hubbell Ave.
(515) 266-4466
www.tursislatinking.com

Since it opened as a simple Italian cafe in 1947, diners have flocked to this restaurant, located just off a gritty stretch of University Avenue on Des Moines's east side. The building has grown since its founding—it now resembles an Italian country villa with numerous dining rooms and a well-appointed wine locker. The menu has plenty of pasta, meat, and seafood choices, and is divided into Italian and American sections. They're known for their steaks, especially the 10-ounce top sirloin and the Des Moines favorite Steak de Burgo, which comes to the table tender and with an excellent, buttery sauce. There are also some nice veal selections, including grilled with mushrooms, peppers, and fresh garlic, and served with potato croquette. The signature Italian dish is chicken spiedini, with a choice of olive oil or Alfredo sauce. Pasta choices include cappellini alla sassi, gnocchi alla sorentina, manicotti al forno, and penne regine with peas, garlic, mushrooms, prosciutto, and tomatoes in cream sauce. Seafood options are fresh and flavorful, like grilled salmon with Roma tomatoes and shrimp with linguine Alfredo. Standard Italian desserts like tiramisu and cannoli, as well as ice cream, and a nice selection of Italian coffee drinks round out the meal. Closed Sunday and Monday.

JAPANESE & SUSHI

HAPPI SUSHI $
Kaleidoscope Mall, Second Floor
555 Walnut St.
(515) 664-9390

Think "McSushi" at this popular lunch-only spot accessible from the downtown skywalk—not due to bland, uniform food, but rather convenience: Combo sushi plates are dished out by a young, enthusiastic staff (this place shares a chef with favorite Des Moines sushi spot Miyabi 9). The standard combo has a choice of sushi rolls including California roll, Alaska roll, and Hawaiian roll, with crab stick, cream cheese, and mango. The sashimi combo has a nice presentation of tuna, salmon, and yellowtail. Combo plates come with miso soup and a choice of salad: squid, ginger, or seaweed. It's hardly a gourmet treat, but it's tasty, quick, and cheap, and a nice alternative to a typical fast lunch.

HOSHI $$
2314 University Ave.
(515) 369-7253
Since opening in early 2010, this Drake University spot has been turning out some innovative touches on sushi. Alongside standard nigiri and sashimi like tuna, eel, octopus, and some especially fine yellowtail are rolls like the Love You Long Time, which includes spicy tuna, spicy octopus, tempura shrimp, and jalapeno—it's very hot—and the Tokyo Bomb, with spicy octopus topped with Dynamite tuna, and spicy mayonnaise. Other rolls include a Caterpillar Roll with shrimp tempura, crab, cucumber, and avocado, a Miami Heat roll with tuna, salmon, yellowtail, crab, cucumber, asparagus, and fried tempura, and a French Roll with crab, cucumber, avocado, and flying fish roe—all wrapped in an egg crepe. The menu also has tempura and other Japanese appetizers, and the liquor bar is as big as the sushi bar and pours an array of creative cocktails. The endless stream of '80s pop songs on the sound system may or may not be your thing.

MIYABI 9 $$
512 E. Grand Ave.
(515) 288-8885

Miyabi "Mike" Yamamoto was a master sushi chef in Osaka before coming to America to work his magic. His background shows in this East Village spot, which takes a more traditional, Japanese approach to sushi. Favorites like tuna and yellowtail are expertly prepared, and the selection of rolls includes whimsical touches like the Captain Crunch roll with crab, shrimp, and Tobiko tempura crunch, or the popular Volcano Roll, a spicy combination of California roll, scallop, crab, scallions, and spicy mayonnaise. The yellowtail special is a great use of one of the more popular Japanese specials. Other Japanese standbys aren't bad either: Miso soup is good and filling, while the tempura comes to the table light and crispy. It's best to stick with the sushi—other entrees are frequently just average, although several of the appetizers are tasty, like deep-fried soft-shell crab, Japanese dumplings, and scallions wrapped in beef with a teriyaki sauce. The decor is a nod to sleek, minimalist stylings that fit right in this hipster neighborhood, with small black tables and a blond wood sushi bar in the back. The open space makes for a noisy dining experience on busy nights. Closed Sunday.

MEDITERRANEAN

*PROOF $$
1301 Locust St.
(515) 244-0655
www.proofrestaurant.com
Ultramodern and ultrapopular, with office workers streaming into this minimalist Western Gateway storefront for lunches with a touch of Spain, Morocco, and Italy. Order at the counter from a menu posted above it—the menu changes seasonally, always bringing in fresh new offerings. Moroccan chicken and lamb burger flatbread sandwiches are

both extraordinarily succulent and tasty. For the less carnivorously inclined, the vegetable falafel flatbread has a good, earthy taste in its chickpea patties, and there's also a tabouli with feta and salads like a spring mix and spinach with apple. Sandwiches are served with a choice of salad or soup, which also changes and may include potato and cheese bisque or a beef stew. The numerous "grains" dishes don't quite measure up to the same standard as the flatbreads, but there's some good there, too, especially the scallops served with a light and fluffy tabouli. Besides lunch, the restaurant also features Fri-night dinners that highlight fresh ingredients and are particularly sought-after—make reservations early. Closed Sat and Sun.

MEXICAN

DOS RIOS CANTINA AND TEQUILA
LOUNGE $$
316 Court Ave.
(515) 282-2995
www.dosriosrestaurant.com
Upscale Mexican food with Iowa touches is the rule at this large, open dining room. This is no corner taco joint: Warm wood accents are complemented by full-length windows that look out on a popular sidewalk patio, which includes outdoor couches and is a wonderful place to sip a beer or margarita on a warm day (it fills up with downtown workers on Fri afternoons). Known for its guacamole, which is mashed tableside in a stone mortar, Dos Rios (the name is an homage to the nearby confluence of the Des Moines and Raccoon Rivers) has an extensive menu of meat and vegetarian dishes of varying spiciness. For those who like their Mexican food simple and straight up, the a la carte taco plate is a nice choice, with a selection of meats or vegetables—the seared mahimahi

---

Tacos on the Cheap

Plenty of locals swear by the cheap, greasy tacos at **Tasty Taco**, which occupies half a dozen fluorescent-lit locations around the Des Moines metro area (the closest location to downtown is at 1418 E. Grand Ave.). Or for even more authentic Mexican street food, hop onto I-235 and head over to E. 14th St. (US 69) to pick up some tacos at two popular taco trucks: **Tacos de Jerez** is parked in a convenience store parking lot across from East High School, at E. 14th and Buchanan Streets, while **Tacos Tarascos** is in a parking lot at SE 14th Street and Edison Avenue (look for the colors of the Mexican flag painted on the side of the truck). Both offer cheap, tasty, and filling tacos, filled with spicy seasoned beef, pork, and other meats, served with a small plastic container of salsa.

---

is especially fresh and tangy, the *carne asada* is juicy and tender, and the chorizo has just the right amount of spiciness. The taco plate also comes with a salsa sampler—be careful with the habanero! Other fish selections are good, too, including wild salmon glazed with agave nectar, the Devil Shrimp in a *hot* tomato sauce, and a fresh fish of the day. There are also choices like a grilled Nieman Ranch pork chop (you're in Iowa, remember), which also has an agave glaze, and an organic half-chicken, spit roasted to perfection and served with vegetables and cilantro rice. They manage to pull off a good flan for dessert. A dizzying array of tequilas fills up a glass case at the back of the bar. Gets a little crowded and noisy, with service slipping a little during the dinner rush—go early or late if you're looking for a more relaxed meal. Closed Sunday and on Monday in the winter.

MIDDLE EASTERN

OPEN SESAME $$
313 E. Locust St.
(515) 288-3151
www.opensesamedsm.com
This cramped yet cozy, tapestry-hung East Village space has some nice basic dishes on its Lebanese menu. Start with a meze like baba ghanouj with light and tasty pita bread or hummus that has just the right amount of garlic, olive oil, and lemon. Grilled meats like the chicken or beef kebab are succulent and tasty, and the tabouli on the side is well-prepared. The kibbe plate of ground beef baked with cracked wheat has an interesting mix of flavors and textures. Other choices include a grilled kofta, or top sirloin flavored with parsley, onion, and spices and grilled with tomatoes and potatoes, and grilled eggplant topped with seasoned ground beef, topped with tomato sauce and garnished with pine nuts. The pita bread is hot and fresh. Order a cup of Turkish coffee or Lebanese iced tea with cardamom and watch the belly dancer who performs on Thurs and Fri nights. Closed Sunday.

PIZZA

BAGNI DI LUCCA $
407 E. 5th St.
(515) 243-0044
Like its sister restaurant, Lucca, a few blocks away, this hole-in-the-wall pizzeria, a popular East Village lunch spot, does one thing and does it well: A short menu of personal pizzas is listed on a blackboard behind the counter, where you step up, order, and a few minutes later receive your pizza, which you eat at tables that sit on a concrete floor, under exposed ceiling tiles. Atop semolina crusts with a distinctive cornmeal taste are toppings like shiitake mushrooms, artichokes, pesto, and ricotta and occasional featured pizzas like smoked salmon with capers and tomatoes (you can also get old standbys like pepperoni and four-cheese). At about 10 inches in diameter, the pizzas are big enough to share, but you'll probably want your own after taking a bite! Calzones stuffed with fillings like ham, bell peppers, or mushrooms are another option. There's a nice wine selection for a pizza joint, and gelato for dessert. Lunch only Tues through Thurs. Closed Sunday and Monday.

CHRISTOPHER'S $$
2816 Beaver Ave.
(515) 274-3694
www.christophers-restaurant.com
This low-key neighborhood place, in the heart of Beaverdale, has a menu featuring pizza and Italian comfort food like baked lasagna and chicken parmigiana. Pizzas have a nice crispy crust with a zesty tomato sauce, and there are some specialty pizzas like marinated grilled chicken and roasted red peppers with white sauce. There are also steaks, including a juicy New York strip and the Des Moines favorite Steak de Burgo, as well as a good selection of fish, including orange roughy, Baja tuna, and pan-seared scallops. Chicken saltimbocca is topped with artichokes, prosciutto, fresh sage, and provolone, and pastas also include an a la Mediterranean option, with roasted red pepper, artichoke hearts, fresh basil, garlic, and Roma tomatoes, or Penne Sophia, in a light cream sauce. They do a decent burger as well

and several other sandwiches, including a nice blackened tilapia. Classic desserts like crème brûlée and cheesecake are rich and delicious. Dinner only. There's plenty of parking in surrounding lots. Closed Monday.

COACH'S PIZZA $
560 S. Prairie View, West Des Moines
(515) 223-2233
www.coachspizza.com
Despite its location among the bars and nightclubs of West Glen, this is actually a nice little neighborhood-style pizza parlor with some tasty pies. It's simple, basic pizza, with a selection of meats and veggies for toppings, as well as some specialty pizzas like bacon cheeseburger and barbecue chicken. The "Crack Pizza" has white sauce, chicken, bacon, fresh basil, and tomato. Salads, including a Caesar and a wedge salad with blue cheese, are a decent accompaniment. Pastas include spaghetti under a blanket of marinara, a thickly layered lasagna, and penne baked with marinara, sausage, onion, mushroom, green pepper, and pepperoni. There's beer on tap and a wine list. Several sandwiches, including an Italian grinder with melted mozzarella, Italian meatball with sautéed red onions, roasted red peppers, and provolone, and an Italian sub that has capocollo, pepperoni, and salami baked with mozzarella on a toasted hoagie bun round out the menu.

PARADISE PIZZA CAFE $$
2025 Grand Ave., West Des Moines
(515) 222-9959
www.paradisepizzacafe.net
Sitting on a wide road among auto shops on the southern edge of West Des Moines, this nondescript little restaurant has some of the tastiest pizza in the metro area. A wide selection of specialty pies, including

barbecue chicken and a Sicilian pizza with several meats, have a zesty sauce and chewy, tasty crust. The signature Crock pizza has a thick crust and generous amounts of tomato sauce and mozzarella and is baked upside-down in a crock (it's a bit like a calzone—try it). Pastas include a Thai chicken option with angel hair, a butternut squash lasagna, and a Cajun Pasta, with shrimp, crab, whitefish, and Cajun ham. Salads are especially good with the restaurant's hot, fresh-baked Italian bread. Desserts include a chocoholic's fantasy: a dense, dark chocolate mousse inside chocolate cake with chocolate sauce on top. Good beer and wine selection. The dining room has a vaguely tropical motif, with potted palms and a surreal mural of island life.

RUSSIAN

IRINA'S RESTAURANT & BAR $$
2301 Rocklyn Dr.
(515) 331-0399
www.irinasrestaurantandbar.com
More like an American menu with Russian accents, there are nonetheless some intriguing choices at this nondescript squat building near Hickman Road. Inside, dim lighting and red curtains separating booths make for an intimate atmosphere. Try the pork shashlik kebabs or beef stroganoff if you're in the mood for Russian dining. There are also steak and seafood selections, including shrimp prepared in a tasty marinade of fresh herbs, white wine, garlic, and lemon, and top sirloin grilled and seasoned with spices and served with grilled marinated squash and zucchini. For many the allure here is the 60-plus varieties of vodka, Russian and otherwise. Ask the owner or bartender to choose one for you if you're intimidated by the selection, and have them show you the proper, Russian way to drink vodka—shots are served with a

pickle spear and a wedge of rye bread, which must be consumed in a certain order to fully appreciate the experience. Loud pop music over the sound system may be disconcerting for some. The clublike feel makes this a nice place to start a night out before proceeding to the bars a mile or so to the west.

SEAFOOD

WATERFRONT SEAFOOD MARKET $$
2900 University Ave., West Des Moines
(515) 223-5106
www.waterfrontseafoodmarket.com
Tucked away in the Clocktower Square shopping center in West Des Moines is a classic seafood shack, divided into 3 rooms: a cozy bar and dining room and a fresh seafood market, bringing a wide selection of fish to landlocked Iowa. Grilled fish is a good bet, including halibut, mahimahi, orange roughy, and rainbow trout, which has a rich, meaty flavor. Wild salmon, available when in season, is superb, and very fresh. Oysters on the half shell are a good starter. Other fish options, most available grilled, baked, or pan-fried, include scallops and Gulf shrimp. There's even a sushi bar with some good rolls. Many menu items are based on market price, with some items only available seasonally. Steaks, chicken paillard, and pasta dishes round out the non-seafood choices, and for the lighter eaters there are po'boy sandwiches with oysters, rock shrimp, scallops, and catfish. Friendly service. Closed Sunday. A second location is at 2414 SE Tones Dr., Ankeny; (515) 963-1940.

STEAKHOUSES

801 CHOPHOUSE $$$$
801 Grand Ave., #200
(515) 288-6000
www.801chophouse.com

White tablecloths, high booths, dark wood paneling, and drawings of prize steers on the walls: Hidden behind the steel and glass facade of Des Moines's tallest building is an old-school carnivore's paradise. The menu may seem a little intimidating to first-timers, particularly the 40-ounce Delmonico (for two), but just go with the classics: Big, broiled cuts of meat, like the New York strip or rib eye, are always good choices, as are the lamb chops, which come with a homemade mint sauce. The filet mignon is tasty and a little more manageable than the bigger cuts. You could also try the osso bucco or chicken breast. Stick with the basics with the sides as well, like the hash browns with cheddar or the 1-pound baked potato. The lobster corn chowder is a good start to the meal, as are a jumbo shrimp cocktail or oysters Rockefeller. The dessert list is as lengthy and impressive as the dinner menu, with choices like strawberry crème brûlée, Grand Marnier soufflé, and a banana split with Absolut vanilla ice cream. There's an extensive wine list, including many fine by-the-glass options. The brass-rail bar offers a large selection of martinis and single-malt scotches, as well as happy-hour specials like $1 oysters on the half shell and filet mignon "sliders," or small burgers, with horseradish cream. No lunch. Reservations are a good idea.

JESSE'S EMBERS $$
3301 Ingersoll Ave.
(515) 255-6011
www.theoriginaljessesembers.com
This shoebox of a restaurant is a more affordable place to eat a well-cooked steak—it hosts a large and loyal crowd of regulars, many of whom come in for the Embers Special, a 12-ounce aged prime sirloin that has plenty of tenderness and flavor. All the

steaks are good, as are side dishes such as simply divine french fries or hearty baked potato, included in the modest price. The half-pound Emberburger makes a good dinner as well, grilled just right and served on a firm and tasty bun, while the rack of baby back ribs will make you get Neolithic as you suck as much meat as possible off the bone. There's also a yummy pork chop, a grilled breast of chicken over rice pilaf, and plenty of seafood selections, including beer-battered lobster tails, orange roughy Florentine, and charbroiled salmon, but this is first and foremost a red-meat kind of place. For a lighter choice, try a shrimp or chicken dinner salad. Closed Sunday.

JOHNNY'S ITALIAN
STEAKHOUSE $$$
Radisson Hotel
6800 Fleur Dr.
(515) 287-0847
www.johnnysitaliansteakhouse.com
This Des Moines outpost of a midwestern chain, located in a Radisson hotel near the airport, is perennially popular with locals and out-of-towners alike. Focus on the "steakhouse"—there are plenty of cuts of meat to choose from. The rib eye and porterhouse are huge and tasty and come with salad, bread, and choice of a side dish. Prime rib (available Fri, Sat, and Sun only) is juicy and tender. They do a Steak de Burgo here, Des Moines's signature filet sautéed in garlic and herbs. The Italian dishes are fine as well—try the shrimp scampi, lasagna, or angel hair with fresh basil, garlic, and tomatoes. Other options on the lengthy menu include smothered steak with mushrooms and onions and lots of seafood choices like cedar-plank salmon, tilapia with garlic and fresh herbs, and an 8-ounce broiled lobster

tail. Plenty of salads that work as a light meal, like parmigiano chicken and fresh greens with pecan-crusted goat cheese, red onion, and Roma tomatoes. Desserts include crème brûlée, cannoli, and tiramisu. Service ranges from speedy to slow and the dining room, which has wood floors and brick walls, can get noisy. Check out their website for other area locations.

TAPAS

THE CONTINENTAL $$
428 E. Locust St.
(515) 244-5845
Tapas in a hip bar setting is the highlight at this trendy, dimly lit East Village spot. There's a nice cross-section of small plates: Caponata crostini is a smoky mélange of eggplant, roasted red pepper, and anchovy that does well by its Sicilian roots, while melon and prosciutto crostini is a light and delicate palate-cleanser. *Albondigas* (meatballs) of pork and beef are for those with a taste for the spicy—the tomato salsa packs a wallop. Button mushrooms sautéed in white truffle oil are sublime, and blue cheese crostini gives a nod to Iowa with its Maytag blue cheese. There are entrees like filet au poivre and marinated duck breast with caramelized onion as well as vegetarian polenta lasagna with roasted red pepper, mushrooms, and a marinara sauce topped with mozzarella. Sandwiches and salads, including a good blackened sashimi tuna and a chicken Caesar pita, aren't bad if you're looking for a smaller meal. A popular happy hour knocks a few dollars off the price of tapas and brings in everyone from Capitol Hill staffers to tattooed punk rockers to nosh. Tables in back are quieter than those in the bar area. The kitchen stays open into the wee hours on Fri and Sat. Closed Sunday.

✳TROSTEL'S DISH $$

12581 University Ave., Clive
(515) 221-3474
www.dishtrostels.com

Warm woods and deep banquettes along one wall give this restaurant a welcoming, homey feel. A long bar stands along the other wall in the narrow room. Tapas are organized according to cuisine, with offerings in American, Asian, Latin, and Mediterranean flavors. With new items introduced frequently and so many choices, most involving at least one or two familiar ingredients, it's hard to go wrong (the staff can help if you're having trouble making a selection). Meat and vegetable tapas tend to be better than the seafood selections, with a nice lamb kebab and a tangy crispy fried avocado, prepared with jalapeño sour cream, pico de gallo, and cilantro mayo, particularly good choices. The Boursin mushrooms are very savory in a beef wine sauce. Bigger entrees include a half duck glazed with a maple sauce and roasted on hash, a grilled New York strip steak, and braised pork osso bucco with butternut squash puree and spiced pumpkin seeds. The menu also has "sliders" or little sandwiches, including a Cuban and a Reuben, as well as crispy pizzas with eclectic toppings and antipasto flights with dried fruit, breads, and crackers. Extensive wine list. Closed Sunday.

THAI

COOL BASIL $$

8801 University Ave., Clive
(515) 225-8111
www.coolbasil.com

"Cool" is the correct adjective—the muted colors, track lighting, and friendly black-clad servers help make this a fun dining experience. The menu, with a large selection of dishes, helpfully includes descriptions of different herbs, spices, and flavors in Thai cooking. The extensive selections include curries with a choice of meat, tofu, or vegetables, as well as a roasted duck curry tossed with pineapples, grapes, tomatoes, and fresh peppers. The herbal crispy catfish is one of the chef's specialties, deep-fried and covered with a special herbal curry sauce and sweet basil leaves. Peppers in the other curries are nice and crunchy, while the panang curry is silky smooth, cooked with coconut milk and sparkling with Kaffir lime leaf and a creamy peanut sauce. Pad thai and other noodle dishes are good, and the *tom ka kai* soup is infused with lots of lemongrass, giving it a peppy kick. There are many stir-fried options, including some vegetarian choices like sweet basil, bamboo shoots,

---

Takeout Spots

Three small Vietnamese restaurants are clustered along a stretch of 2nd Avenue, about 6 blocks north of I-235 and downtown, that are recommended spots to pick up takeout: **Pho Ha Do** (1521 2nd Ave.; 515-288-1277), **Lucky Dragon** (1452 2nd Ave.; 515-288-3936), and **Le Paris Cafe** (1517 2nd Ave.; 515-288-3800), are all good places to swing by if you have a hankering for a meaty banh mi sandwich on a crusty French baguette or a bowl of hot, steaming pho full of spices and vegetables alongside strips of beef.

and mushrooms. Dishes can be prepared on a spiciness scale of 1 to 6—3 and greater will make your eyes water at least a little.

NUT POB   **$$**
3322 Indianola Ave.
(515) 246-8055
Hidden away in a nondescript strip mall on a busy commercial road a few miles south of downtown, this hybrid Thai-Vietnamese restaurant turns out solid, tasty versions of favorite dishes from both cuisines. Both the *pho* and *tom ka* soups are good, as is the pad thai. There's a wide selection of both meat and vegetarian dishes. The Angry Catfish is an entire fish deep-fried with garlic and hot chiles—it's quite a meal. There's also Angry Chicken, Beef, and Pork.

VIETNAMESE

A DONG   **$**
1511 High St.
(515) 284-5632
This low-key, unassuming Western Gateway restaurant is a nice, cheap spot to order up a big bowl of *pho,* or Vietnamese beef noodle soup. The steaming bowl arrives at your table with a full plate of bean sprouts, herbs, and lime wedges, which you then strew liberally in the spicy broth. Beyond *pho,* the menu runs for several pages and close to 100 dishes, including such Vietnamese specialties as fried squid stuffed with ground pork or deep-fried sea bass or catfish with ginger and tomato sauce. For the less adventurous, noodle dishes with beef, pork, chicken, or shrimp are a good choice. Coffee is served "French style" with condensed milk, and there are some interesting Vietnamese drinks, like Pickled Lemon Ice Drink or Club Soda with Condensed Milk and Egg Yolk on Ice" (hmmm . . .). Closed Monday.

NIGHTLIFE

Des Moines nightlife is concentrated in a few areas, especially the Court Avenue District downtown, the blocks around 86th Street and Hickman Road in Clive, and the newer West Glen area, just off I-35 in the western part of West Des Moines, east of the Jordan Creek Mall. In all three you will find plenty of bars, ranging from simple set-ups that pour tap beer and strong mixed drinks, to much more sophisticated cocktail lounges that feature mood lighting, luxurious surroundings, and multi-page drink menus with all sorts of martinis, cosmopolitans, and other mixologists' creations. Plenty of these bars feature live music. All three areas also feature a selection of restaurants, with Court Avenue and West Glen having more variety and higher-end dining spots.

There are also plenty of neighborhood bars found throughout the city. These are the "shot and a beer" kind of places that attract loyal regulars. You may draw a few initial stares when you take a seat at the bar, but most of these places are genuinely friendly, and a nice place to relax with a beer, watch sports on television, and play a game of pool or darts.

For an idea of what's going on entertainment-wise, pick up a copy of *Juice* or *CityView*, both of which can be found at locations all over downtown and other parts of the city and suburbs and feature extensive listings of live music, movies, and other nightlife. Bars with live music often charge a cover, although it's often very modest; higher on the weekends and for better-known local acts. Bigger acts, of course, are more expensive and may require advance ticket purchase. Some dance clubs may charge a cover as well. Tickets can be purchased through ticket agencies including Ticketmaster and MidwestTix, as well as through the websites of individual venues and at their box offices (this last option is usually the cheapest, as many venues don't charge service or processing fees).

Under the Iowa Smokefree Air Act of 2008, smoking is prohibited in bars as well as restaurants—you'll have to step outside to light up, which can be quite a challenge in the winter months.

CONCERT VENUES

✳HOYT SHERMAN PLACE
1501 Woodland Ave.
(515) 244-0507
www.hoytsherman.org

A beautiful old theater just north of Des Moines in the Sherman Hill neighborhood, open since 1877 and lovingly restored to its current impressive state. The redbrick exterior, velvet curtains, parquet floors, and intricately carved arched ceiling are almost worth a visit in and of themselves, but the theater also hosts an eclectic array of music acts: rock, jazz, and other artists have all played here, from famous musicians to up-and-coming groups, with plenty of them getting people out of their seats and dancing in the aisles. With a capacity of just over 1,200 for its main floor and balcony, there isn't a bad seat in the house, and the acoustics are pretty good, too. The theater has also been home to various theater and dance productions. Ample free parking is available in the lot on the side of the building, near the box office entrance.

7 FLAGS EVENT CENTER
2100 NW 100th St., Clive
(515) 276-003
All sorts of music groups have played this suburban arena, including plenty of nationally known acts in rock, country, and other genres. The nearly 25,000-square-foot facility has somewhat infrequent concerts, due to its use as a multipurpose meeting facility, but it has still packed in fans for the likes of Ted Nugent, Bret Michaels, Puddle of Mudd, and other hard-rockin' bands, as well as numerous sporting events and expos.

VAL AIR BALLROOM
301 Ashworth Rd., West Des Moines
(515) 223-6152
www.valairballroom.com
The exterior of this music venue just west of 63rd Street will send you into a time warp: The huge, stylized neon letters, including ones that read simply DANCING will remind you of a swank 1940s soiree, and indeed, Glenn Miller, Duke Ellington, and Lawrence Welk all played the Val Air in the heyday of ballroom dancing. Inside it's still a big, open space with

a stage rising at one end, but the music focus has shifted to rock, country, and hip-hop—numerous local and national acts have played here, and it can definitely get a little loud and crazy as fans pack the open space in front of the stage. The room holds at least 2,000 people. Dancing still goes on in open areas farther back from the stage, and there's a raised area with seating off to the side. The ballroom has also become the spot for Latino musical acts in Des Moines. There's a large parking lot with space for plenty of vehicles.

Shriek Heard 'Round the World

The Val Air has played a role in the campaigns of politicians who have sought to use Iowa as a springboard to the presidency, including being the site of at least one Democratic fund-raiser in 1971. More notoriously, the Val Air stage was the site of Howard Dean's infamous "scream," which he delivered the night of January 20, 2004, after finishing a disappointing third in the Iowa caucuses. Dean mounted the stage and let loose with an off-the-cuff speech that culminated in an uninhibited shriek heard 'round the world . . . or at least all through the ballroom (look it up on YouTube and hear it for yourself).

VETERANS MEMORIAL AUDITORIUM
833 Fifth Ave.
(515) 323-5400
www.iowaeventscenter.com

Connected to Wells Fargo Arena as part of the Iowa Events Center, "Vets" or "The Barn" became Des Moines's main music and entertainment venue after it was built in 1954, hosting all kinds of music shows, sporting events, and political confabs. Elvis Presley, Neil Diamond, and Van Halen are just some of the top names who graced the stage before Vets was eclipsed a few years ago by the newly opened Wells Fargo Arena. With a capacity slightly over 7,000, today it showcases acts that may not play next door in Wells Fargo—John Mellencamp, Hall & Oates, Larry the Cable Guy, and Rob Zombie have all played here in recent years, and it sees its fair share of sporting events and trade shows, too.

The biggest names in entertainment play here when they come to Des Moines—everyone from Carrie Underwood to AC/DC to Coldplay to Tom Petty has taken the stage at Wells Fargo, which opened in 2005. Part of the Iowa Events Center and holding up to 17,000 fans, the concert arena is known for its excellent sight lines. It has also hosted circuses, rodeos, monster truck shows, and numerous other sporting events. It is also home to both the Iowa Energy basketball team and the Iowa Barnstormers arena football team.

i MidwestTix.com is a local ticket company that usually has cheaper service charges than Ticketmaster. It's also a lot cheaper to pick up your tickets in person at a venue's box office than to go through a ticket company.

Batty Behavior

Des Moines's former downtown Veterans Memorial Auditorium was the site of an infamous 1982 incident where rock star Ozzy Osbourne bit the head off a live bat during a concert. As part of his tour supporting the *Blizzard of Ozz* album, Ozzy regularly bit the head off rubber bats that were tossed at him from backstage. On this particular night, however, a fan tossed a real bat. Ozzy managed to finish the show and was rushed to a local hospital to be tested for rabies. It is not known if he bit the heads off any more bats during shows.

WELLS FARGO ARENA
730 3rd St.
(515) 564-8000
www.iowaeventscenter.com

BARS WITH LIVE MUSIC

BLUE MOON DUELING PIANO BAR
5485 Mills Civic Pkwy., West Des Moines
(515) 564-7300
www.bluemoonduelingpianobar.com

You may get a kick out of this place, even if noisy sing-alongs by crowds guzzling potent mixed drinks don't sound like fun. On a small, open stage two piano players sit facing each other and take song requests from patrons. The tunes lean toward schlocky '70s and '80s nostalgia, and the performances aren't unlike what you'd see on an episode of *Glee* ("Don't Stop Believin'"!).Try as you might, you may soon find yourself singing and dancing along with the crowd, a mixture of locals and out-of-towners who pack the place, filling up every available surface, including the upstairs balcony, and even spilling onto the stage. Big, foofy drinks are the rule, with the standard bearer a 1-gallon fishbowl filled with vodka and mixers. Shows on Thurs, Fri, and Sat.

HOUSE OF BRICKS
525 E. Grand Ave.
(515) 727-4730
www.thehouseofbricks.com

This corner cubbyhole of a bar in the East Village appears to be just another drinking spot when you first walk in. Behind a garage door that runs down the middle of the room, however, is one of Des Moines's more popular live music venues. All types of bands have played here, including both national and local acts, and in genres from rock to country to anything else. They also have a regular open-mic comedy night and a poetry slam. There's music every weekend and plenty of weeknights as well. Tickets are available ahead of shows through the bar's website or via local ticket outlets.

PEOPLE'S COURT
216 Court Ave.
(515) 244-0038
http://peoplesdsm.com

One of the premier smaller live music venues in Des Moines, this shoebox bar in the Court Center complex has two areas, both of which have hosted bands. There's a focus on rock, but country and other types of bands have played here as well, including even soul singers crooning while banging on the piano. The intimate setting allows fans to get close to the stage, and it can get hot and sweaty when the room fills up, but the bar is well-situated for dispensing beer to the thirsty crowd.

VAUDEVILLE MEWS
212 4th St.
(515) 243-3270
www.vaudevillemews.com

This narrow, low-ceilinged room with a small stage in the back may not look like much at first, but it's one of Des Moines's hottest live music venues. An eclectic selection of rock, everything from fast punk and hardcore to more mellow offerings, spills out of the redbrick storefront and onto nearby Court Avenue. Ticket prices can range from under $10 to more than $20 for more well-known acts.

BARS & TAVERNS

BOMBAY BICYCLE CLUB
8410 Hickman Rd., Clive
(515) 270-6274
http://bombaydsm.com

A stop on the suburban bar scene, with little subtlety: Big, 40-ounce bottles of beer and malt liquor are popular here, and there are some two dozen varieties of suds on tap (cocktails are available as well, but you'll see far more patrons with beer). All types hang out amid the scruffy furniture and large outdoor patio, everyone from white-collar types to tattooed bikers. The bar frequently features live music on its small stage, while tasty burgers and wings are among the food offerings. Gets loud, even during the week.

COSMOPOLITAN LOUNGE
800 Locust St.
(515) 288-5800
www.800locust.com/lounge

Located off the lobby of the Suites at 800 hotel, this upscale cocktail room is a great spot for a martini or other fancy drink. Dim lighting and dark woods add to the subtle elegance of the room, which along with the small bar has several tables for seating, some of which can accommodate around half a dozen people. Peruse the lengthy cocktail menu and try a gin fizz in the summer or a hot buttered rum or Irish coffee in winter as you watch snowflakes drift down outside the windows. Jazz combos set up and play around the piano in the corner. Is that Don Draper sipping a martini at a table in the back? The bar stays open at least until midnight and sometimes later. Closed Sunday.

COURT CENTER
216 Court Ave.

This large complex holds several bars and entertainment venues on several floors, each with a unique character and clientele. **Sinners & Saints** (515-243-2322) is a fairly standard drinking den with a vaguely rock 'n' roll theme, while **Liar's Club** (515-237-5427), up on the second floor, has a big, open layout with hard-rockin' music blaring through the sound system and a young, fun crowd—it's a good spot to start a night of bar hopping, but not for a low-key quiet evening. **Heroes** (515-288-9432) *is* a more low-key joint, with a large selection of beers, while **People's Court** is known for its live music scene (see separate listing). Although the address is on Court Avenue, most of the bars can be accessed through the side door on 3rd Street.

i There are numerous other bars along Court Avenue, offering a variety of atmospheres and drink selections—try Legends American Grill (216 Court Ave.) if you're in the mood for a sports bar, or the Surf Shack (319 Court Ave.) for a wild, college party scene.

DUCKTAIL LOUNGE
1809 NW 86th St., Clive
(515) 727-5670

Dark wood paneling, plaid wallpaper, and framed hunting scenes may make you think you've stumbled into a stodgy private club, but this is actually a cozy, laid-back bar with an impressive selection of martinis and scotches. Drinks are a little on the pricey side, but the bartenders are master mixologists who pour them just right. A fireplace surrounded by couches and comfy chairs is a nice spot to kick back with friends, as well as just a good place to sit and watch the hearth while you sip your drink. Play a game of pool on the red-felt table. A heated outdoor patio accommodates smokers.

EL BAIT SHOP
200 SW 2nd St.
(515) 287-1970
www.elbaitshop.com

When you first walk into this rambling shack covered with all variety of junk and memorabilia, you are greeted by a staggering number of beer taps behind the bar, everything from American bocks and pilsners to German wheat beer, Belgian ale, and Barleywine beer, which has a complex, heavy flavor. There's also a 4-page (!) beer menu that may take you awhile to get through—there must be over 100 beers listed on it, including many microbrews (you can also ask the bartender for a recommendation). The "Jimmy Carter Happy Hour" every Thurs honors a 1979 law that led to the explosion of craft brewers, and local homebrewers have offered their product to be sampled here. There are also beer flights with a selection of beers based on type or country of origin, and beer cocktails that mix together different kinds of beer. They even find room for a menu with classic bar food like burgers, onion rings, and fish tacos. This is a favorite watering hole for local cyclists, who can get a little rowdy at times, but it's just the place if you're looking for a beer-soaked blowout.

✳FONG'S PIZZA
223 4th St.
(515) 323-3333
www.fongspizza.com

It's ostensibly a pizza joint, but what this place *really* is is a tiki bar, with some of the freakiest, most inventive drink presentations (and pizza) you'll find anywhere. The narrow space's green vinyl booths and Chinese lamps give it a sort of '70s kung fu–flick vibe, while the indie rock on the sound system lends hipster cachet. The drinks are headspinning, like the Suffering Bastard, a mixture of several rums, juices, and almond flavor, or the Skull Splitter, which has vodka, guava, and other juices and is served in a "tiki god" mug. Many of the drinks, in fact, come in various theme mugs, like the Funky Monkey in a giant ape bowl or the Scorpion in a blue skull. Classic tiki drinks like the Singapore Sling and mai tai are available as well. And those fighter pilot helmets on the wall? Well, if you want to wear one while downing kamikaze shots, the staff will gladly indulge you. Can't forget the menu: Numerous pizzas include the Fongolian Beef and Thai chicken, which have just the right combination of classic pizza flavors and Chinese spices. Check out the moo shoo pork, kung pao chicken, and crab rangoon pizzas as well. Gets hopping late at night and on weekends with spillover from the nearby Court Avenue Entertainment District.

G2 ROCK'N PARTY BAR
1871 NW 86th St., Clive
(515) 334-7350

A small, loud, no-frills drinking den on the Clive nightlife circuit. There's a pole here for dancing, but most patrons' attention is focused on the bar, where servers pour Bombs—strong, multi-liquor concoctions with secret ingredients that are eagerly sucked down by the largely young, partying crowd. Lots of tap beer gets quaffed here as well, and a disc jockey spins records on Fri and Sat nights. The kitchen turns out cheap, greasy bar food that may help you soak up the liquor.

GINO'S RESTAURANT & LOUNGE
5513 Mills Civic Pkwy., Suite 100, West Des Moines
(515) 226-2320
www.ginosfoods.com

A recently opened outpost in the heart of West Glen of a long-running family-owned Italian restaurant, this location is more of a sleek cocktail lounge, with red crushed-velvet booths and a curving zinc bar. More than 40 different martinis are available, many made with fresh-squeezed juices. Gino's is also known for their fancy ice cream drinks, and there are numerous drink specials throughout the week. Of course, it is a restaurant, with a menu featuring everything from Italian specialties such as seafood Alfredo and veal Marsala to comfort food like fried chicken, as well as big, juicy steaks. Entrees average about $20.

HESSEN HAUS
101 4th St.
(515) 288-2520
www.hessenhaus.com

Get some *gemutlichkeit* at this long, narrow bar with a German flavor, housed in an old train station just south of Court Street. The timbered ceiling adds to the beer-hall atmosphere, as do the many German brews on tap, including Spaten, Hacker Pschorr, Paulaner, and Warsteiner. The Boot is a 2-liter boot-shaped glass of beer, to be shared with friends per drinking rules printed in the bar's menu. There's an unbelievable assortment of bottled beers, too. When the train goes by outside, bartenders ring a bell and offer $3 Jägermeister shots. Food items include Wiener schnitzel, *Kassler Ripchen* (smoked pork chops), and sauerbraten, as well as hybrid items like Black Forest Pizza. There's a good selection of sandwiches as well. *Die Grosse Platte* is a family dinner platter with a smorgasbord of dishes, including bratwurst, Jaeger schnitzel, *Schweinshaxe* (pork shank), and four shots of Apfelkorn liquor. Polka bands play here occasionally, and there's an impressive display of beer steins. Needless to say, this is ground zero for Des Moines's annual Oktoberfest celebration, held in late Sept.

THE KEG STAND
3530 Westown Pkwy., West Des Moines
(515) 327-7249

A large, rambling club right next to I-235 and just across the street from Valley West Mall. Kegs serve as bar stools at some tables, and the bar offers "keg service"—you get your own keg to drink from, at $100 for a half keg or $200 for a full keg. Go ahead, if you feel nostalgia for your college days. Another funky drinking option is the Flabongo, a pink plastic flamingo filled with either beer or a specialty drink with a complex combination of liquor and juices. There's a good selection of tap and bottled beers, and lots of interesting appetizers from the kitchen, including a daily food special. Pool tables, foosball, darts, and even a shuffleboard machine provide ample diversion. There's occasional live music on a small stage.

LOCUST TAP
434 E. Locust St.
(515) 243-9399

There are bars, and then there are *dives*, and this is definitely the latter, its worn brick facade looking all the more incongruous on an East Village block stocked with hip shops and restaurants. The grotty ceiling and graffiti-covered walls inside affirm you're not in an upscale lounge. Plenty of cheap beer is quaffed by enthusiastic regulars, and this is actually a friendly, laid-back spot to have a beer with friends. The building formerly housed a bank and the vault is now used as a beer cooler.

MICKEY'S IRISH PUB
206 3rd St.
(515) 288-8323

One of a few Mickey's in central Iowa, this bar has a trove of Irish-American bric-a-brac on the walls, including a vintage "Kennedy for President" poster hanging prominently in the middle of the narrow room. There are carved shamrocks and a stag's head above the dark wood bar, and this is the place to enjoy a Harp with a shot of Jameson's. It feels like a workingman's pub, with a convivial bartender and a big jar of hard-boiled eggs on the bar, but also attracts plenty of downtown professionals. An eclectic mix of rock 'n' roll from the '70s through the '80s plays over the sound system. There's a shelf of board games in the corner if you don't want to watch sports on the 2 big-screen TVs.

PELICAN BAR & GRILL
208 3rd St.
(515) 243-4456

Televisions ring the entire room in this no-frills drinking bar just off Court Avenue. A regular crowd of young professionals hunkers down over bottled beer and strong mixed drinks, pondering the funky lights over the bar and soaking up the bass-heavy hip-hop pouring out of the stereo. Full-length windows give an unobstructed view of the street. This is a good spot to either start or end your evening out. The menu has pizza, pasta, and some nice sandwiches, including chicken pesto, Italian sausage, and meatball.

RACCOON RIVER BREWING COMPANY
200 10th St.
(515) 362-5222
www.raccoonbrew.com
Though it's primarily a restaurant, this downtown brewpub is also a nice spot to grab a beer. The brew comes out of giant copper tanks on display in the dining room, with several varieties available, including an IPA, cream ale, red beer, and stout. All the beers are fairly thick and hearty, so if a pint is too much you may want to try a flight, or sampler of beers in smaller glasses (you can also ask the bartender for a taste of one of the beers before you decide which one you'd like). Not a beer drinker? They also do a delicious homemade cream soda and root beer. There's a menu of late-night bites, with yummy choices like skillet nachos, french fries with melted cheese, and several pizzas. The upstairs pool room is very nice, with plenty of tables in a cool, retro-ish setting, with redbrick walls and exposed ductwork. The bar stays open until 2 a.m. Fri and Sat nights.

ROYAL MILE
210 4th St.
(515) 280-3771
www.royalmilebar.com
This place really does feel like an authentic British pub, with an extensive selection of porters and stouts on tap and walls cluttered with Brittania: a Union Jack, multiple British

football banners, and malt vinegar on the tables (no smoking, alas). The food menu has bangers and mash, Guinness stew, Scotch eggs, and shepherd's pie, as well as entrees like orange-glazed salmon and Bombay curried chicken. There's a narrow patio outside. Hidden away upstairs is the Red Monk, a dark little cubbyhole open Wed through Sat nights and serving an impressive number of Belgian beers.

SIDESHOW LOUNGE
1408 Locust St.
(515) 288-3672
http://desmoinessocialclub.org
Part of the Des Moines Social Club art center, this space with windows looking out on the street is a comfortable rumpus room full of old tables and chairs that is a nice place to kick back and relax with friends. In addition to a full slate of beer and wine and fairly cheap, strong drinks, there's all kinds of stuff going on here, from weekly trivia contests to comedy shows and dance nights. Definitely not your typical bar scene. Check ahead to see what's happening on any given night, as the schedule may change.

UNDERGROUND
500 E. Locust
(515) 243-4322
http://dsmunderground.com
Hidden away down a flight of stairs in the lobby of the historic Teachout Building (there's also an entrance around the corner on E. 5th Street, in front of Bagni di Lucca pizza), this basement room is the bar of choice for East Village hipsters and young professionals alike. Red vinyl booths line the redbrick walls, with a small stage set up at one end of the concrete floor. You may find yourself stumbling onto an avant-garde

performance of synth-pop versions of classic '70s hard-rock songs, even on a weeknight—it's that kind of place. The small bar stays busy turning out a variety of alcoholic "bombs" chalked up on a nearby blackboard, and there's a range of other drink specials as well. The adjoining large game room has foosball, video games, and multiple pool tables.

UNIVERSITY LIBRARY CAFE
3506 University Ave.
(515) 255-0433
Don't let the name fool you—this run-down little room just west of the Drake campus is a classic college dive bar that happens to make the best nachos in the city—as they inform passers-by with a large outdoor sign. The nachos really are quite good, with several varieties available, including a yummy smoked chicken. Pretty good burgers and fries as well. It's a nice spot for lunch, or to have a beer or two with friends. No credit cards. Closed Monday.

ZIMM'S
3124 Ingersoll Ave.
(515) 277-9929
A friendly crowd of regulars will most likely be on the bar stools at this large yet low-key pub. The atmosphere is vaguely sports bar, with several televisions and sports bric-a-brac on the walls. Classic rock plays in the background and there are numerous drink specials throughout the week. Besides the main bar just inside the entrance, there's a smaller bar in the pool room in back. They even have a shuffleboard table. The outdoor patio is a nice spot to unwind on a sunny afternoon. The food is a cut above the typical pub grub, including a Philly cheese steak (called a "Des Moines" here) and several other

sandwiches and salads, as well as steak and seafood.

i Several no-frills "dive" bars line Ingersoll Avenue and are nice places to go if you just want a low-key evening of beers with some friends. Try Greenwood Lounge (3707 Ingersoll Ave.; 515-277-1219), Alpine Tap Room (2720 Ingersoll Ave.; 515-245-9717), or Des Moines Yacht Club (2617 Ingersoll Ave.; 515-245-9208). A good reason to head over to Ingersoll during a night out is to pick up a slice at Big Tomato Pizza Co. (2673 Ingersoll Ave.; 515-288-7227). Though slices should be available anytime, you're more likely to get one late, late in the evening, so this might be a good end-of-night stop.

CASINOS

PRAIRIE MEADOWS RACETRACK
** & CASINO**
1 Prairie Meadows Dr., Altoona
(515) 967-8544 or (800) 325-9018
www.prairiemeadows.com
A large gambling establishment located just northeast of Des Moines on I-80. Try your luck at nearly 2,000 slot machines, as well as table games like poker and blackjack. Thoroughbred and quarter horse racing runs Apr through Oct on the track, and there's simulcast racing throughout the year from Churchill Downs, Saratoga, and other famous tracks. Numerous entertainment and restaurants are found throughout the complex. Top acts like B. B. King and Kenny Rogers have taken the stage here. Free parking and valet service, as well as a free shuttle from the parking lot to the main entrance.

CINEMA

FLEUR CINEMA & CAFE
4545 Fleur Dr.
(515) 287-4545
www.fleurcinema.com

This multiscreen theater in a south-side strip shopping center is as close as it gets to an "art house" in Des Moines, with occasional showings of offbeat and independent films. Actually, they do a good job most weeks of having a mixture of current Hollywood releases with more obscure selections, including foreign films. The lobby cafe has beer and wine as well as coffee drinks and snacks. Plenty of parking in the lot right outside.

VARSITY THEATRE
1207 25th St.
(515) 277-0404

A wonderfully old-school movie house across the street from the Drake campus, with a single screen and a popcorn machine wedged in just behind the ticket window. Prices are reasonable, and they usually have something interesting playing on any given weekend—often an independent or overlooked film, although they do show mainstream Hollywood fare as well. It may take you several minutes to find parking on the street—plan accordingly with your movie's starting time.

COMEDY CLUB

THE FUNNY BONE
560 S. Prairie View Dr., West Des Moines
(515) 270-2100
www.funnybonedm.com

A West Glen comedy club that features numerous touring comedians, including the

---

Movie Theaters

The following Des Moines–area cinemas show more mainstream Hollywood releases. Many have stadium seating and expanded concession stands.

- Century 20, 101 Jordan Creek Pkwy. (Jordan Creek Mall), West Des Moines; (515) 267-8981.
- Cobblestone 9, 8501 Hickman Rd. (Cobblestone Market), Urbandale; (515) 331-3456.
- Copper Creek 9, E. University Avenue and Copper Creek Drive, Pleasant Hill; (515) 266-2676.
- Merle Hay Mall Cinema, 3800 Merle Hay Rd.; (515) 252-0804.
- Nova 10 Cinemas, 4353 Merle Hay Rd.; (515) 270-8221.
- Southridge 12, SE 14th Street and Army Post Road (south of Southridge Mall); (515) 331-3456.
- Wynnsong 16, NW 86th Street and I-35/80; (515) 331-3456.

---

occasional celebrity appearance. It's a typical comedy club setup, with tables surrounding a small, low stage. The room is small enough that you should have a good view no matter where you sit. Seating is first-come, first-served. The club is completely nonsmoking. There's an extensive food menu and full bar. Shows run Wed through Sun nights, with two shows nightly on Fri and Sat, and typically cost $10; more for the big names.

DANCE CLUBS

515 ULTRA LOUNGE
5535 Mills Civic Pkwy., Suite 100, West Des Moines
(515) 564-7010

Inside this sleek, futuristic, dimly lit space in West Glen, there's little more than a bar and couches along the walls, leaving plenty of room to groove to the pounding bass beat on the DJ's sound system. Swirling colored lights and the sparse decor give this space a chic, big-city vibe, which is further fueled by the fact that it doesn't get going until late in the evening. Have a drink, preferably something vodka-based, chill out, and ease into your own personal dance zone.

MISS KITTY'S DANCE HALL & CYBER SALOON
8800 Swanson Blvd., Clive
(515) 327-1303

A big, cavernous dance club inside a suburban strip mall that at first glance resembles a honky-tonk—the saddle hanging from the ceiling is a tip-off, and there is plenty of line dancing to country tunes here. Hang out awhile, however, and you'll hear an incredibly eclectic mix of music, with rock and hip-hop in addition to country (you'll probably catch all three styles of music in a single night, sometimes one after the other). On weekends the line to get in can snake out the door, and the dance floor fills up as the night grows later with a young, stylish crowd that likes to party while slamming down drinks. Closed Sunday, Monday, and Tuesday.

UNCLE BUCK'S
1720 25th St., West Des Moines
(515) 221-2317

A hangar of a dance club with an airport-size parking lot. The huge dance floor has a mechanical bull at one end and an actual beer truck pouring drafts. On weekend nights it's virtually indistinguishable from a college-town meat market, with a young crowd and suitably loud music. Doesn't really get going until late at night, but packs 'em in once it does—expect to get hot and sweaty. The adjoining sports bar is a somewhat more low-key scene, with plenty of televisions on which to watch a game.

GAY & LESBIAN NIGHTLIFE

Des Moines gay nightlife is not as developed even as much as some other midsize cities—some bars and clubs have closed in recent years. The LGBT comes together every June for **Pridefest** (www.capitalcitypride.org), a weekend festival held in the East Village.

BLAZING SADDLE
416 E. 5th St.
(515) 246-1299
www.theblazingsaddle.com

If not for the clientele, which is largely (though not entirely) male, this nondescript redbrick building on an East Village side street could be any dark, narrow bar with a pool table and a crowd of loyal regulars. There's a welcoming atmosphere here, with friendly bartenders pouring beer, wine, and mixed drinks. Attracts a mixed crowd of young gays and older, more buttoned-down professionals, as well as its share of lesbians. There are drink specials throughout the week. Hosts drag shows and can get a little carnival-esque on the weekends, but overall it's a pretty low-key spot.

THE GARDEN NIGHTCLUB
112 SE 4th St.
(515) 243-3965
www.grdn.com

Local Entertainment Guides

CityView
www.dmcityview.com
A free weekly newspaper that has several pages of listings of upcoming acts at music clubs, bars, and other venues. They also have quite a few restaurant listings, as well as a weekly news summary and some rather opinionated political columnists. This paper not only helps you find out about nightlife options in Des Moines, but gives you a sense of the overall state of affairs in the city as well.

Juice
http://dmjuice.desmoinesregister.com
Published by the *Des Moines Register,* this is another free weekly with extensive listings of music shows and other goings-on in Des Moines and the surrounding area, as well as restaurant reviews and guides to different types of shopping. There's a feature article every week, some weeks with more depth than others, and, like *CityView,* plenty of photos of twenty- and thirtysomethings on the town. Both *Juice* and *CityView* can be found at numerous locations downtown and throughout the city.

Datebook
www.desmoinesregister.com/datebook
In addition to *Juice* (see above), the *Des Moines Register* also publishes this weekly entertainment guide, with the paper version included in the paper's Thursday edition. There are plenty of restaurant, movie, and music listings, as well as feature articles on entertainment options (some of the coverage is duplicated between *Juice* and *Datebook*). The restaurant reviews tend to be especially well-written, while movie reviews are often syndicated or reprinted from other publications. There are plenty of family-friendly events listed as well, like community parades and holiday goings-on, especially from Halloween through Christmas, and lots of summertime events, too. The online version is well organized in terms of dining, movies, music, and other nightlife possibilities.

Metromix
http://desmoines.metromix.com
A large online clearinghouse of information, one of many on different cities nationwide, that lists restaurants, nightlife, and other things to do in Des Moines. It's easily searchable and fun to browse through the long lists of local hot spots, although some entries may be out of date.

Housed in a converted warehouse space out past the southern end of the east village, this bar and dance club attracts a younger crowd of both men and women, gay and straight. During the week, the ground-level video bar is a fairly low-key spot to grab a drink, with friendly, energetic bartenders moving to the pulsating bass of dance tracks that play on the room's many screens. The dance floor heats up on weekends, and there are regular karaoke nights and drag shows. Drinks are reasonably priced, and there's usually no cover charge earlier in the evening or on weeknights.

RITUAL CAFE
1301 Locust St., Suite D
(515) 288-4872
www.ritualcafe.com
Not explicitly a gay/lesbian spot, but one that is very LGBT friendly, this funky little cafe in the Western Gateway section of downtown has a full vegetarian menu of healthy meals and snacks like quiche, hummus, and panini, as well as some yummy breakfast items. It also has a full complement of coffee drinks and other hot beverages, and hosts music acts on its small stage. The decor gives a definite international vibe, with Tibetan prayer flags, tie-dyed items, and similar accoutrements. Closed Sunday.

SPORTS BARS

DOWN UNDER BAR & GRILL
8350 Hickman Rd., Clive
(515) 278-6718
www.greatestbar.com
Though it has a vaguely Australian theme, this place is really a sports bar on steroids: Endless televisions showcase games in every sport and with every team you might possibly imagine (and some you haven't).

Abundant drink specials throughout the week make this a favorite of both regulars and the weekend party crowd. Lots of dartboards are in constant use by local sharpshooters. There are pool and video games as well, and a respectable menu with a wide selection of appetizers, pizza, and sandwiches.

THE LONGEST YARD
122 5th St., West Des Moines
(515) 274-1710
All the sports bar touchstones can be found here: memorabilia cluttering the walls, a generous selection of tap beers, and, most important, wall-to-wall televisions to watch games. However, there are some atypical features as well: the pressed-tin ceiling and carved, dark wood back bar make for a somewhat more sophisticated drinking spot, and the crowd can be a little more low-key than a typical sports bar (although not during Hawkeyes games). A lengthy menu has plenty of burgers and sandwiches to choose from and munch on while cheering on the team. The name may be a sports reference, but it also refers to the signature drink: A "yard" of beer, served in a long, thin glass. Located on the main drag of Valley Junction, and a good spot to take a break from shopping in nearby stores.

WELLMAN'S PUB
2920 Ingersoll Ave.
(515) 245-9737
These two sports bars may be siblings, but they differ significantly in tone and atmosphere: The original location on Ingersoll is a somewhat low-key bar and grill where folks from the neighborhood go to have a pint and watch the game. The new location, out just past West Glen (597 Market St., West Des

Moines; 515-222-1100) is a rather different story: Rising up out of the surrounding flat landscape, it is packed with young professionals most nights, and may set a record for the number and size of television monitors, including 2 giant screens that hang over the middle of the large, open room. There's also a ticker running scores above the bar. The rooftop patio is *the* place to hang out on a warm evening, sipping a cold drink as you look out over this rapidly developing frontier of Des Moines. (The Ingersoll location has outdoor seating as well.) Food is served at both spots, the usual pub grub of burgers, pizza, sandwiches, and appetizers.

THE ARTS

D es Moines has a thriving art scene, and you don't have to look too hard to find it: From the fabulous Pappajohn Sculpture Park in a refurbished Western Gateway section downtown to the city's free art museum, with a fine collection of contemporary works, art is easily accessible. In addition, artists have set up shop in studios around the city, especially in converted downtown buildings, creating all sorts of works, while there are numerous storefront galleries in major shopping areas like the East Village, Ingersoll Avenue, and Valley Junction in West Des Moines.

Performing arts include a symphony, a ballet, and an opera that mounts ambitious productions every summer, bringing in singers from all over the world, as well as numerous live theater options, offering everything from light comedies and musicals to serious drama and including a good selection of children's shows.

In addition to always having something going on in both visual and performance art, the Des Moines Social Club, 1408 Locust St. (515-288-3672; www.DesMoinesSocial Club.org), home to the Instinct Gallery (see below), is a centrally located clearinghouse of information on artists working in Des Moines—if you're serious about exploring the city's art scene, you might want to drop by or give them a call to find out what you might check out, artwise. (The Social Club is moving to a new downtown location sometime in 2011, so call or check their website for details.) Metro Arts Alliance, 500 E. Locust St., Suite 201 (515-280-3222; www.metroarts.org), maintains a directory of area artists as well as a calendar of upcoming arts events.

The Des Moines Arts Festival, held every June in and around Western Gateway Park and the Pappajohn Sculpture Garden, is a three-day celebration of the visual arts. Artists come from all over to showcase their wares in booths set up on city streets that are closed to traffic, and there's a juried exhibition of artworks in various media, as well as a film festival. A performing arts stage and live music add to the festive atmosphere. Admission is free. Artstop, usually held in September, consists of two days of special events at galleries and studios throughout the city, including sites in the East Village, Western Gateway, Ingersoll Avenue, and Valley Junction, and includes free bus service to different locations, as well as an extensive guide to local art options.

ART MUSEUM

✳DES MOINES ART CENTER
4700 Grand Ave.
(515) 277-4405
www.desmoinesartcenter.org

A free museum with numerous contemporary art pieces, including works by Picasso, Matisse, Edward Hopper, and Francis Bacon. Andy Warhol and Georgia O'Keeffe have works here as well, as do more recently recognized artists like John Currin. There's a good mix of painting, sculpture, and other media, all laid out in spacious, well-lit galleries that are arranged for a nice stroll through the museum. Additional sculptures are displayed on the museum grounds. Visitor guides are available, including audio guides. The outside of the building is worth a look as well: The white structure is a combination of designs by three world-renowned architects, with the original part of the building, designed by Eliel Saarinen, joined with additions by I. M. Pei and Richard Meier. Each part stands out and adds to the building's overall style, even in areas where the different architects' visions seem to clash. The museum is closed Mon.

ART GALLERIES & STUDIOS

ARTDIVE
1417 Walnut St.
(515) 245-9000
www.artdive.com
Located on the southern edge of Western Gateway, along a stretch still dominated by warehouses and auto garages, this 1,600-square-foot space serves as a gallery and studio for local artists. A good selection of art is on display, with paintings in styles such as pop art and post-impressionism, as well as some landscapes. Many of the works are very colorful and playful. A selection of jewelry and wood and metal decorative pieces are on display as well. Open Thurs, Fri, and Sat afternoons and early evenings, or by appointment.

INSTINCT GALLERY
1408 Locust St.
(515) 288-3672
www.instinctgallery.com

Located just past the front entrance of the Des Moines Social Club, this small space has shown plenty of modern and experimental art, including the work of numerous local artists, as well as themed shows with works by nationally known artists. The gallery sometimes has artists come in and "paint live" and has hosted competitions where artists must create work in an hour or less—these can get pretty intense, as artists square off to create compelling pictures, with spectators watching and choosing the winner. In addition, there is an annual photography show. Open Tues through Fri from 5 to 8 p.m. and by appointment.

MOBERG GALLERY
2921 Ingersoll Ave.
(515) 279-9191
www.moberggallery.com
Artist Tom Moberg's gallery has featured his work in landscape sculpture, with an emphasis on trees and nature designed to blend in with their surroundings, as well as more abstract work in painting and multimedia. The gallery has also hosted numerous rotating shows by other modern artists working in a variety of media. Open Tues through Sat and by appointment.

OLSEN-LARSEN GALLERIES
203 5th St., West Des Moines
(515) 277-6734
www.olsonlarsen.com
This Valley Junction storefront is full of canvases and other works from the more than 70 artists represented by the gallery. Painting, photography, sculpture, and mixed media are all part of the collection here, and represented artists have displayed work in major museums as well as created pieces for numerous commissions. Regular shows have

featured new works from numerous artists. Open Tues through Sat.

POLK COUNTY HERITAGE ART GALLERY
2nd Avenue and Walnut Street (Polk County Building)
(515) 286-2242
www.polkcountyheritagegallery.org
Tucked away inside the northwest corner of the Polk County Building, in a space that was once the city's post office, this ornate, high-ceilinged gallery has rotating shows of Iowa artists working in different styles and media. The high, arched windows provide plenty of natural light, and the smooth marble floors add to the calmness and serenity as you stroll past landscapes, portraits, and other works. Open Mon through Fri 11 a.m. to 4:30 p.m. Free admission.

ROBERT SPELLMAN GALLERY
1727 Grand Ave.
(515) 979-6158
www.robertspellmangallery.com
A small, spare storefront gallery in Western Gateway that showcases the work of a Des Moines artist who paints mainly in oils and acrylics. His work has touches of landscape painting as well as more abstract styles, and often features a wide palette of colors. Open by appointment only.

STUDIO 3
2925 Ingersoll Ave., Third Floor
(515) 491-5312
www.hnndesign.com
This top-floor space is located in a sleek, fairly new glass tower—to reach the studio, take the elevator by the back door of Red China Bistro, next to the parking lot. The two artists-in-residence specialize in colorful

acrylic paintings, with both contributing to many of the canvases on display. There are also numerous hand-painted silk scarves and handbags and colorful mobiles and other household products. They also offer art classes in the space. Open Tues through Thurs from midmorning to midafternoon, and by appointment.

i Some Des Moines artists open their studios to the public on select dates, allowing them to get an up-close look at their work. One of the best opportunities for this is at Fitch Studios (304 5th St.; 515-288-1185), which has a number of artists working in different media. They typically open to the public twice a year, for the city's Artstop gathering in September and then again in early December. Contact the studio to find out exact dates when studios will be open.

PERFORMING ARTS

Live Music

CIVIC MUSIC ASSOCIATION
1620 Pleasant St., Suite 244
(515) 280-4020
www.civicmusic.org
For nearly a century Civic Music Association has offered an annual lineup of top performers in a wide variety of music styles. Wynton and Branford Marsalis, Marian Anderson, Beverly Sills, and Yitzhak Perlman have all been brought to Des Moines by CMA. So have well-regarded combos like the Berlin Philharmonic Wind Quintet, the Wycliffe Gordon Quartet, and the Boston Brass & Brass All-Stars Big Band. Contemporary acts like jazz singers are found on the schedule alongside folk musicians and classical ensembles and

choirs. They have also taken a stab at holiday music with a Christmas concert that had big-band arrangements of offbeat Christmas tunes. All concerts are held in Sheslow Auditorium at Drake University. Individual ticket prices range from roughly $5 to $45, with ticket packages available for multiple shows.

✳DES MOINES SYMPHONY
221 Walnut St.
(515) 280-4000
www.dmsymphony.org
A not-for-profit professional orchestra in operation since 1937, the Des Moines Symphony performs 6 pairs of Masterworks concerts annually and has played pieces by composers including Dvorak, Beethoven, and Tchaikovsky. The symphony has over 75 musicians and is conducted by Maestro Joseph Giunta, who has conducted orchestras around the world and has been with the Des Moines Symphony since 1987. The symphony performs downtown at the Des Moines Civic Center, in a large auditorium that has good sight lines and acoustics. A well-attended New Year's Eve pops concert has in recent years combined classical music with performances by circus acrobats. The annual Yankee Doodle Pops Concert, held right around the Fourth of July, takes place on the State Capitol grounds. Individual tickets cost from $15 to $70, with significant discounts available for students.

DES MOINES VOCAL ARTS ENSEMBLE
(515) 961-1578
www.dmvae.org
Dedicated to bringing choral performance to Des Moines in a chamber choir setting, the ensemble has been performing since 1992 and has covered works by Beethoven and Bach as well as contemporary composers. The ensemble has worked with internationally renowned conductors as well as collaborated with other choirs. It performs 3 to 5 concerts a year, including a highly anticipated holiday concert in December. Performance venues vary and have included several local churches. Tickets are often no more than $15 and can be purchased through the ensemble's website.

Dance

BALLET DES MOINES
712 E. 2nd St.
(515) 440-1177
http://balletdesmoines.org
A ballet company that has been rebuilding since the mid-2000s and is looking to move forward as a professional company, this troupe has many promising young dancers, with guest dancers in many productions. For nearly 20 years, the ballet has put on a popular production of *The Nutcracker* every Christmas season, which features many children dancing in supporting roles. Several dancers with the company have gone on to have successful professional dancing careers. There are occasional shows the rest of the year, such as *Alice in Wonderland*, which was performed in the winter of 2011, accompanied by the Des Moines Community Orchestra. The ballet performs *The Nutcracker* at Sherman Place Theater and also performs at the Des Moines Civic Center downtown. The company also makes an effort to do previews and shorter versions of performances in the community, performing at all sorts of locations including malls and schools. Ticket prices for individual performances can vary widely—check to see prices for each show.

Live Theater

BLACK BOX THEATER
1408 Locust St.
(515) 288-3672
www.desmoinessocialclub.org
Another part of the Des Moines Social Club arts complex, this wide-open theater, which seats up to 200, puts on around a dozen shows a year. It is home to the Repertory Theatre of Iowa (see below), as well as 2 other resident theater companies, one of which puts on more experimental works and the other performs several works by one chosen playwright a year. The performance schedule varies—contact the Social Club for more details.

CIVIC CENTER OF GREATER DES MOINES
221 Walnut St.
(515) 246-2300
http://civiccenter.org
In addition to its in-house theater company, StageWest (see below), the downtown Civic Center presents an annual season of numerous theater productions, as well as music, dance, and other shows—it has begun running dance shows featuring internationally renowned companies of ballet and modern dance, including the Martha Graham Dance Company. The theater shows are generally a mixture of touring plays and musicals, pop music acts and family-friendly shows, like children's theater and music productions. Shows take place on one of three stages— make sure you know in which space your performance is located! At the Civic Center building, a main hall seats nearly 3,000, with seating sloping steeply upward from the stage, thus giving a good view of performances from throughout the auditorium; a much smaller black box theater seats

about 200. Many music shows take place at the Temple Theater, a 4,000-square-foot room that seats about 300 and has excellent acoustics, and is actually located in the Temple for Performing Arts at 1011 Locust St. Tickets for all shows are available at the Civic Center box office, as well as via telephone and online.

CLASS ACT PRODUCTIONS
201 1st Ave. S, Altoona
(515) 967-7950
www.captheatre.org
This community theater does nothing but shows for children, and features productions with a large number of children onstage. Shows have included musicals, comedy, and holiday-themed plays. Ticket prices can range from around $10 to around $25 for adults. Open auditions allow children to try out for several shows over the course of the year.

✳DES MOINES PLAYHOUSE
831 42nd St.
(515) 277-6261
www.dmplayhouse.com
Home to 2 stages, including a main auditorium and a smaller children's theater, this long-running community theater, one of the oldest in America, is located in a castle-like structure across the street from an elementary school and always has an interesting lineup of plays. Productions have included longtime favorites as well as lesser-known plays, including adaptations of popular books and movies. Serious drama and experimental, off-Broadway-style shows have been followed onstage by musicals, comedy, and other lighter fare. The children's theater has delighted younger theatergoers with works from some of the more popular

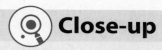

Close-up

Bill Bryson, Bard of Des Moines

Des Moines doesn't really have any sort of literary scene, but Iowa has produced a few well-known authors, and perhaps the most popular is contemporary writer **Bill Bryson,** who grew up on the west side of Des Moines and graduated from Roosevelt High School before moving on to college and a career as a newspaperman in the United Kingdom. He eventually began writing books, with his writing marked by a sometimes biting wit and dry sense of humor. He often relies on personal experience for his material, including his time in Des Moines: He offered up some tidbits about the city, not always flattering, in his first book, *The Lost Continent,* which detailed a meandering driving trip he made around America in his mother's car. Subsequent books found him continuing the travel theme, with a journey around Europe in *Neither Here Nor There* and Australia in his book *In a Sunburned Country,* as well as *A Walk in the Woods,* a recounting of a memorable, error-plagued trek down the Appalachian Trail with an old Iowa friend from his youth. Bryson has also focused on more general books that explored science and history. His memoir of growing up in Des Moines in the 1950s and '60s, *The Life and Times of the Thunderbolt Kid,* was adapted into a play that had a short run at the Des Moines Playhouse in 2009.

children's books as well as tales of adventure and adaptations of Broadway hits. There are also regular children's theater classes. Tickets are available at the theater's box office, as well as through its website and by telephone.

REPERTORY THEATER OF IOWA
1408 Locust St.
(515) 779-0994
www.rtiowa.com
This professional company has been around since the mid-2000s and has presented plays by theater giants like Tennessee Williams, Arthur Miller, and Horton Foote, as well as Beckett, Chekhov, and Shakespeare, and numerous productions by lesser-known playwrights. Recent shows have included *Agnes of God* and *Cat on a Hot Tin Roof,* as well as seasonal favorites like *A Christmas Carol.* There are over a dozen actors

in-residence in the company. Performances are held at the Des Moines Social Club, in their intimate black box theater. They have also presented shows at other locations including the Iowa governor's mansion and the annual Shakespeare on the Lawn Festival. Tickets are usually around $15–$20 and can be purchased via www.MidwestTix.com, which is also linked to the theater's own website.

STAGEWEST THEATRE COMPANY
P.O. Box 12127, 221 Walnut St.
(515) 309-0251
www.stagewestiowa.com
Since 1995 this theater company has brought some offbeat and experimental shows to Des Moines, showcasing works by Neil LaBute and other cutting-edge artists and mounting some ambitious productions like *Angels in America.* They have also put

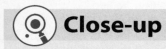 **Close-up**

Outdoor Shakespeare

Two summer theater events have brought the works of the Bard of Avon to alfresco performances in central Iowa. For several years **Shakespeare on the Lawn,** www .salisburyhouse.org/events_shakespeare_on_the_lawn.html, has featured the Repertory Theater of Iowa's performances of *The Merry Wives of Windsor, Twelfth Night,* and other plays at Salisbury House (4025 Tonawanda Dr.; 515-274-1777), on the west side of the city. Wine for sale adds to the festive atmosphere as theatergoers relax on lawn chairs on the house's spacious grounds. Meanwhile, **Iowa Shakespeare Experience,** www.iowashakespeare.org, takes to the stage at Simon Estes Riverfront Amphitheater downtown, putting on a festival with unique takes on Shakespeare over several days, leading up to the main production, which recently has included an adaptation of *A Midsummer Night's Dream.* You can expect to see lots of music, dance, and special effects. Picnicking on the lawn is a highlight for many attendees—some go all out with tents and champagne chilling in a bucket alongside gourmet cheese, antipasto, grilled meats or fish, and fresh-baked bread from one of Des Moines's signature bakeries. Local favorite Chocolaterie Stam has proffered yummy desserts at the festival, too, and the wine flows freely.

on numerous premieres by many different playwrights. The full season of plays runs from roughly Oct through July. Shows take place at the Stoner Theater, a 180-seat black box theater located in the Des Moines Civic Center downtown. Ticket prices are around $20–$25, and are available at the Civic Center box office, as well as through the center's website and by telephone. The company also has a tradition known as "Scriptease," a regular event that usually takes place the last Tues of the month and is held at a venue other than their theater. It includes unrehearsed readings of scripts as well as new material. Works by local playwrights have been included in the mix.

TALLGRASS THEATRE COMPANY
P.O. Box 301, Dallas Center
(866) 745-4535
www.tallgrasstheatre.org

Since its founding in 2000 by two local theater artists, this community theater company has put on an interesting array of shows, staging 3 to 5 productions each year, specializing in dramas. The company has also put on an annual playwriting workshop that features an Iowa playwright. Shows are usually held at the Rex Mathes Theatre (1401 Vine St.) in West Des Moines, a short drive from the Valley Junction shopping area. Ticket prices range from $10 to $15, and can be purchased through the theater's website.

OPERA

DES MOINES METRO OPERA
106 W. Boston Ave., Indianola
(515) 961-6221
www.desmoinesmetroopera.org
In a quiet college town a half-hour drive from Des Moines, this opera company has

taken to the stage for nearly 40 years and has become one of the more respected regional opera companies in America. Each season, which runs June through July, the company presents 3 operas, which are usually a mix of a classic, well-known opera, a more contemporary opera, and a more challenging work. Under its longtime director, Robert Larsen, the opera performed many of the standards of grand opera, including *Madame Butterfly, Carmen, Don Giovanni, Othello,* and many, many others. Its new director now oversees a company of singers and musicians who come from all over to perform in central Iowa. The opera performs in the Pote Theatre, which has less than 500 seats and is located in the Blank Performing Arts Center on the campus of Simpson College. The center has undergone renovations and now has over 1,500 square feet of additional lobby and other space, as well as adjustments to the seating that have improved the opera experience. The smaller theater space makes for a more intimate performance, and you may have the opportunity to hear a talk from the director before the show or to meet the singers afterward, a rare opportunity to discuss the craft of opera with those who practice it. Tickets for individual performances range from about $50 to about $90 and may be purchased online, via telephone, or at the opera's box office.

SHOPPING

Major shopping areas in Des Moines include the East Village, which is bounded roughly by E. Court Avenue on the south, the State Capitol on the east, I-235 on the north, and the Des Moines River on the west and has many shops along Grand Avenue and Locust and Walnut Streets, and Valley Junction, with several blocks of shops packed tightly along 5th Street in West Des Moines. There are a ton of boutiques and unique shops in these two neighborhoods, and they're both good places to make "finds" of unique items, antiques, and both high-end and funky jewelry. They also have numerous good eating spots that can be very pleasant places to take a break from searching for that perfect gift or tchotchke. Though it's known more for its nightlife, West Glen, on the western side of West Des Moines, right off Mills Civic Parkway and to the east of Jordan Creek Mall, has some interesting shops located amid its bars and clubs. Ingersoll Avenue is another area that has some low-key shops that are well worth poking around in to find hidden treasures.

More mainstream shopping can be found at Des Moines's quartet of large malls, as well as along many major east–west arterial roads like University Avenue in West Des Moines, where you'll find every type of big-box store imaginable, including stalwarts Best Buy, Barnes & Noble, Borders, and many others. But if it's a shopping adventure you want, stick to the East Village or Valley Junction—you'll be surprised what you can find just by coming back for a second day!

ANTIQUES

A-OK ANTIQUES
124 5th St., West Des Moines
(515) 255-2525
This Valley Junction shop has a large selection of modern items mainly from mid-20th-century America, as evidenced from the neon signs cluttered above the doorway and hanging in the front room. There are a lot of retro household items—need a pea-green Hamilton Beach milk shake mixer? The womb chairs on the second floor are far-out, man, especially the model with a built-in sound system, and the Warhol artwork on the walls adds to the vibe. Check out the

vintage stereo systems scattered among the sleek tables and other furniture. A small backyard serves as an impromptu sculpture garden, with some geometric, modernist pieces. This shop has the same owners as Atomic Garage, across the street, and both are fun places to check out.

FOUND THINGS
520 E. Grand Ave.
(515) 265-8624
www.foundthingsdsm.com
An interesting jumble of antiques and other old stuff spread over 2 floors. There's lots of

antique furniture as well as kitchen items—you may find some old cast-iron appliances if you root around enough. Downstairs you'll find vintage clothing and a nice collection of vintage books, including a bunch of children's titles. There are some neat vintage postcards as well.

PORCH LIGHT
526 E. Grand Ave.
(515) 255-5900

A treasure trove of retro housewares, such as vintage glass food containers and pottery teapots, is stuffed inside this shop on one of the East Village's more popular street corners. There's an entire cabinet of milkglass, done up in the old "bubble" style. Some fun vintage toys are scattered throughout the long, narrow space as well. Take a few minutes to flip through the cubbyholes stocked with wonderful old metal diner signs, and check out the selection of jewelry at the sales counter.

BOOK STORES

BARNES & NOBLE BOOKSELLERS
4550 University Ave., West Des Moines
(515) 221-9171
www.barnesandnoble.com

BORDERS BOOKS, MUSIC, AND
MOVIES
4100 University Ave., West Des Moines
(515) 223-1620
www.borders.com

These are the Des Moines outposts of the two big national bookstore chains. Although there is a Barnes & Noble at 101 Jordan Creek Pkwy. at the Jordan Creek Mall in West Des Moines (515-453-2980), the University Avenue Barnes & Noble probably has the widest selection. If you don't find what you're looking for there, you can always check at the Borders just down

the road (which is remaining open, despite many recent store closures throughout the country). Both chains, of course, have a wide array of fiction and nonfiction titles as well as music, magazines, and cafes where you can sip a hot drink while browsing through your purchases. You can also find plenty of deals on the discount and bargain shelves, and this may be the place to go if there's a hard-to-find book you can't locate at one of the smaller bookshops—if they don't have it in stock they may be able to order it for you.

*BEAVERDALE BOOKS
2629 Beaver Ave., Suite 1
(515) 279-5400
www.beaverdalebooks.com

An intimate little bookshop in a strip shopping center at the heart of Beaverdale. Covers all the usual genres in fiction and nonfiction, with popular authors and best sellers alongside some undiscovered gems. There's also a section devoted to Iowa authors, where you can pick up works by Bill Bryson and other native scribes, as well as some nice coffee table and picture books on the state. The shop hosts the occasional reading and is a popular gathering spot for local book lovers.

THE BOOK STORE
606 Locust St.
(515) 288-7267

A classic, hole-in-the-wall independent bookstore, in business since 1961 and located in a storefront in the Equitable Building downtown. The store has a good mix of fiction and nonfiction, with strong cookbook and travel sections, among other genres. The owner is a book aficionado who can help you find what you need or make recommendations. Occasionally hosts readings. Closed Sunday.

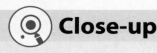 # Close-up

Eating and Shopping in Valley Junction

Valley Junction, a former railroad hub in the older part of West Des Moines, has become well-known as a shoppers' paradise—it's a place where you can pick up all sorts of unusual and unique items ranging from international arts and crafts to vintage clothing and accessories to fine arts and jewelry to homemade pet food (and that's just a start). All that shopping makes one hungry, however. Fortunately, there are several places to grab a quick bite before resuming your search for the next hidden treasure:

Sandwiches and soups are tasty and filling at **The General Store** (206 5th St.) or **Paula's** (501 Elm St.). A much longer menu, with plenty of fried items, can be found at the **Longest Yard** (122 5th St.), which has some great burgers. This is a first-rate sports bar, known for their long, thin glasses dispensing "yards" of beer, and has lots of televisions tuned to various games (you may have difficulty finding a seat here if the Hawkeyes are playing). Stop in at another spot for a cold brew, **Giff Wagner's Fifth Street Pub,** housed in an old VFW post. Finally, pick up some sinfully sweet treats at **Carefree Patisserie** (516 Elm St., just off 5th Street), with a scrumptious selection of cupcakes. The lineup of flavors changes occasionally, giving you the opportunity to try some new ones.

PLAIN TALK BOOKS & COFFEE
602 E. Grand Ave.
(515) 283-1230

This cozy little room on the edge of the East Village stocks a wide variety of books, including titles on Des Moines and Iowa and novels by local authors. The selection is somewhat limited, but you're sure to find something that interests you, plus there are comfy chairs where you can sit and read and snacks for sale. The staff is friendly and helpful.

BOUTIQUES & SPECIALTY SHOPS

ANCIENT WAYS
3029 Ingersoll Ave.
(515) 274-9034
www.ancientwaysdsm.com

New-age books and items are available at this modern-day corner store on a busy stretch of Ingersoll Avenue. Tomes on Eastern thought, mysticism, holistic health, and other spiritual disciplines can be found on the shelves, as can crystals, incense, oils, and other paraphernalia. There are also classes offered on a wide variety of topics, including astrology and shamanic healing, as well as tarot card readings. The staff can advise you if you're looking for a book or item in a particular field that you aren't able to find.

FAIR WORLD GALLERY
116 5th St., West Des Moines
(515) 277-7550
www.fairworldgallery.com

A funky little shop with an assortment of items from around the world, as well as by local artisans. There are some beautiful wood and metal folk art pieces from Africa and Latin America, and a nice selection of colorful dresses, scarves, and other clothing.

A small jewelry counter has glittering bracelets, earrings, and necklaces. Also a good spot to pick up some interesting soaps or lotions, as well as some world music CDs in a wide range of genres.

GONG FU TEA
414 E. 6th St.
(515) 288-3388
www.gongfu-tea.com
On a busy street in the East Village sits this oasis of serenity: Every type of tea imaginable in a spare, minimalist room, with leaves stored in glass containers on shelves that line the shop. The tea ranges from old standbys like Darjeeling and Chinese Gunpowder to decidedly more offbeat blends like Erin Go Bragh or Blue Spring Oolong. A lengthy booklet explains the flavors of the teas for sale, and the staff is happy to answer any questions—the owners travel the globe looking for interesting varieties of tea to bring back to Des Moines. There's a small tasting room if you want to enjoy your tea on the spot, including a Japanese area with woven mats. A formal Chinese tea service is available as well. The store also sells plenty of other tea-related items, like different types of teapots and tea drinking accessories.

JETT AND MONKEY'S DOG SHOPPE
503 E. Locust St.
(515) 244-4211
www.jettandmonkey.com
Named after two of the canines who hang out in their own space behind the counter, this East Village shop offers dog items that are both practical (organic dog foods and shampoos) to the more extravagant (doggie sweaters in a variety of colors). A countertop case holds fresh-baked doggie cookies and biscotti. Being dog lovers, the staff are good for recommendations for local vets and other pet professionals.

KITCHEN COLLAGE
400 E. Locust St.
(515) 270-8202
http://mykitchencollage.com
This East Village shop is chock-full of all sorts of kitchen gear, including a wide array of baking pans and every type of kitchen accessory you might need, whether preparing a small, intimate supper or a major feast. There's a nice selection of knives as well. High-end coffeemakers and coffee accessories are piled on shelves in the middle of the room. The test kitchen in back hosts occasional cooking classes as well as other classes on topics like knife skills. A knowledgeable staff can help you sort through the vast array of items and pick out the cooking gear you need. Closed Sunday.

LIGHT THE EARTH
125 5th St., West Des Moines
(515) 271-7625
www.lighttheearth.com
A fine selection of oil lamps built from different types of stones, as well as incense burners and jewelry, can be found at this Valley Junction shop. All items are handcrafted in-house, with many of the lamps fashioned out of stones the owners have collected on their far-ranging travels. There are also lamps made of petrified wood and other materials. Closed Mon as well as Sun from Jan through Mar.

THE QUILT BLOCK
325 5th St., West Des Moines
(515) 255-1010
www.iowaquiltblock.com
Lots of fabrics, plus complete quilts, are for sale here at the north end of Valley Junction.

Numerous patterns and notions are available as well. The shop features Bernina sewing machines and offers regular classes on using them and creating various projects, and also serves as a clearinghouse of information on local and area quilting shows.

✳RAYGUN
400 E. Locust St.
(515) 288-1323
www.raygunshop.com
This funky East Village T-shirt shop, run by a scrappy young entrepreneur, specializes in offbeat screen-printed shirts with sayings that have an often mischievous and decidedly local edge. Samples: DES MOINES: FRENCH FOR "THE MOINES," or "IOWA CITY: ALL OUR CREATIVITY WENT INTO THE NAME." (There are other designs that probably can't be mentioned here.) Many shirts have a decidedly political bent. The selection of shirts can change, with new shirts coming onto the racks that line the narrow, minimalist space, and the young staff will probably be hard at work printing shirts when you drop by. The store also has other hipster wear like jackets and sweatshirts and an eclectic selection of books and novelty gifts.

SEED
500 E. Grand Ave.
(515) 244-3277
A funky, boutique-y garden shop, with its stock about evenly divided between plants and garden decor items. Among the plants are some interesting tulip bulbs and a wide selection of herbs, including rosemary, Greek oregano, and grapefruit mint. Some gardening implements are available, as well as a whole rack of gardening gloves. The staff are a good source of information, particularly if you have questions about garden design and which plants are best for your garden.

SQUIGGLES
3200 Ingersoll Ave., Suite B
(515) 277-1120
Entering this storefront in a strip shopping center set back from the street, you are greeted with a riot of color—there are all sorts of home decor items and jewelry in a rainbow of hues. Many of the items would make a nice yet funky addition to your dining table or living room—plenty are by local artists, with some pieces cleverly constructed out of found or salvaged objects. The store also has many seasonal themes, making this a good place to go if you're looking for stuff to decorate your home for Halloween, Christmas, or other holidays.

STICKS AMERICAN CRAFT GALLERY
521 E. Locust St.
(515) 282-0844
www.sticks.com
This rambling, tasteful storefront in the East Village houses a cornucopia of furniture, household decorating items, and accessories. Many of the pieces have a distinctly folk art look, with bright colors and whimsical touches a feature of many items. The store grew out of the work of a local abstract painter who designed small decorative items. Today all pieces are designed and crafted by a team of artisans in the shop's own design studio, who use birch, poplar, and driftwood to turn out everything from armoires to dresses and beds, and also create mirrors, lamps, and candlesticks and everything in between—you can spend a lot of time in the store perusing the selection. The staff will also build custom pieces based on different themes and colors.

THEATRICAL SHOP
145 5th St., West Des Moines
(515) 274-3661
www.theatricalshop.com
A treasure trove of costumes, from historical figures to superheroes and everything in between, is piled high in the aisles and along the walls at this store, which announces itself with a large marquee in the heart of Valley Junction. There's a wide selection of kids' costumes, as well as wigs, makeup, accessories, and some risqué items for adult costume parties. Also sells standard theater and dance supplies.

VITAE DESIGN COLLECTIVE
400 E. Locust St., Suite 4
(515) 288-1349
www.vitaedesign.com
A shoebox of a boutique in the East Village that has lots of interesting items, such as T-shirts with printed designs and batik-pattern dresses. There are some nice tote bags and kids' items too, as well as a good jewelry selection. Most of the items come from local artisans and designers. Poke around the clothes and accessories that line the walls—you should be able to make some good finds.

WANDER THIS WORLD
333 E. Grand Ave.
(515) 279-0371
www.wanderthisworlddsm.com
A cornucopia of neat items from around the world is found in this small shop. This is the place to pick up African woven baskets or an Andean panpipe, and there are plenty of items that would make great gifts. Several musical instruments are among the offerings, including a good selection of drums. One display case holds a fragrant array of

soaps and lotions, and there are plenty of kids' T-shirts with colorful designs. Pick up a tote bag made from all-natural fibers or a bag of fair-traded coffee. Closed Monday.

WEST END ARCHITECTURAL SALVAGE
22 SW 9th St. (corner of Ninth and Cherry)
(515) 243-4405
www.westendarchsalvage.com
This redbrick warehouse in the shadow of a traffic overpass is 4 stories of recovered vintage treasures for the home. Stuffed in the high, open rooms is everything from basic building materials to fine antiques. Whole sections are devoted to lamps, doors, and furniture, including pieces made from recycled materials in the in-house workshop. Stained-glass windows stand alongside old advertising signs. Retro decorative objects stand on every available flat surface. Telephones on each floor put you in touch with the staff, who will run your finds down in the freight elevator. There's a coffee bar on the first floor—you'll need it to take a break from your hunting!

CAMERA & PHOTOGRAPHY STORES

ALEXANDER'S PHOTO
3313 Ingersoll Ave.
(515) 288-6888
Located in the heart of the Ingersoll Avenue commercial strip, this small shop has a pretty good selection of camera and accessories, with all the major brands represented. They also carry a full line of photography guides if you're looking to brush up on your technique or just need some tips on shooting better. Several of the sales staff are photographers themselves, and they can advise you on everything from camera selection to

lighting to the proper filter to use to get the shot you want. Closed Sunday and Monday.

CHRISTIAN PHOTO
6721 Douglas Ave.
(515) 270-8030
www.christianphoto.biz
This family-owned camera store near Merle Hay Mall has a good selection of photography items. In addition to all the major camera models, including the newest digital cameras, they also carry darkroom supplies and lighting equipment, and do digital printing for customers. The store offers photography classes that are a good introduction to the basics of digital photography. They also take trade-ins on used cameras. Closed Sunday.

H. B. LEISEROWITZ CO.
213 13th St.
(515) 244-5195
In business for over 100 years, this shop in a brick warehouse on the edge of the Western Gateway carries a full line of cameras and accessories, including a wide selection of Canon and Nikon models, everything from point-and-shoot cameras to more professional outfits. Offers lots of accessories as well, like lenses, flashes, and camera bags. The sales staff knows their stuff, and they can help track down more obscure equipment and order it for you. Closed Sunday.

COMIC BOOKS & COLLECTIBLES

COFFEE & COMICS
4521 Fleur Dr., Suite F
(515) 974-0515
Wedged into a small shopping center by Fleur Cinema and near the Des Moines airport, this shop has a small but varied mix of comics and graphic novels. Cardboard boxes on the front counter hold older and vintage books and are worth a look if you're looking for classic D.C. or Marvel titles. As the name indicates, there's a full coffee bar, as well as comfy chairs at the front of the store for perusing your purchases. Open until 10 p.m. Mon through Sat.

JAY'S CD & HOBBY
3315 SE 14th St.
(515) 287-4578
www.jayscdandhobby.com
A *huge* pop culture smorgasbord, occupying an 11,000-square-foot space, of thousands of used CDs, DVDs, comics, video games, sports cards, action figures, and many other hidden treasures, plopped down alongside a supermarket and large thrift store at one of the busiest intersections in the city. Items are not organized in any particular fashion—expect to spend a lot of time hunting through the racks and bins. This place is run by a crew of young enthusiasts who will gladly jump in to try to help you find what you want, as well as buy your old stuff. Prices are very reasonable. Open 7 days a week.

MAYHEM COLLECTIBLES
7500 University Ave., Suite D, Clive
(515) 271-8104
www.mayhemcomics.com
A well-stocked comic lovers' paradise, with a large back room offering hundreds of used comics, very nicely organized by title. Everything from classic superhero books to more esoteric titles can be found here if you look hard enough. There are plenty of new comics as well, with a wall of new releases up by the front counter, and the staff can help you find what you're looking for. They also carry card and board games, videos, and novelty items, including all sorts of comic-related

collectibles. An adjoining room has long tables where local gamers gather to do battle in fantasy worlds.

CLOTHING STORES

Men's Clothing

BADOWER'S ON INGERSOLL
2817 Ingersoll Ave.
(515) 283-2121
An upscale yet relaxed haberdashery behind a low-key facade, with a nice selection of casual and dressy clothes, including sport coats, pants, shirts, and accessories. Some stylish designers on the racks, including Hugo Boss and Robert Talbott. The fashion intimidated need not worry—the salesmen here know their clothes, and they'll set you up with everything from a single piece to a complete outfit, putting together the best combination of fabrics and patterns.

MR. B
1995 NW 86th St., Clive
(515) 276-8589
www.midwestclothiers.com
A long-standing presence on the local clothing scene, this suburban shop carries multiple lines including Hart Schaffner Marx, Allen Edmonds, and Ike Behar, as well as many others. Their selection of suits and ties is impressive, and there are plenty of casual clothes with elegant touches. They have a reputation for great customer service. On-site tailoring is top-notch as well. There's also a women's shop at the same location.

Women's Clothing

AIMEE
432 E. Locust St.
(515) 243-0045

This East Village boutique is the place for couture—new dresses, tops, and other items arrive almost weekly, with many lines coming from the UK. The owner will pour you a glass of wine or champagne and help you pick out a piece or a whole outfit, but it's also fun to just browse through the racks of cashmere, fur, wool, and other fabrics. Lots of nice accessories, like scarves and hats and locally designed jewelry, too. Closed Monday.

DORNINK
518 E. Grand Ave.
(515) 255-7528
www.dornink.com
Run by a mother-daughter team who together have spent decades in the fashion industry, including time in New York, this elegant little East Village shop offers custom-made bridal and cocktail dresses in colorful silks and other fabrics. Dresses are inspired by top designers yet have their own unique touches and accents. Celebrities and local notables have turned up in Dornink's work, and you can easily outfit a full bridal party here, including accessories. The designers will work with you throughout the process of creating your dress. Closed Sunday.

CYCLING SHOPS

BIKE WORLD
6600 Douglas Ave., Urbandale
(515) 255-7047
www.bikeworldiowa.com
A mecca for local bike enthusiasts, Bike World has 2 floors of bikes and gear at their main shop near Merle Hay Mall. Stocked among the bikes are helmets, jerseys, gloves, and shoes in all sizes for kids and adults. Upstairs are bike racks for vehicles as well as a complete maintenance and repair shop. Most of the staff are bike fanatics, and they

know bikes down to the most minute technical specs (the shop isn't only for serious bike riders—if you just want to pick up a modest bike, you can do that here too). The staff is also a good source of information on local spots to ride and local cycling events. In addition to the flagship store, there are also locations in West Des Moines and Ames. Open 7 days a week "in season," from spring through fall.

ICHI BIKE
311 E. Walnut St.
(515) 274-0397
www.ichibike.com
If you want to take a nostalgia trip, bike-wise, then you *must* check this place out. Salvaging old bike frames, workers here slap on new tires and components to create fully functional rides. Classic Cruisers, Fastbacks, and Stingrays from the '60s and '70s are in stock here, with high-riser handlebars, banana seats, and springer forks. Some bikes even have the old stick-shift mounted on the frame, and you may also find some original Schwinns from the Chicago factory. Prices vary, and the staff can fix up and trick out your old bike if you bring it in. They also sell new bikes and accessories.

RASMUSSEN BIKES
301 Grand Ave., West Des Moines
(515) 277-2636
www.rasmussenbikehome.blogspot.com
Just past 63rd Street, on the western edge of Valley Junction, this modest-size shop is crammed full of bikes and accessories. Plenty of major brands and models are here, with a knowledgeable sales staff to help you pick out the bike that's right for you. Also carries helmets, clothing, and shoes, and has a full in-house maintenance and repair shop. Chat up some of the staff to find out about good places to ride in the area. Open 7 days during the height of riding season, from spring through fall.

OUTFITTERS & SPORT SHOPS

*BACKCOUNTRY OUTFITTERS
2702 Beaver Ave.
(515) 255-0031
http://theoriginalbackcountry.com
All sorts of camping and outdoor equipment is available at this family-owned Beaverdale shop, from ultralight, high-tech outdoor stoves to an extensive selection of sleeping bags, tents, and accessories. The majority of the store is devoted to clothing, both rugged outdoor gear and more fashionable pieces. Poke around on the sales racks—you can find some really great deals on clothes and shoes. The sales staff includes outdoor buffs who can explain to you the finer points of the gear for sale.

FITNESS SPORTS
7230 University Ave., Windsor Heights
(515) 277-4785
www.fitnesssports.com
This unassuming storefront in a strip mall just off 73rd Street has an impressive selection of shoes for both serious runners and more casual types. They also carry swimming gear, including suits and accessories. Plenty of local triathletes stock up here in preparation for their next event, but if you just need a new pair of shoes for running or walking, the staff is happy to help you out, and very knowledgeable about the different models of shoes they have for sale. The store also serves as a clearinghouse for information on running races of all lengths all over the Des Moines area and Iowa.

Shopping Malls

Des Moines is amply served by malls, with four good-size ones offering a wide variety of stores, as well as food courts and in some cases movie theaters. The two malls located in West Des Moines are fairly easily accessible from interstate highways, while the two older malls, located in the city proper, require a bit more of a drive along busy city streets. The malls are listed here from newest to oldest.

Jordan Creek Town Center
101 Jordan Creek Pkwy., West Des Moines
(515) 224-5000
www.jordancreektowncenter.com

This is the big kahuna of Des Moines malls: A 2-million-square-foot complex that is one of the largest malls in the Midwest, with numerous restaurants and entertainment options in addition to over 150 small stores. The mall's anchor stores are Dillard's, Younkers, and Scheels All Sports. The mall's movie theatre has 20 screens. Outside, there's a 3.5-acre lake with walking, jogging, and bike paths and many restaurants. Nearby are several big-box stores.

Southridge Mall
1111 E. Army Post Rd.
(515) 287-3881
www.shopsouthridgemall.com

On the southern edge of Des Moines alongside US 69/SE 14th Street, this mall has a JCPenney, Sears, Target, and Younkers and many smaller stores, as well as a food court and stand-alone restaurants. There's also a movie theater and a children's carousel and play area.

Valley West Mall
1551 Valley West Dr., West Des Moines
(515) 225-3631
http://valleywestmall.com

A quick hop off I-235 brings you to this 2-story mall just south of University Avenue, with anchor stores JCPenney, Von Maur, and Younkers spread out evenly along the mall's central corridor. The large food court is located on the lower level, and there are some interesting specialty shops here, including an outpost of sweet shop Chocolaterie Stam.

Merle Hay Mall
3800 Merle Hay Rd.
(515) 276-8551
www.merlehaymall.com

Des Moines's oldest mall, open since 1959, has a more modest selection of stores spread out over a fairly large mall, including anchor stores Kohl's, Sears, Target, and Younkers. There's a food court, a movie theater, and a bowling alley in the basement. (In case you're wondering, Merle Hay was the first Iowa soldier to be killed in World War I, and possibly the first American soldier to be killed in the war.)

RECORD STORES

ZZZ RECORDS
2200 Ingersoll Ave.
(515) 284-1401
www.zzzrecords.com

A very cool record store that has managed to hold on even in the face of dwindling interest in recordings—they still have long rows of bins containing used vinyl LPs. There's even *new* vinyl here—the store has plenty of aficionados of this older format, and the owner gladly stocks it for them. They also carry CDs, new and used, and a small selection of DVDs. There's a listening station where you can cue up a record for a spin before you decide to buy it. They buy used LPs, which are then added to the stock of thousands. The shop is a little tricky to find—it's the storefront at the eastern end of a building housing a large audio store. Closed Monday.

SPECIALTY FOOD STORES

ALLSPICE
400 E. Locust
(515) 868-0808
www.allspiceonline.com

Step inside this bright East Village storefront and you are confronted with a roomful of shelves of clear glass containers holding every spice imaginable, from your basic cinnamon and nutmeg to *much* more exotic choices, including every type and intensity of chili powders and other spicy seasonings. In the back of the room are metal kettles with a wide selection of olive oils and chile peppers, with flavors ranging from the spicy to the sweet, including chocolate (try a free sample!). The helpful staff can provide recommendations, recipes, and cooking tips,

and there are occasional cooking classes offered. Closed Sunday.

✳CHOCOLATERIE STAM
2814 Ingersoll Ave.
(515) 282-9575

This unique chocolate shop started in the Netherlands and now has locations in both that country and all over the American Midwest. Glass cases are filled with chocolate creams, marzipans, bonbons, truffles, and many other delights. There's also a full selection of gelato, which is a bit pricey, but it's velvety smooth, with flavors like berry, lime, and mango peach as well as several chocolate-based varieties. The shop sells wines from Iowa wineries as well. The Ingersoll location has an elegant indoor seating area, as well as some outdoor seating by a tranquil fountain, which is a nice place to hang out on warm evenings. An additional location is at the Valley West Mall, 1551 35th St., West Des Moines, (515) 457-8464.

HEART OF IOWA MARKET PLACE
211 5th St., West Des Moines
(515) 274-4692
www.HeartofIowa.com

The focus here is on foods from Iowa, with shelves of hearty bread, pancake and soup mixes, Amana Colonies jams, preserves, and mustards, Iowa salsas (some of which can pack a punch!), and wines from local and state wineries. Homemade fudge, made right in the shop, is sinfully delicious—try a free sample. There's also a full array of Iowa-themed gifts, including plenty of toys and licensed items from the University of Iowa, Iowa State University, and John Deere. They do plenty of gift baskets if you're having trouble picking out an item.

SUZETTE HOMEMADE CANDIES
2837 Ingersoll Ave.
(515) 288-1405
http://suzettecandies.com
A longtime neighborhood confectioner, specializing in chocolate and fudge, with lots of rich varieties of the latter. Decadent truffles peer out from the display cases, and there's a large selection of yummy roasted nuts. Ice cream is available—the flavors aren't anything extraordinary, but they're tasty, and the shop does seasonal treats like homemade caramel apples in the fall. There are also suburban locations in Altoona and Urbandale.

TOY STORES

ANGIE'S KID ZONE
228 5th St., West Des Moines
(515) 277-6832
www.angieskidzone.com
A bright, airy shop in a former bank building (the first-floor vault now holds a collection of stuffed animals). Lots of wooden toys for sale, including items like a build-your-own log cabin. Plenty of educational toys as well, with a wide selection of Melissa & Doug items, and theme toys like Thomas the Tank Engine. Good choice of board games and puppets, too.

BRILLIANT SKY TOYS AND BOOKS
699 Walnut St., Suite 233
(515) 288-4689
www.brilliantskytoys.com
Located in the Kaleidoscope at the Hub atrium mall on the downtown skywalk, this shop's selection is somewhat modest, but it has some intriguing toys, including plenty of unique board games, action figures, and educational items, including plenty of "brain teaser" puzzles and other logic games. They

also have a nice selection of somewhat offbeat items like View-Master disks and some nice kites. Friendly and helpful staff.

VINTAGE SHOPS

✴ATOMIC GARAGE
127 5th St., West Des Moines
(515) 274-8787
Walk through the front room at this dusty Valley Junction shop to find a back room overflowing with vintage clothing arranged by era, from the roaring '20s to the swinging '60s and disco '70s (they don't seem to have made it up to the '80s yet). This is the place to pick up go-go dresses and boots, *Mad Men*–style loungewear, paisley shirts, Nehru jackets, and all sorts of other kitsch duds. There are numerous racks of vintage T-shirts as well, with all sorts of designs available, and plenty of jewelry and accessories.

DOROTHEA'S CLOSET VINTAGE
1733 Grand Ave.
(515) 991-3516
www.dorotheasclosetvintage.com
An impressive array of retro dresses and other clothes are crammed into this storefront on the edge of Western Gateway. Clothes here range from the 1880s (!) to the 1980s, with all sorts of pieces available, including hats, purses, and accessories, including costume jewelry. The shop has outfitted actors in period films, and it's not hard to put together an ensemble that will make you look like you just stepped out of the pages of a fashion magazine from the 1940s. In stock are so many great names of 20th-century fashion: Halston, YSL, Lagerfeld, and Dior are just some of the labels you'll find on the racks. Open Wed through Sat or by appointment.

ATTRACTIONS

Des Moines has attractions for all sorts of interests, from sports and local history to fine art and science, including a working observatory where visitors can do some stargazing under the guidance of an astronomy professional. The Iowa State Capitol is perhaps Des Moines's most prominent attraction, with many interesting architectural features both inside and outside the building, although the state historical museum, just a few blocks away, also has a rich trove of items to peruse during a long or short visit. When visiting the Capitol, don't forget to check out the rolling grounds around the building with their numerous monuments. The city's art museum is a true gem, with free admission to its respectable collection of contemporary art well-arranged in a winding series of galleries inside a building that bears the stamp of three world-renowned architects. Other art attractions, including many galleries, can be found in the arts chapter.

There's an appreciable amount of green space and outdoor attractions in the Des Moines area, including some surprisingly scenic vistas. Information on these and other outdoor attractions can be found in the Parks chapter. The Kidstuff chapter includes some attractions not listed here that may appeal especially to younger visitors.

Attractions are grouped below according to location, beginning with those located in downtown neighborhoods, then moving into the rest of the city, and finally covering the outlying areas outside the city limits.

Price Code

Price codes are based on the cost of a single adult admission.

$	Less than $5
$$	$5 to $10
$$$	$10 to $20
$$$$	More than $20

DOWNTOWN

DES MOINES BOTANICAL CENTER $$
909 Robert D. Ray Dr.
(515) 323-6290
www.botanicalcenter.com

This glass geodesic dome on the east bank of the Des Moines River has numerous displays of plants and trees, including an interesting bonsai collection and lots of tropical and subtropical plants, with palm trees arching overhead. Orchids and desert plants are some of the more intriguing displays. There are a few animals here as well, including birds, fish, and other water life. An adjacent outdoor garden has some nice shrubs and water features. Brochures are available for self-guided tours. Children's programs are featured throughout the year, including tours and story presentations. Free parking in the center's lot.

IOWA HALL OF PRIDE $$
330 Park St.
(515) 280-8969
www.iowahallofpride.com
Located on the ground floor of Hy-Vee Hall at the Iowa Events Center, this large, open room is largely focused on Iowa athletics, with extensive displays on football, basketball, baseball, softball, volleyball, and other sports. The achievements of Iowa high school and college athletes are highlighted in the many interactive displays and video presentations, including a 180-degree panoramic theater that lets viewers relive some of Iowa's most storied sporting events. Other video screens contain interviews with legendary Iowa players. In an adjoining room are sporting games, including a quarterback challenge where participants try to complete as many passes as possible, and a basketball free-throw challenge (a limited number of free game tokens are provided to visitors). There are also displays on the achievements of Iowans in other fields, like science, music, and the arts. Free parking is available in the lot right outside the entrance. Closed Sunday.

*IOWA STATE CAPITOL $
East 9th Street and Grand Avenue
(515) 281-5591
www.legis.state.ia.us/pubinfo/tour
Perched atop a hill, with its dome gilded in 23-karat gold leaf and rising to a height of 275 feet, the Capitol is perhaps the most striking site in the entire city. Free tours are given Mon through Sat and cover an impressive amount of space, giving the visitor plenty to see (there is a lot of walking on this tour, including climbing some long staircases). Saturday tours run every hour on the half hour beginning at 9:30 a.m. and ending at 2:30 p.m. Weekday tour times may vary—it's best to make arrangements ahead of time. Weekend tours do not include the governor's office, and tours do not go onto the floor of the House or Senate when they are in session, from mid-Jan through mid-Apr.

Tours begin at the tour desk on the first floor, one level above the ground floor where you enter the building. Next to the tour desk is a display on the construction of the Capitol, which began in 1871 after the state government moved from the original capital at Iowa City Twenty-nine types of marble were used in the building, as were 13 types of wood. Much of the original interior was painted over in the 1930s and '40s, and interior restoration began in the late 1970s, with paint scraped away to reveal the original paint scheme. There has also been renovation work on the sandstone and limestone exterior, including the 5 statues over the pediment. The secretary of state's office includes the Iowa Constitution, which was signed in 1857 and is displayed in a specially designed case. Down the hall is the old, ornate Supreme Court Chamber, where justices heard cases for nearly 120 years until the new Supreme Court building was completed in 2003. You can see the intricately carved judicial bench, which features whimsical touches like griffins and the "wheels of justice."

The governor's office is a 4-room suite with both working and formal offices and containing many of its original furnishings dating back to 1885. A huge chandelier hangs over the reception area. A grand staircase rises at the east end of the first floor. Intricately carved alabaster entwines around marble column at the foot of the staircase—look closely to see "fighting lizards" and other details of the carvings. The bronze statues of nymphs, one on each column, were originally intended for the Illinois State Capitol but ended up in Iowa after Illinois found them too risqué! Once you reach the top of the staircase on the second floor, you have a view of the large, majestic mural *Westward*, which covers an entire wall. The mural measures 40 feet wide by 14 feet high and depicts the arrival of pioneer settlers in Iowa by covered wagon. A female angel figure holds the great seal of Iowa, another holds a book symbolizing learning and enlightenment, and two more hold a basket symbolizing Iowa's rich agricultural heritage. Two more angels, behind the wagon, hold a model of a steam engine and a dynamo, respectively, representing the coming of the machine age. Above the mural are 6 colorful mosaics, created out of Murano glass from Venice, Italy. Ask your tour guide to point out the optical illusion in the mosaics—it's hard to see if you don't know where to look. Higher up in the rotunda are 12 golden statues Below the statues are 8 lunettes, or half-moon-shaped paintings by 19th-century American artist Kenyon Cox.

The House chamber, finished in black walnut with marble wainscoting, is decorated with portraits of notable Iowans and US presidents and still has its original wooden desks. In 1904 a fire broke out when a worker who was part of the building's conversion from gas to electric light left a candle burning above the chamber. The chamber's ceiling was destroyed and the Capitol's lower floors suffered water damage.

The Senate chamber is not quite as high as the House chamber, but, like the House chamber, it is finished in walnut and marble. Large brass chandeliers and Corinthian columns, add elegant touches.

The second-floor law library is notable for the iron grillwork spiral staircases that snake up 4 levels of bookcases. At each level, grillwork balconies hide passageways that allow staff to circulate around the entire room. Books are still delivered from the upper levels by dumbwaiter, and the entire room has a hushed, scholarly feel. The windows give a nice view down Locust Street to downtown.

The climb up inside the dome is about 130 steps from the second floor, with the last 9 steps up a narrow, ladder-like staircase that leads to a "whispering gallery" (ask your guide to demonstrate how it works) directly under the inner dome. Above is stretched a banner with the emblem of the Grand Army of the Republic, including an early American flag and a bald eagle. Round windows evenly spaced along the whispering gallery actually give a view: To the south is the copper dome of the Supreme Court building, and all around are the 4 smaller copper domes at each corner of the Capitol. After leaving the Capitol, check out the main dome from outside. The gold leaf that covers the dome is so thin that 250,000 sheets pressed together would measure only 1 inch thick. The dome also has a lantern and was regilded in 1998–99 at a cost of nearly $500,000.

JOHN AND MARY PAPPAJOHN SCULPTURE PARK FREE
13th Street and Grand Ave.
(515) 277-4405
www.desmoinesartcenter.org
One of downtown's newer gems, this lovely, free sculpture garden in Western Gateway, operated by the Des Moines Art Center, is a lovely place to stroll among an eclectic selection of artwork. The pieces here

The Capitol Grounds

The grounds around the Capitol are festooned with monuments, especially to the south of the building, where the column rises of the soldiers' and sailors' monument, honoring Union forces in the Civil War. Memorials to other wars are nearby. The *Shattering Silence* sculpture, across Court Street from the Capitol and to the west of the copper-domed Iowa Supreme Court building, is a stylized wheel design by Iowa artist James Ellwanger that commemorates an 1839 Supreme Court ruling that said that former slaves who came to Iowa were free people with equal protection under law. In front of the Capitol's west entrance, a statue of Abraham Lincoln and son Tad sits in the shadow of the building's limestone friezes. The East Village and downtown unfold to the west, with streets moving downhill toward the river. To the north is the state library, formerly the state historical building, which in turn has moved into the large, modern structure on Locust Street just past the Capitol grounds.

are largely modern, including William de Kooning's *Reclining Figure*, a fine example of abstract expressionism, and Barry Hannah's whimsical *Thinker on a Rock*, which may give children visions of *Alice in Wonderland*. Take your time moseying along to appreciate the sculptures along the winding paths. One of the most popular spots is at Jaume Piensa's

Nomade, a large, open figure where you can stand and examine the pileup of painted white metal letters that make up the sculpture (although touching the sculptures is not allowed, with the exception of Scott Burton's *Seating for Eight* and *Cafe Table I*, a minimalist circle of chairs that's a nice place to take a break from walking).

Guided tours of the sculpture garden are available Apr. 1 through Oct. 1—contact the art center at (515) 271-0328 to arrange a tour. Three or more weeks' advance notice is required to schedule a guided tour, for which there is a fee.

i Guided tours of downtown are offered throughout the summer by the Iowa Architectural Foundation (400 Locust St.; 515-244-1888; www.iowaarchfoundation.org). Tours typically begin at 5:30 p.m. on the third Thursday of May, June, July, August, and September, and depart from the foundation's office at Capital Square. Cost is $10.

SCIENCE CENTER OF IOWA   **$$**
401 West M. L. King Jr. Pkwy.
(515) 274-6868
www.sciowa.org
Two floors of hands-on science activities for kids of all ages are found at this museum, located downtown just south of the Court Avenue Entertainment District. There's an outer-space room with telescopes to look through and examine stars and planets, and a planetarium-style theater where you can choose the shows you want to watch from a long list of astronomy topics. In the adjoining hands-on room, kids can build a paper rocket and shoot it up to 40 feet using a compressed air gun, build a miniature dam

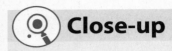# Close-up

Downtown Walking Tour

Downtown Des Moines is a fun spot for architecture enthusiasts and history buffs, with numerous interesting buildings and hidden treasures in the details of some of the bustling blocks of office towers. Start out at the **Polk County Courthouse** (500 Mulberry St.), facing the Court Avenue Entertainment District to the east, which is also the site of the **Saturday farmers' market** (this tour, in fact, can be a fun excursion to take after a stroll through the market). The courthouse is a prime example of Beaux Arts architecture and was built as part of Des Moines's participation in the City Beautiful movement of the late 19th and early 20th century. Look closely at the courthouse and you will see nearly 30 "grotesques," or carved faces, nestled in among the building's Corinthian columns.

Heading west on Mulberry into the core of the downtown business district, you soon reach one of downtown's more intriguing structures: the **EMC Insurance Companies.** The main lobby is around the corner at 700 Walnut St., but take a moment, step back from the building's south facade, and look up: It's easy to imagine that the back of the building resembles an Absolut vodka bottle. Now walk north to Walnut Street—inside the main lobby is a large sculpture by the artist Mac Hornecker, entitled *Prairie Wind.* The curved black steel lines evoke both the weather and topography of the Great Plains. The more intriguing aspects of this building are not quite as explicit: The exterior is constructed of recycled aluminum equal to almost 17 million soda cans, while the building's nearly 1,400 windows are extremely thermal resistant. The granite foundation was built to last 100 years, and the heating and cooling systems make and store ice that cuts down on energy costs.

Across Walnut Street is the **Hub Tower** (699 Walnut), which has a row of carved lions along its redbrick exterior and is the home of **Kaleidoscope at the Hub,** an indoor shopping center along the downtown Skywalk, with numerous shops and restaurants. Head one block up 7th Street and turn right onto Locust to reach the **Equitable Building** (604 Locust St.). This gothic revival structure was the tallest building in Des Moines for much of the 20th century, at 319 feet tall, with 19 stories and a distinctive tower on top. Numerous concrete pillars support the building, which used a plethora of materials, including polished granite, brick, cast iron, and terra cotta. Look up at the building's north and east sides to catch a glimpse of terra cotta gnomes holding up the roof (the hotel **Suites of 800 Locust,** 2 blocks to the east, also has figures along the roofline). Above the gnomes are small alcoves, like those found on the exterior of cathedrals to display statues of saints. This is the core of the downtown business district—the **Ruan Center** is to the west on Locust, and just across 7th Street is the back end of the Marriott Hotel—together, these are two of the taller buildings in downtown (the tallest, both in Des Moines and Iowa, is the spire-like tower at 801 Grand Ave.).

As you head north up Sixth toward Grand, you pass the **Des Moines Building** (405 Sixth Ave.) and the **Liberty Building** (418 Sixth Ave.), both of which have interesting facades. The **Catholic Pastoral Center** (601 Grand Ave.) is a modern building designed by Mies van der Rohe, and perfectly reflects its minimalist aesthetic. Note the strong lines formed by steel I-beams, and the stone paving at the base.

Walk east 1 block to 5th Street, turn right, and walk 2 blocks, passing under a corridor of the downtown skywalk, to Walnut. To your right, the **US Bank building** (520 Walnut St.) is a prime example of Art Deco style, with ornamental lighting featuring geometric designs. The exterior also has brass and nickel decorative features, and black granite and marble.

From here, go east on Walnut, walking toward the Des Moines River and passing the Capital Square building across the street and an adjacent concrete plaza that has sculptures by Claes Oldenburg and Coosje van Bruggen. Crossing 3rd Street, you pass the glass-enclosed **Federal Building** on the right, while across Walnut is the downtown **Civic Center,** performance venue for all sorts of music and live theater shows. Just across 2nd Avenue is the **Polk County Building,** another example of Beaux Arts style, with simple, elegant lines. Just inside the door on the corner of Walnut and Second is an entryway leading to the **Heritage Gallery,** a handsome, high-ceilinged showcase for local artists. After you check out the gallery, return to Walnut Street—just north is the former central library, a salmon-colored Beaux Arts structure of Minnesota sandstone. It is a scale model of the Library of Congress, built in 1900 as part of the City Beautiful movement. Shuttered in 2006 with the opening of the new central library in Western Gateway, it is the future home of the **World Food Prize,** an annual award bestowed on individuals who have made contributions to fighting world hunger (see the History section for more details).

The Beaux Arts legacy in Des Moines continues on the other side of the river—cross the Walnut Street bridge and come to the **US Courthouse** (123 E. Walnut St.), then go 1 block north on E. 1st Street to reach **Des Moines City Hall** (400 Robert D. Ray Dr.). Inside, City Hall has an arched, ornate ceiling on the second floor, as well as a little sitting garden facing the river—it's a nice place to sit on sunny days. Just to the south is the **Simon Estes Riverfront Amphitheatre,** which hosts a popular summer concert series. Looping back south, walk 2 blocks to Court Avenue and the **Des Moines Police Department** (25 E. 1st St.), a fine neoclassical building. The gold-domed Iowa State Capitol rises in the background, as does the more modest copper dome of the Iowa Supreme Court building.

Re-crossing the river on Court, you are just about back to the starting point. There's one last stop—before reaching the courthouse head up Fourth to **Hawkeye Iowa Insurance Building** (209 4th St.). A bit of a change from what you've seen so far, the 4-story redbrick Italianate structure, which dates from 1868, is the oldest surviving commercial building in Des Moines, and features decorative molding and elaborate cornices. The building is listed on the National Register of Historic Places. If you're a little worn out, Court Street has numerous dining options, as well as a popular outdoor patio area at **Dos Rios,** which makes a mean margarita, too.

There's even more to see while strolling downtown, notably the **Pappajohn Sculpture Garden,** located in the Western Gateway area, between 13th and 15th Streets and along Grand Avenue and Locust Street, adjacent to the copper-skinned central library, and the nearby **Temple for Performing Arts** (1011 Locust St.), a century-old former Masonic Temple saved from the wrecking ball to become the site of theatrical performances and rehearsal space for local classical music groups. The nearby complex of buildings making up the Meredith Corporation include an original redbrick structure as well as some outdoor gardens accented with large sculpture. Another nice walk downtown is along the river—a new pedestrian bridge connecting the east and west sides of downtown has opened in the shadow of Wells Fargo Arena on 2nd Avenue, part of a plan to create a downtown riverwalk, and an easy way to get to the East Village and its numerous shops and restaurants.

to learn about hydroelectric power, and wrap a simulated egg in padding to see if it will survive a high fall from an elevator tower. There's a natural-world room with displays of native Iowa plants and animals, including a replica bat cave and a tornado simulator that creates the swirling winds of a funnel cloud.

Downstairs, another hands-on room has lots of levers to pull and buttons to push in demonstrations of properties of physics. An open area hosts scientific demonstrations throughout the day, while an IMAX theater, which has a separate admission charge, presents shows on undersea life and outer space, as well as feature films (several of the Harry Potter movies have played here). Outside the IMAX, a Foucault pendulum sways back and forth endlessly—stoop down and follow its path as it comes closer and closer to knocking over a pin in the ring that surrounds the pendulum.

The museum occasionally hosts temporary exhibits examining great scientists or various scientific phenomena (these may shut down some of the permanent exhibits). Paid parking is available at meters on surrounding streets or in a city garage just north of the museum entrance on the east side of 4th Street.

✳STATE HISTORICAL MUSEUM   FREE
600 E. Locust St.
(515) 281-5111
www.iowahistory.org
This airy, multistory free museum in the building housing the state historical society contains a huge wealth of information on Iowa history. Displays extend all the way back to prehistoric times, including a look at the great inland seas and early creatures once found in what is now Iowa. The state's early years are examined with exhibits on

---

Stargazing in Des Moines

For those who want more of a stargazing experience beyond looking at the exhibits and star theater at the downtown museum, there are observatories in the Des Moines area where you can take a closer look at the night sky. The **Drake Municipal Observatory** (www.drake.edu/artsci/physics /observatory.html), located on the grounds of **Waveland Golf Course** (4908 University Ave.; 515-248-6302), hosts free public programs on Friday nights in spring, summer and fall, which include presentations on astronomy followed by an opportunity to look through the large refracting telescope in the dome, as well as smaller telescopes set up outside. The **Des Moines Astronomical Society** (515-255-1585; www.dmasonline .org) has public nights from April through June and August through October at **Ashton Observatory** (8755 W 122nd St. N, Mingo), located in Ashton-Wildwood Park, about a 30-minute drive from downtown Des Moines, which also feature astronomy presentations and sky viewing.

---

native cultures, immigration, and taming the land for agriculture. You can push a plow and try to move a two-person saw, as well as watch videos about the challenges faced by pioneer settlers. Nearby, another room showcases all sorts of archived treasures,

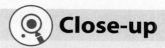 **Close-up**

The Iowa Caucuses

Every four years presidential hopefuls, campaign staffs, and the national and international media faithfully make a pilgrimage to Iowa to enact one of the most prominent rituals of American politics: the Iowa caucuses. Many of the candidates set up shop in Des Moines and then fan across the state, hopscotching from farm to coffee shop to church pancake breakfast and getting up close and personal with the voters who get first shot in the nation at choosing the man or woman who may become president.

The caucuses first assumed importance in the 1972 campaign, following the efforts of young Democratic activists who pushed the party to bring the nominating process out of the archetypal "smoke-filled rooms" by limiting the influence of powerful party bosses in selecting nominees. Following an influential series of newspaper articles, the Iowa caucuses became the first opportunity for candidates to try to pick up delegates on the way to the nomination.

Today the Iowa caucuses are a regular feature of each presidential campaign season. Candidates spend weeks or even months visiting Iowa hoping to gain voters' support. Yet how the caucuses work and what voters actually do at them sometimes gets lost in the shuffle. Voters gather across the state on appointed days, in high school gyms and other public spaces, to select delegates for candidates. Each party has different rules for how they conduct their caucuses: Republicans take a straw poll by secret ballot, while Democrats have a more open, raucous process that must be seen to be believed, with groups of supporters of different candidates clustering in spaces throughout the caucus room and attempting to persuade uncommitted voters in joining them.

While the caucuses ultimately select only about 1 percent of the delegates who nominate the Democratic and Republican presidential nominees, they are seen as an early bellwether of the front runner for each party, and have in some cases given candidates whose campaigns were sagging a boost that carried them to a strong showing in the New Hampshire primary, which shortly follows the caucuses, and ultimately to the nomination. Yet the caucuses are not always so clear-cut, for either the winners or losers: George McGovern finished second to Edmund Muskie in 1972 before going on to win the Democratic nomination. Likewise, George H. W. Bush beat out Ronald Reagan in a caucus that saw Reagan do limited campaigning in Iowa, before Reagan went on to the White House (in 1992 Bill Clinton skipped Iowa entirely, preferring to focus on New Hampshire). Even with such unpredictable results, the caucuses have become a litmus test for candidates to see if they have a realistic hope in the race, as well as one of the purest displays of American democracy in action.

including historical household items and military relics dating back to colonial times.

Large artifacts dominate the lower floor, including a stagecoach and a casting of a woolly mammoth skeleton, as well as vintage airplanes hanging in the building's atrium. The exhibit "Patten's Neighborhood" examines the history of African-American life from the early 1900s until the 1960s in Des Moines's old Center Street neighborhood.

While African-American residents of Des Moines never accounted for more than 5 percent of the city's population, even with the influx of African-American officer candidates at Fort Des Moines during World War I, there were still two newspapers and numerous businesses serving the community, including a printing business operated by Robert E. Patten, collector of many artifacts presented in the exhibit. A display of photos of prominent Iowans on the other side of the gift shop includes Herbert Hoover, Grant Wood, and renowned opera singer Simon Estes. One of the museum's most interesting exhibits is a large room of wildlife dioramas, featuring all sorts of stuffed animals posed in simulated native habitats: Check out the different birds and wildlife in strikingly lifelike displays. Another exhibit gives visitors a front-row seat to the Iowa caucuses, which bring presidential hopefuls to Iowa every four years. You feel like you're actually walking alongside the candidates through the whirlwind of campaigning and media appearances all across the state.

Temporary exhibits have examined notable moments in history and their impact on Iowa, including wars and other historic events as well as more low-key aspects of history, such as domestic life and education.

The museum is closed Mon and has a gift shop. There's a cafe in the building, open Mon through Sat.

WALLACE HOUSE   FREE
756 16th St.
(515) 243-7063
http://wallace.org
This modest Victorian Italianate home in the Sherman Hill neighborhood was home to the Wallace family beginning in the late 1800s, when patriarch Henry Wallace moved his family to Des Moines, living in the house while editing *Wallaces' Farmer* and *Iowa Homestead*, influential newspapers and agricultural journals. Many other Wallaces passed through the house, including future US Secretary of Agriculture and presidential candidate Henry A. Wallace. The home remained in the Wallace family until the 1940s, then was repurchased in the 1980s and largely restored to its original floor plan and appearance, with period furniture and other items. Tours of the house are available Tues through Fri, 9 a.m. to 2 p.m. Donations are suggested. The Wallace Centers of Iowa, which maintains the house, also operates the Country Life Center, located on the old Wallace Family Farm near Orient, Iowa, about an hour and a half drive southwest of Des Moines. It includes a restored farmhouse and barn as well as a flower garden and displays and artistic exhibits. There's also a restored Iowa prairie with native grasses.

AROUND TOWN

BLANK PARK ZOO $
7401 SW 9th St.
(515) 285-4722
www.blankparkzoo.com
A midsize, respectable zoo, the only one accredited in Iowa, with numerous animals divided into geographical areas like Wilds of Africa and the Australian Outback, which has giant kingfisher, plumed whistling duck, and wallabies hopping around. The Great Cats area features a rare snow leopard alongside the lions and tigers. New animals are brought in regularly—check out some of the newer arrivals, like red pandas and golden-headed tamarins. There's a wide variety of birds, too, including a large parakeet enclosure where the winged creatures will hop on your hand and nibble on food purchased for

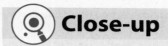

Close-up

Henry Wallace, Iowa Statesman

Scion of a prominent Iowa family, **Henry A. Wallace** was a successful farmer who went on to become a hugely influential secretary of agriculture before running for president on the Progressive ticket in 1948. Born on a family farm in rural Iowa, he moved to Des Moines as a child and while still a teenager began experimenting with growing varieties of corn that would produce higher yields. After college he farmed just outside Des Moines while also writing for his family's agricultural newspaper. Eventually he founded Hi-Bred Corn, a hybrid seed company (the company today is known as Pioneer Hi-Bred and is still based in the Des Moines area). Wallace stepped onto the national political stage when he was selected to become secretary of agriculture in 1933 by Franklin Roosevelt. In this role he oversaw numerous New Deal programs and also represented the United States on extensive world travels. Roosevelt then selected Wallace as his running mate in 1940, and he served one term as vice president.

Wallace served as secretary of commerce under Harry Truman, but that ended after a disagreement with Truman over relations with the Soviet Union—Wallace favored dialogue with the Soviets rather than the Cold War strategy that became official US policy.

As the Progressive Party's presidential candidate, Wallace was an unabashed left-ist who spoke out against big business and Wall Street and continued to stress his vision of peace and reconciliation, but he was soundly defeated in the four-way contest. After the election he returned to farming, and died in 1965. His ashes were interred at Glendale Cemetery in Des Moines. In 1999 he was named the most influential Iowan of the 20th century by the *Des Moines Register* newspaper.

a small additional charge. A train ride winds halfway around the zoo's perimeter, and a petting zoo area offers kids the opportunity to feed animals including goats and llamas. Hours and days open vary by season.

✴DES MOINES ART CENTER   **FREE**
4700 Grand Ave.
(515) 277-4405
www.desmoinesartcenter.org
An outstanding collection is found at Des Moines's free art museum, located in a building whose design was created by three world-renowned architects that sits along

a winding stretch of road on the edge of a residential neighborhood. The focus is on contemporary art, with Matisse, Jasper Johns, and Edward Hopper just a few of the many artists whose work is on display. Paintings, sculptures, and other works are arranged in a series of galleries that are laid out in a way that provides for a nice stroll around the museums, with some pieces located on the main floor and others on smaller upper and lower levels. Temporary exhibits have showcased the work of emerging artists, and the museum has also highlighted works by some of the artists featured in the city's Pappajohn Sculpture Garden downtown. The museum also shows free films year-round and has numerous education programs, as well as "art backpacks" available for free at the entrance, with lots of activities for kids to do throughout the museum. Audio guides are also available, giving further insight into some of the works on display.

The large white museum is really three buildings combined into one structure: a 1948 design by Eliel Saarinen, a 1968 addition by I. M. Pei, and a 1985 addition by Richard Meier. The styles of all three architects are readily apparent: Saarinen's understated work in regional limestone and Pei's low structure of limestone-based concrete have some similarities, but Meier's really stands out: The building's most recent architect used porcelain-coated steel tiles to create sweeping curves that can be a little jarring at first but also have quite a bit of flair.

There's a restaurant and gift shop in the museum. Closed Monday.

FORT DES MOINES MUSEUM
& EDUCATION CENTER **$$**
75 E. Army Post Rd.
(Corner of South Union and Army Post Road)
(515) 282-8060 or (888) 828-3678
www.fortdesmoines.org
Inside a redbrick building just beyond the gates of this historic military fort, a 20,000-square-foot museum showcases Fort Des Moines's pioneering role in training America's first African-American officers during World War I and the formation of the first female military units during World War II, when 72,000 women were trained here for military service, including commissioned female officers. The extensive exhibits,

including some interactive displays, do a good job of telling the stories of the men and women who went on to lead troops and perform other critical tasks, and they don't shy away from the tensions that accompanied the introduction of blacks and women into leadership roles in the military, as well as examining general social conditions of the era. There are also displays covering the service of women and African-Americans in other wars, as well as looking at Fort Des Moines between the world wars as a center for training cavalry officers, including a young Ronald Reagan, who learned horsemanship at the fort while serving in the army reserves during his time working as a radio broadcaster in Des Moines in the 1930s.

Outside, a reflecting pool and memorial sculpture stand next to a granite wall that commemorates the fort's first graduating class of officers of 639 men in 1917. The fort, which was originally built in 1901, has shrunk in size since the end of World War II. Some of the land has been sold off and developed into the city's Blank Park Zoo, among other developments. Today the remaining fort still serves as a training center for the army reserves.

Admission to the museum is $5 for adults, $4 for children. Seniors are admitted free. The museum is open Mon through Sat 10 a.m. to 4 p.m.

HISTORIC JORDAN HOUSE **$$**
2001 Fuller Rd., West Des Moines
(515) 225-1286
www.thejordanhouse.org
Built by a pioneering settler of the area now part of West Des Moines, this Victorian home of Italianate gothic design in the older part of the suburb has 16 rooms full of period furniture and antiques. The formal parlor has a

large settee and Chickering piano. There are 2 kitchens in the house, one from the house's original construction in 1850, the other from additions built in 1870. The newer kitchen has been restored with a cast-iron stove and old appliances and cooking items. Upstairs the master bedroom has a burled walnut bedroom set made especially for the Jordan family. The other bedroom, also part of the original construction, is more modest, with a small stove for heat.

The Jordan House was built by James Jordan, a cattle farmer who came to Iowa from Virginia, settling in the Des Moines area and building a log cabin near the Raccoon River. He eventually served in both the Iowa House of Representatives and Senate and was instrumental in bringing the railroad to Valley Junction, as West Des Moines was then known, ensuring the young town's growing prosperity and development. After first settling in a lean-to tent, he built his cabin in 1848, then in 1850 began building the house. His family, which included 6 children, lived in the basement as construction progressed. When finished, the house included a large entryway as well as a center hall and 2 large rooms on the first floor. At the top of a walnut staircase, 2 bedrooms dominated the second floor. The house's kitchen was located in the basement and porches faced to the east and south.

Jordan expanded his house as his family grew, adding several rooms. The house became a way station for travelers making the trek west, and also served for a time as a stop on the Underground Railroad, providing shelter to escaping slaves. Abolitionist leader John Brown stayed at the Jordan House at least twice as he led slaves through Iowa toward freedom. The house is listed on the National Register of Historic Places.

The house, which is operated by the West Des Moines Historical Society, is open to visitors May through Sept, from 1 to 4 p.m. Wed and Sat and from 2 to 5 p.m. Sun. The nearby **Bennett Schoolhouse,** also operated by the historical society, is a one-room school and is also worth a visit. Also nearby is **Jordan Cemetery,** on the south side of Fuller Road, ½ mile west of Grand Avenue, which includes the graves of many early residents of the area, as well as the Jordan family's plot.

LIVING HISTORY FARMS $$$
11121 Hickman Rd., Urbandale
(515) 278-5286
www.lhf.org

Get an up-close look at pioneer and Native American life in Iowa at this sprawling, outdoor living museum on the northwest edge of the city. Reenactors bring to life different historical periods, demonstrating farming techniques and showcasing other aspects of daily life. There are 3 farms spread over 500 acres: At the circa 1700 farm, where Ioway Indians grew beans and corn, visitors get a look at deer hides tanning in the sun and food cooking over an open fire. An 1850 farm, from a time when many Iowa farm families raised corn, wheat, potatoes, and pigs, shows farmers taming the prairie with teams of oxen and just becoming aware of the coming changes in farming. You can watch reenactors utilize draft horses for the hard labor required in farming, and observe the new machines that allowed farmers and their families to thrive across Iowa.

Reenactors throughout the site demonstrate a wide variety of skills used by Indians and pioneers, including hunting, toolmaking, and domestic arts like cooking and cleaning. Next to the farms, the 1875

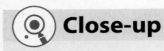

Close-up

Valley Junction

Though it's known today as a cute little shopping mecca, **Valley Junction** was for several decades an important railroad center, as well as the oldest part of the thriving suburb of West Des Moines. Once the rural outskirts of Des Moines, the area began to grow after a train roundhouse and railroad shop were built in 1891. Within a few years 26 passenger trains were arriving and departing daily, with a switching yard handling trains along several tracks. Population grew steadily, and a town grew up around the local depot, with businesses and city buildings along present-day 5th Street. You can still see the facade of the old city hall at 137 5th St., as well as the former First National Bank at 228 5th St. After Valley Junction's name was changed to West Des Moines in 1938, not long after the railroad left town, businesses began moving to newer developments. However, the high school in West Des Moines, established in 1905, retains the name Valley High, and just east of the archway at 5th Street and Railroad Avenue marking the entrance to Valley Junction stands a bright red caboose, the one tangible reminder of the bustling railroad days.

town of Walnut Hill has numerous places to explore, including a blacksmith, broom maker, and millinery, as well as a general store, drug store, office, and other pioneer-era businesses, giving visitors a taste of town life before the coming of the railroads, which dramatically altered the Iowa landscape.

Allow at least two hours to see the farms and town, more time if you really want to soak up all there is to see here. Closed from mid-Oct until the beginning of May, with limited hours in Sept and the first half of Oct.

SALISBURY HOUSE & GARDENS $–$$
4025 Tonawanda Dr.
(515) 274-1777
www.salisburyhouse.org
A brick, Tudor style country estate tucked away in Des Moines's tony South of Grand neighborhood, the Salisbury House has room after room filled with thousands of items collected by the Weeks family, who

occupied the house for many years. Artworks, over 1,000 rare books, including numerous first editions, and precious objects of every sort are just some of the treasures found here. Many of the objects were acquired during the Weeks's extensive world travels. There are also personal mementos from notable Americans like Twain, Sargent, and Hemingway.

Modeled after the King's House, a 15th-century manor in Salisbury, England, the house was built in the 1920s by Des Moines cosmetics magnate Carl Weeks. When built, it measured 22,500 square feet on 9.5 acres and included 17 bedrooms and 16 bathrooms on 4 stories, as well as a caretaker's cottage, gardens, and grounds.

The house later served as headquarters for the Iowa State Education Association. Guided and self-guided tours are available, with guided tours slightly more expensive. Closed Jan and Feb.

TERRACE HILL $$

2300 Grand Ave.
(515) 281-3604
www.terracehill.org

The Victorian tower peeking out from south of Ingersoll Avenue leads you to Terrace Hill, since 1976 the official residence of Iowa's governor and family. Originally built by Iowa's first millionaire on a bluff overlooking the Raccoon River, the house was later purchased by the Hubbell family, who donated it to the state after nearly a century. It is considered one of the finest examples of Victorian Second Empire architecture in the United States.

As you enter through the grand vestibule, the first rooms you see are the reception room, with its ornate fireplace adorned with intricate grillwork, then the drawing room across the hall, which has a 7.5-foot crystal chandelier and hand-carved rosewood furniture and is used for entertaining visiting dignitaries and other formal events. The music room features a Steinway grand piano, while the main hallway is impressive for its grand, arching 14.5-foot ceilings. Other rooms on the first floor include a library and sitting room. Upstairs, past a grand staircase framed by 2 large decorative lamps and backlit by a large stained-glass window, are offices for the governor and First Lady, and a bedroom for overnight guests. The first family's actual living quarters are on the third floor, which is not open to the public.

Guided tours are available Mar through Dec, Tues through Sat at 10:30 and 11:30 a.m., and 12:30 and 1:30 p.m., and take about an hour. A gift shop and visitor center are located in the carriage house on the grounds.

OUTLYING AREAS

ADVENTURELAND $$$$

305 34th Ave. NW, Altoona
(515) 266-2121 or (800) 532-1286
www.adventureland-usa.com

An old-fashioned amusement park and waterpark, located just northeast of Des Moines off I-80. Dozens of rides offer something for visitors young and old, such as 2 wooden roller coasters that carry the cars up to a view over Iowa cornfields before sending riders down a scream-inducing drop. If those don't get you dizzy, there are plenty of other thrill rides up for the challenge, including the twisting and turning Dragon roller coaster. Numerous water rides include a log plunge and a "raging river," which gives you the whitewater experience on round rafts that bounce down the channel. Old favorites like bumper cars, a Ferris wheel, and a carousel are here also, and there are plenty of rides for younger children as well. Adventureland's waterpark, included in the general admission ticket, has lots of water slides and pools, as well as a "lazy river" where you can kick back and float on an inner tube, and plenty of space for just lounging in the sun. In the park's game rooms you can try your luck at Skee-Ball or other games. There are numerous food concessions throughout the park.

An on-site hotel offers pools, spas, swim-up bar, and poolside rooms. RVers may want to stay at the site's campground, which has full hookups, showers and restrooms, and a large swimming pool, as well as spots for tent camping.

Multi-day passes are available. Children ages 3 and under are admitted free. There's a fee for parking. The park opens on weekends beginning in late Apr and then the entire week beginning late May through the end

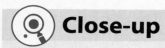 **Close-up**

Bob Feller: Iowa's "Rapid Robert"

One of the most legendary pitchers to ever don a major league uniform, **Bob Feller** emerged from a real-life field of dreams to become one of the titans of baseball. Growing up on a farm in tiny Van Meter, Iowa, west of Des Moines, Feller could throw a scorching fastball by age nine. A few years later he and his father built a baseball diamond on the farm, including bleachers, a scoreboard, and a concession stand, where Feller played exhibition games with local teams. Major league scouts showed serious interest in the teenage Feller, who in addition to his high school team played for a local amateur team alongside future University of Iowa star quarterback Nile Kinnick. He signed with the Cleveland Indians and joined the club for the 1936 season as a 17-year-old. With the help of his blazing fastball, which earned the nickname the **"Heater from Van Meter,"** he struck out 15 batters in his debut game, one short of the record, which he broke later that season with 17 strikeouts. Returning to Van Meter High School for his senior year, Feller was elected president of his class of 19 students, and his graduation was broadcast live on NBC radio. Heading back to Cleveland, Feller led the league in strikeouts and wins for the 1938 season, a year he also set a new record for strikeouts when he fanned 18 batters in one game. Two years later Feller threw a no-hitter on the first day of the 1940 season, the only player ever to achieve that feat on an opening day. Enlisting in the navy immediately after Pearl Harbor, Feller became a chief petty officer and led a battleship gun crew that saw action in both the Atlantic and Pacific. Returning to baseball after four seasons away, Feller continued to pitch for the Indians, throwing his career-best and season record 348 strikeouts in the 1946 season, and playing on the World Series Champion Indians team in 1948. He retired after the 1956 season. One of baseball's most exciting players to watch, he threw a curveball that was nearly as devastating as his "heat" and he was known for his high left-leg kick when pitching. He retired with 266 wins and 3 no-hitters and led the American League in strikeouts 7 times. He was elected to the hall of fame in 1962 and died in 2010 at the age of 92.

of Aug, when it is open only on weekends until late Sept.

BOB FELLER MUSEUM   **$$**
310 Mill St., Van Meter
(515) 996-2806
www.bobfellermuseum.org
Located in a small town about 20 miles west of downtown Des Moines, and just a few miles away from the farm that was the boyhood home of Bob Feller, one of the greatest baseball pitchers ever. There are 2 rooms

of artifacts, including uniforms Feller wore during his career, trophies for his numerous achievements in baseball, and numerous photos and newspaper clippings chronicling his career and life, including his four years of navy service in World War II. There are also balls and bats signed by Feller and other players, including the bat Babe Ruth was holding during the famous photograph taken of him at his retirement ceremony at Yankee Stadium. The museum is closed Mon through Wed in the winter, and open 7 days the rest of the year.

IOWA GOLD STAR MILITARY MUSEUM
FREE
7105 NW 70th Ave., Johnston
(515) 252-4531
www.iowanationalguard.com/museum
/museum.htm

Located at Camp Dodge, north of Des Moines, this free museum features memorabilia from wars stretching back over 100 years. Detailed displays throughout the 6,000-square-foot museum are divided among several galleries and include uniforms, weapons, and other military paraphernalia. Displays focus on legendary Iowa military units, and some dioramas re-create battlefield conditions, with, for example, a mannequin outfitted for combat and waiting behind sandbags. The Korean War exhibit is housed in an actual tent from that era. There's even a display of military rations from the Civil War to the present day. A special room is dedicated to prisoners of war and soldiers missing in action. Outside are old howitzers, tanks, and helicopters, including a UH-1 "Huey" and an F-84F fighter plane. Enter Camp Dodge through the gate off NW 70th Avenue (photo ID required) and follow the sign to the museum. Closed Sunday.

NATIONAL BALLOON MUSEUM $
1601 N. Jefferson Way, Indianola
(515) 961-3714
www.nationalballoonmuseum.com

Believe it or not, Indianola, Iowa, is a mecca for hot-air ballooning. It hosts the National Balloon Classic every summer, and multiple balloons can be seen in the sky on sunny days. The airy, high-ceilinged museum has exhibits on the history of ballooning, unique balloons, including some rather odd designs, and notable flights. Peer into an actual balloon gondola in one room. There's a hall of fame and a children's area where young visitors can feel balloon fabric and pilot a balloon on a virtual simulator. The museum's library has extensive holdings of ballooning books and other materials, including some rare volumes. A small theater shows ballooning videos. Closed the entire month of Jan.

NATIONAL SPRINT CAR HALL OF FAME
& MUSEUM $
One Sprint Capital Place, Knoxville
(641) 842-6176
http://sprintcarhof.com

Located at the Knoxville raceway, a mecca for sprint car racing, this museum displays artifacts related to the high-powered, superfast dirt track racing cars. Included are some actual cars, both with and without the distinctive "wing" mounted above the car's body. Other displays feature prominent drivers, including a hall of fame stretching back many years, and there's a small theater as well.

SPECTATOR SPORTS

hat Des Moines lacks in big-time professional or college teams, it more than
makes up for in spirit and enthusiasm: Principal Park, which sits at the confluence of the Raccoon and Des Moines Rivers, is home to the Iowa Cubs and is regularly
packed on game days as fans pour into central Iowa's version of the friendly confines,
with a view past center field of the Iowa State Capitol. North of downtown, the Iowa
Energy, part of the NBA's development league, take to the hardwood inside Wells Fargo
Arena, as do arena football's Iowa Barnstormers, who play a fast-break, high-scoring
version of the gridiron classic that never fails to excite fans. Even ice hockey has plenty
of partisans in Des Moines, with the local team, the Buccaneers, skating out in their
old-school ice shed near where the city fades into the suburbs. More obscure sports
are popular as well, including two roller derby leagues. Des Moines is also a running-
mad town, and large numbers of both local and out-of-town runners go all out for the
annual city marathon and triathlon, with huge crowds of spectators cheering them on,
as well as numerous smaller races. Crowds also turn out en masse for the Drake Relays
every spring to watch some of the world's most elite runners compete for a championship and a possible shot at the Olympics.

BASEBALL

✳**IOWA CUBS**
Principal Park
1 Line Dr.
(515) 243-6111
www.iowacubs.com
A Triple-A affiliate of the Chicago Cubs playing in the Pacific Coast League, the Cubs
are a much-loved institution in Des Moines,
regularly filling the stands at Principal Park,
an 11,000-seat stadium just south of the
Court Avenue Entertainment District at the
confluence of the Des Moines and Raccoon
Rivers. The golden dome of the Iowa State
Capitol looms behind center field, and there
really isn't a bad seat in the house. Players
are approachable for autographs before the
first pitch gets thrown—just go hang out
by the dugout. The Cubs have had some

excellent players in recent years, and former
Chicago slugger Ryne Sandberg did a stint
as manager before leaving the team after the
2010 season. All kinds of goofy games and
contests go on between innings—the club
does like to keep fans entertained. There's a
plethora of concessions stands, and prices
are reasonable by major league standards, as
are tickets: No ticket will cost you more than
about $25, and that's for the most expensive
seats right behind home plate—tickets for
the rest of the ballpark cost much, much
less. The lines at the ticket windows can get
long right before game time, so try to arrive
early. Paid parking is available in lots right
next to the ballpark, with just a short walk
to the gates.

BASKETBALL

IOWA ENERGY
833 Fifth Ave.
(515) 462-2849

The Energy take to the hardwood in Wells Fargo Arena, where they square off against other teams in the NBA development league and regularly draw several thousand fans. The Energy are an affiliate of the Chicago Bulls and Phoenix Suns, and have had players called up by both teams. Since winning their first game ever in 2007, they placed first in their division in both the 2008–09 and 2009–10 seasons, and advanced to the semifinals of the playoffs in 2010, when they entered as the number-one seed. There have been some thrilling moments, including a comeback when the Energy were 30 points down to win the game in 2009, and fans really get into the games, cheering on their favorite players as they dribble down the court. Tickets range from under $10 to around $20. The season runs from late Nov to late Mar.

FOOTBALL

IOWA BARNSTORMERS
833 Fifth Ave.
(515) 633-2255

An arena football team that counts NFL legend and Iowa native Kurt Warner among their alumni, the Barnstormers shake up Wells Fargo Arena from Mar through July, playing against the likes of Chicago, Milwaukee, and Cleveland. The Barnstormers have a history in Des Moines going back to the early 1990s. In this earlier incarnation, the team placed first in their division several times and has come very close to winning the Arena Bowl. Since coach John Gregory resurrected the team in 2007, he has made them a contender in arena football, leading them to the second round of the playoffs in 2009. If you've never seen arena football before, you may be in for a shock—the players bounce down the enclosed space like pinballs, rather than the athletic ballet and crushing hits one sees in the NFL. Still, it's fun to watch, and the ridiculously high scores drive the fans wild with excitement.

IOWA CRUSH
3204 SE 24th Court
(515) 783-6229
www.theiowacrush.com

The Crush is a women's tackle football team that has been fighting down the gridiron since 2006. They are part of the Independent Women's Football League, which has over 30 teams spread throughout every part of the country and runs a full season of games, including playoffs and a championship. This isn't powder-puff football—players wear helmets and pads just like the men's game, and they are just as aggressive and block and hit just as hard, too. Several players on the team have been named league all-stars. Their season runs Apr through June.

ICE HOCKEY

DES MOINES BUCCANEERS
7201 Hickman Rd., Urbandale
(515) 278-2827
www.bucshockey.com

Part of the Des Moines sports landscape since 1981, the Bucs face off Sept through Apr against teams from across the Midwest in the US Hockey League. Teenage prospects from the United States, Canada, and Europe fill out the roster and give it their all on the ice. The team has won several championships, and several former Bucs are now on NHL teams. Games are fast-paced and feature some great skating and puck handling. Lots of promotions keep fans entertained and make the Bucs a good option for families as well. Tickets are very reasonably priced, with even center-ice seats costing around $15. The Bucs' home arena is a wonderfully old-school ice rink located amid the commercial bustle of Hickman Road—look for the pirate logo on the side of a large shedlike building.

SOCCER

DES MOINES MENACE
6400 Westown Pkwy.
(515) 226-9890
www.menacesoccer.com

The Menace have been in Des Moines since 1994 and are currently part of the Premier Development League, an entry level of the minor league United Soccer League. An international roster of players has brought the team to the playoffs 10 times, including 3 final-four appearances and a national championship in 2005. The Menace's Casey Mann was named PDL coach of the year in 2009, when the Menace finished first in their division and made it to the playoff quarterfinals. They regularly finish in the top three of their division. Enthusiastic crowds turn out for games from May through July at Valley High School Stadium. Tickets are usually no more than $10 and can be purchased through the team's website as well as at the game.

COLLEGE SPORTS

DRAKE UNIVERSITY BULLDOGS
www.drake.edu/athletics

The "true blue" bulldogs compete at the Division I level in several sports, including traditional college favorites football and men's and women's basketball, but also other sports including soccer, tennis, softball, swimming, golf, volleyball, and even women's crew. They attract plenty of fans to games played at facilities in the heart of Des Moines, especially football at Drake Stadium and basketball in the Knapp Center, both located along Forest Avenue just past the main part of the Drake campus.

Several Drake athletes have gone on to pro careers, including in the less spotlighted college sports, with former Drake golfer and Iowa native Zach Johnson winning the Masters in 2007 and playing on two US Ryder Cup teams. Teams at Drake play in different leagues, with the football Bulldogs a member of the Pioneer Football League, which includes teams stretching from San Diego to Jacksonville, Florida, to Dayton, Ohio, while Drake basketball is part of the Missouri Valley Conference, which is more regionally focused, including teams from Iowa, Illinois, Indiana, Kansas, Missouri, and Nebraska. The football Bulldogs won a conference championship in 2004.

Drake University Sports Facilities

DRAKE STADIUM
2719 Forest Ave.

This redbrick stadium, with a capacity of around 15,000, sits at the north end of the Drake campus and is home to Drake football and track and field. Since opening in 1925 it has also hosted the Drake Relays, as well as several collegiate and professional track and field championship meets, as well as the annual Iowa high school track and field championships. The stadium underwent a $15 million renovation in 2005, which focused on improvements to the track and reduced the stadium's seating capacity somewhat. Olympic gold medalists including Jesse Owens, Bruce Jenner, Carl Lewis,

Big-Time College Sports in Iowa

While local fans may cheer on Drake teams, often their real loyalty is to their chosen college team: The **University of Iowa Hawkeyes** hit the gridiron at Kinnick Stadium in Iowa City, a mere 2-hour drive away, while **Iowa State**'s stadium in Ames is even closer—barely a half-hour from Des Moines. Both schools' basketball teams have large, rabid fan bases in Des Moines as well, and any given Des Moines bar, sports or otherwise, that you walk into at game time will be showing either the Hawks or the Cyclones. The wrestling teams from both universities are popular, too—Iowa is the physical and spiritual heart of college wrestling, and fans love to cheer on top grapplers.

Michael Johnson, and Bob Hayes have all streaked down the Drake Stadium track. High school football games are held here on fall Fri nights. Parking can be tricky once the small lot fills up—you'll have to search on nearby residential streets.

KNAPP CENTER
2601 Forest Ave.
Located just east of Drake Stadium on Forest Avenue, the Knapp Center is a 7,000-seat arena that has been home to Drake basketball since it opened in 1992. It is also home to Drake women's volleyball. Previously the basketball Bulldogs played at Veterans Memorial downtown. The Knapp Center's

location just off the main part of the Drake campus makes it much easier for students to attend games. The center underwent an extensive renovation in 2007 and now has top-line scoreboards, video displays, and lighting.

BUEL FIELD
1500 27th St.
Drake's home softball field is just north of Drake Stadium and the Knapp Center. The well-maintained field looks out over a residential neighborhood that borders the Drake campus and has an updated press box and sound system, as well as a top-of-the-line drainage system to maintain the outfield.

ROGER KNAPP TENNIS CENTER
2525 Clark St.
Home to Drake tennis since 1992, this well-equipped facility has 6 indoor and 6 outdoor courts. It is clustered in with the other Drake athletic facilities at the north end of campus, just north of Forest Avenue and west of 25th Street.

OTHER COLLEGE SPORTS

Grand View University in Des Moines, **Central College** in Pella, and **Simpson College** in Indianola all play at the lower levels of college sports, yet the crowds are just as enthusiastic as you'll find in big-time college stadiums, while the smaller facilities make for a more relaxed experience (but not when the game is close and the clock is ticking!). Central's football team has done very well in recent years, while Simpson has had successes over the years with its softball and wrestling programs. Central and Simpson have facilities for all sports on campus, while Grand View plays its home football games at Williams Stadium, just south of campus. Grand View's basketball, baseball, and other teams play home games at facilities on campus. Tickets are very reasonably priced at all three schools, and parking is pretty easy right up to game time.

ROLLER DERBY

DES MOINES DERBY DAMES
www.dmderbydames.com

MID-IOWA ROLLERS
www.midiowarollers.com

Roller derby has caught on in a big way with these two clubs stocked with female skaters who go by names like "Elbow MacPhearson," "Minnie So Tuff," and "Anna Killakova." Both clubs offer the usual bruising brouhaha as they zip around the track, while an appreciative crowd cheers from the stands. The Mid-Iowa Rollers first strapped on skates in 2006 and were 8–0 in 2010.

TRACK & FIELD

✳DRAKE RELAYS
www.godrakebulldogs.com

A legendary track and field meet for university and Olympic-caliber talent that brings competitors to Drake Stadium for three days every year in late Apr, the Drake Relays began in 1910 on the university campus and have been there ever since. From modest beginnings, they now encompass a full slate of track and field events, including sprint and distance runs, hurdles and steeplechase, high, long, and triple jump, shot put, discus throw, pole vault, and heptathlon. The stands of Drake Stadium fill up with fans eager to watch competitors move down the sky-blue track. Many top American

Cricket

If you're out at Holiday Park in West Des Moines on a Saturday between May and September, you may blink twice when you spot a large group of men dressed in cricket whites. Yes, this genteel British sport has made it to central Iowa, with a club made up of players largely of South Asian descent, as well as from other former British territories. The **Knights Cricket Club** has had a presence in Des Moines since 1999 and maintains a fairly active schedule, playing matches against clubs from other cities and winning some tournaments. Their concrete pitch and wicket was the first of its kind in the Midwest. Hang out at the matches and chat up the players when they're not playing—they may be able to give you some insight into the sport's byzantine rules. For more information, check out the Knights' website, www.knightscricket.org.

athletes have competed at the relays, including sprinter Michael Johnson, high-jumping pioneer Dick Fosbury, and homegrown track star Lolo Jones. Jesse Owens set a record in the broad jump and won the 100 meters at the 1935 Drake Relays, a year before his timeless performance at the Berlin Olympics.

Ticket packages range from around $45 to $85 and cover various days and times. Single-day admission is available as well. Drake Stadium is located on Forest Avenue north of campus.

AUTO RACING

IOWA SPEEDWAY
333 Rusty Wallace Dr., Newton
(641) 791-8000
www.iowaspeedway.com
This ⅞-mile, asphalt-paved tri-oval track holds over 25,000 fans and was designed by NASCAR champion driver Rusty Wallace. It's located about a half-hour drive from Des Moines and hosts IndyCar and NASCAR races from May through Aug. The arena also features concerts and other events. Camping is permitted and several hotels are nearby. A Fan Walk pass allows spectators to get even closer to the action. Racing usually starts in May and runs for several months.

KNOXVILLE RACEWAY
1000 N. Lincoln St., Knoxville
(641) 842-5431
www.knoxvilleraceway.com
A ½-mile dirt-track raceway at the Marion County Fairgrounds in Knoxville, a short distance from the Dutch village and popular tourist destination of Pella. The track is the self-proclaimed "Sprint Car Capital of the World," with over half a million dollars in prizes awarded as part of its championship series, and it's worth attending just to see the wild shapes and styles of the cars, many of which resemble souped-up go-karts with a large "wing" jutting out over the driver's safety cage. Races are held regularly on Sat nights as well as on other nights during the season, which starts in Apr and culminates with the Knoxville Nationals, a series of races for different types of cars held from Aug through Sept. The on-site **National Sprint Car Hall of Fame,** (515) 842-6176, http://sprintcarhof.com, gives visitors the opportunity to see more cars, as well as numerous displays on famous racers and races and the history of the sport.

HORSE RACING

PRAIRIE MEADOWS
1 Prairie Meadows Dr., Altoona
(515) 967-8544 or (800) 325-9018
www.prairiemeadows.com
Play the ponies from Apr through Oct at this 1-mile thoroughbred and quarter horse track located just east of Des Moines off I-80. There's also simulcast racing from top tracks all over the country. Just as big an attraction is the large casino with slots, poker, and blackjack. The **Iowa Derby** is a race for 3-year-olds, held every June and with a purse of $250,000.

RECREATION

The Des Moines area has a seemingly endless number of things to do year-round, from long afternoons of boating on area lakes and pedaling along the miles of cycling trails as the sun dips over the cornfields, to wintertime fun like ice skating at the city's popular downtown outdoor rink, which at times gets so crowded you are practically moved along by the force of the crowd. Summer also means swimming at the city's popular pools while come winter, plenty of locals strap on their cross-country skis or snowshoes and head on down the miles of local trails, or grab a sled and head over to the nearest hill for a thrilling ride down to the bottom (no, the land is not completely flat here!). Hiking and other activities are popular at area parks, and duffers can be found on local golf courses until the cold finally drives them inside in the late fall.

This chapter focuses mainly on recreation spots that offer a specific activity—other sources for more general recreation options include the chapter on parks, which has information on hiking and cycling opportunities in the Des Moines area as well as general parks information.

BOATING & FISHING

BANNER LAKES AT SUMMERSET STATE PARK
13084 Elkhorn St., Indianola
(515) 961-7101
www.iowadnr.gov/parks/state_park_list
/banner.html
Central Iowa's only trout fishery, at the state's newest state park, located about 6 miles south of Des Moines. The south lake is stocked from Oct through Mar with trout weighing up to 10 pounds. All people fishing for trout must pay a fee. There are also bluegill, crappie, catfish, and largemouth bass in both lakes at the park. Shoreline fishing is available, and there are boat ramps on both lakes.

BIG CREEK MARINA
12397 NW 89th Court, Polk City
(515) 984-6083
www.bigcreekmarina.com

Located right on the water inside the entrance to Big Creek State Park, which is known for the great fishing in the clear waters of its lake, this marina has all types of boats for rent, including pontoon boats, smaller fishing boats, and sailboats, as well as canoes, kayaks, and hydro bikes. They also sell fishing licenses and bait. In addition to the marina, there are 5 boat ramps in the park, each of which also has sailboat rigging facilities.

DES MOINES RIVER WATER TRAIL
www.desmoinesriver.org or
www.iowadnr.gov/riverprograms/files
/map_polk.pdf
This 19-mile stretch of the river, from Cottonwood Access in the north, just south of the Saylorville Dam, to Yellow Banks County Park in the south, is a paddlers' paradise, with

the river flowing past some very peaceful stretches of wilderness in the heart of the city. Bald eagles, beavers, great blue herons, and American white pelicans are just some of the wildlife that have been spotted along stretches of the river. The final segment, from Pleasant Hill Access to Yellow Banks, is perhaps the most scenic—paddlers have spotted as many as 70 eagles in a single trip. Keep your eyes peeled for the high, wooded bluffs of loess as you reach the end—you'll see how the park got its name. Powerboats use the water trail as well, and fishermen cast lines downstream of the dams at Saylorville, Center Street, and Scott Street in the spring and fall. A 2-mile section of the river downtown is closed to boaters due to low-head dams, requiring a portage around the Center Street Dam, just south of I-235, and the Scott Avenue Dam, just past the confluence with the Raccoon River.

The **Des Moines Rowing Club,** www .desmoinesrowing.org, which trains on the river as well as offering novice rowing classes at Gray's Lake, is headquartered at the boathouse at Birdland Park marina, on the north section of the River Water Trail. **Central Iowa Paddlers** (515-284-6910 or 641-363-4451; www.paddleiowa.org). is an informal group of paddling enthusiasts, both novice and experienced, who share information on paddling opportunities.

GRAY'S LAKE
Fleur Drive and George Flagg Parkway
(515) 237-1386
www.dmgov.org
Part of the City of Des Moines park system, Gray's Lake, a 96-acre lake just south of downtown with a maximum depth of around 14 feet, is the main boating facility within the city limits. Only electric trawling

motors are allowed on motorboats, and sailboats must not be taller than 24 feet, due to overhead wires. Sailboats must also remain more than 30 feet from the bridge that crosses over the southern edge of the lake.

Canoes and sailboats are available for rent beginning in mid-Apr, and canoeing and sailing lessons are offered during the summer. The park also rents paddleboats, kayaks, catamarans, and hydro bikes. There is fishing on the lake for catfish, crappie, and largemouth bass.

Gray's Lake also has a swimming beach, playground, and pavilion. The area around the pavilion at the southwest corner of the park is popular for kite flying. The lake is open for boating Mar through Oct.

LAKE AHQUABI STATE PARK
1650 118th St., Indianola
(515) 961-7101
www.iowadnr.gov/parks/state_park_list /lake_ahquabi.html
Boats, canoes, kayaks, and paddleboats are available for rent at this 770-acre state park, located south of Indianola and about 22 miles south of Des Moines. The 115-acre man-made lake also has numerous fishing jetties and a fishing pier spread throughout the park for shoreline casting. There are a couple boat ramps, too. The park's name comes from a Sauk and Fox word meaning "resting place," and it's a wonderful spot for a picnic or a swim, too. Many of the park's structures were erected by the Civilian Conservation Corps in 1935 and are standing to this day.

SAYLORVILLE LAKE MARINA
6170 NW Polk City Dr., Polk City
(515) 984-6541
http://saylorvillemarina.com

The only marina on Saylorville Lake, a large reservoir north of Des Moines, with boat rentals, hundreds of slips, indoor storage, and a full slate of boat services. The lake, which covers over 25,000 square miles, is managed by the Army Corps of Engineers and has numerous opportunities for camping, boating, fishing, hiking, and cycling, as well as a visitor center that has exhibits on the geology and wildlife around the lake. For more information, contact Saylorville Lake Administration Office (515-276-4656; www2 .mvr.usace.army.mil/Saylorville).

BOWLING

Iowa is one of the bigger states for bowling—must be all those long winters driving people indoors to the lanes. Many bowling alleys are major social centers, with multiple leagues and bars, restaurants, and other activities.

AIR LANES BOWL
4200 Fleur Dr.
(515) 285-8632
www.airlanesbowling.com

AMF DES MOINES
3839 NE 14th St.
(515) 265-0315
www.amf.com/desmoineslanes/center homepage.htm

PLAZA LANES
2701 Douglas Ave.
(515) 255-1111
www.plazalanesdm.com

VAL LANES
100 Ashworth Rd., West Des Moines
(515) 274-0493
www.vallanes.com

CLIMBING

CLIMB IOWA
3605 SE Miehe Dr., Grimes
(515) 986-2565
http://climbiowa.com
Practice your climbing and rappelling skills at this fully equipped climbing center north of Des Moines. The large climbing wall has every type of challenge and hazard, with sections designed from beginning climbers all the way up to the most experienced. An introduction to climbing class fills in new climbers on basic techniques and safety procedures before they hit the wall. The cost of the intro class includes climbing gear and safety equipment. Gear is also available for rent for all climbers. Climbers 13 and under must have an adult with them unless they are enrolled in a specific program.

CROSS-COUNTRY SKIING

Many parks throughout the area offer groomed ski trails. Here are a few of the best options:

Jester Park (11407 NW Jester Park Dr., Granger) and **Chichaqua Bottoms Greenbelt** (8700 NE 126th Ave., Maxwell) are both operated by Polk County Conservation (515-323-5300; www.conservationboard .org). Jester offers some 5 miles of skiing trails, starting at shelter 2 near the main park entrance. Ski rentals are around $10 a day, and you can pick them up Mon through Fri and keep them over the weekend. Chichaqua has 3 miles of groomed trails, beginning near the park ranger's residence just east of the longhouse next to the parking area.

Raccoon River Park (2500 Grand Ave., West Des Moines; 515-222-3444; www.wdm-ia.com), part of the City of West Des Moines's park system, has a 3.2-mile crushed rock skiing trail encircling Blue Heron Lake, plus additional wooded trails winding through the 631-acre park.

Big Creek State Park (8794 NW 125th Ave., Polk City; 515-984-6473; www.iowadnr .gov/parks/state_park_list/big_creek.html) has a 3-mile groomed trail, located on the east side of the park's lake. Pick up the trail near the park's disc golf course.

Des Moines YMCAs

Des Moines has several branches of the YMCA scattered throughout the city and nearby suburbs. Facilities vary, but most have gyms, exercise equipment, and indoor pools, some of which have zero-depth entry, which can be especially good for younger children. Day passes are available, and overall it's a good value. For general info: **www.dmymca.org.**

John R. Grubb YMCA
1611 11th St.
(515) 246-0791

Riverfront YMCA (downtown)
101 Locust St.
(515) 282-9622

South Suburban YMCA
401 E. Army Post Rd.
(515) 285-0444

Walnut Creek Family YMCA
948 73rd St.
(515) 224-1888

Waukee Family YMCA
210 N. Warrior Lane, Waukee
(515) 987-9996

GOLF

Des Moines has a nice selection of courses to choose from—in fact, too many to provide a comprehensive listing here. Listed below is a sampling of courses throughout the metro area. Rates vary, even on Des Moines municipal courses, where a round of 18 can run anywhere from just over $15 to around $30, depending on the course and day. Among the municipal courses, Waveland and Grand View are both a short drive from downtown and easily accessible from the interstate.

A. H. BLANK GOLF COURSE
808 County Line Rd.
(515) 248-6300
www.blankgolfcourse.com
One of three municipal courses in Des Moines, this course, adjacent to Blank Park Zoo on the city's far south side, has a challenging front nine, with numerous sand and water traps. Lots of hills and trees further add to the challenge of the game, and curious zoo animals may poke their heads over the course fence as you play through. There's a well-tended minigolf course as well for the kids. The course is open Mar through Nov.

BEAVER CREEK GOLF COURSE
11200 NW Towner Dr., Grimes
(515) 986-3221
www.beavercreek-golf.com
This 27-hole course northwest of Des Moines is a *Golf Digest* four-star course, with numerous trees, hills, and water hazards. The course specializes in golf outings, and does them either with tee times or shotgun starts. There's a nice driving range as well as a clubhouse and pro shop.

COPPER CREEK GOLF CLUB
4825 Copper Creek Dr., Pleasant Hill
(515) 263-1600
http://golfcoppercreek.com
This public 18-hole course offers a scenic round set among rolling hills. There are plenty of trees along the fairways as well. It's just a short drive east on I-80 and then south on US 65 to reach the course in the growing town of Pleasant Hill. The large clubhouse has a pro shop, bar, and food service.

COUNTRYSIDE GOLF COURSE
3089 North Ave., Norwalk
(515) 981-0266
www.countrysideiowa.com
This is one of a handful of courses nestled in the countryside south of Des Moines. There aren't as many trees as on other area courses, but there are bent-grass fairways and water hazards on most of the front nine.

GRAND VIEW GOLF COURSE
2400 E. 29th St.
(515) 248-6301
www.dmgov.org/departments/parks/pages/golfcourses.aspx
This is considered the easiest of the city's municipal courses, with a flat layout and fairly open fairways. Trees fill in most of the open space, but it's still not a difficult course to play, with a shorter distance of around 5,500 yards. There are a few challenges, including a pond on the 11th hole, several bunkers on the 6th hole, and a few hills scattered throughout the course.

JESTER PARK GOLF COURSE
11949 NW 118th Ave., Granger
(515) 999-2903
www.jesterparkgolf.com

A full-service complex that fills up with golfers tackling the 27-hole course or taking swings at the driving range or practice facility. The 18-hole championship course has four sets of tees on each hole, while the par 3 nine-hole course is ideal for beginning or younger golfers to improve their game. The practice facility includes bunker areas and chipping and putting greens. Located just down the road from Jester Park, about 30 minutes north of Des Moines.

LEGACY GOLF CLUB
400 Legacy Pkwy., Norwalk
(515) 287-7885
www.thelegacygolfclub.com
This public course sits alongside new residential development south of Des Moines. The par 72 course has bent-grass fairways and four tees at each hole, and has won numerous local and national awards for its play. It's a challenging course, with bunkers and water hazards popping up along the fairways. The clubhouse features a nice outdoor patio and full food service as well as a pro shop.

LONGVIEW GOLF CENTRE
10300 NW 54th Ave., Grimes
(515) 986-9799
www.longviewgolf.com
Look for the giant golf ball rising from the countryside north of Des Moines—this is a large, year-round indoor golf practice facility. The 40,000-square-foot, two-level driving range has a full complement of hitting and landing surfaces, and there's a putting green for practicing your short game. In addition, there's an outdoor driving range and both indoor and outdoor miniature golf courses.

TOURNAMENT CLUB OF IOWA
1000 Tradition Dr.
(515) 984-9440
www.tcofiowa.com

This Arnold Palmer Signature Course, laid out around a residential community north of Des Moines, has a picturesque setting, with scenic bluffs and hills winding around Big Creek and a pair of lakes. There are plenty of trees framing the bent-grass fairways as well. The par 71 course ranges from around 5,000 to 7,000 yards. A practice tee area includes a putting green.

WAVELAND GOLF COURSE
4908 University Ave.
(515) 248-6302
http://wavelandgolfcourse.org

In the heart of the city and within view of I-235, this is the oldest municipal course west of the Mississippi River, built in 1901. The course, which measures just over 6,500 yards, is rather popular—on any given day you'll see endless carts zooming up and over the numerous hills. The hills can be very steep and make a round here quite a challenge—patience is required on many of the holes. The stately redbrick clubhouse adds to the old-school atmosphere, and at the far west end of the course the domed observatory, which holds a large telescope, is a unique touch.

WOODLAND HILLS GOLF COURSE
620 NE 66th Ave.
(515) 289-1326
http://golfwoodlandhills.com

This privately owned course, one of the oldest in Des Moines, is open to the public and has 18 holes plus a driving range. The rolling hills of the course's location on the northern outskirts of Des Moines make for

Disc Golf

Des Moines has a thriving disc golf scene, with several nice courses laid out in local parks. Listed below are three courses in the city, as well as two in outlying areas. Details on the city courses can be obtained from **Des Moines Parks & Recreation** (515-237-1386; www.dmgov.org). For more information on disc golf in general, including course descriptions and lists of other area disc golf courses, check out **www.disc golfdesmoines.org.**

Pete Crivaro Park
1012 E. 14th St. (US 69)

Ewing Park
5300 Indianola Ave. (at McKinley Avenue)

Grand View Golf Course
3226 University Ave.

Big Creek State Park
8794 NW 125th Ave., Polk City
(515) 984-6473
www.iowadnr.gov/parks/state_park_list/big_creek.html

Southwoods Park
S. 39th Street at Mills Civic Parkway, West Des Moines
(515) 222-3444
www.wdm-ia.com

Water Works Park
2201 George Flagg Pkwy.
(515) 283-8791
www.dmww.com

a fairly quiet round on the fairways. A large water hazard loops around holes 5, 6, and 7, and there's a smaller one at hole 14. Decent rates, especially on weekdays, make this a nice choice.

HORSEBACK RIDING

JESTER PARK EQUESTRIAN CENTER
11171 NW 103rd Court, Granger
(515) 999-2818
www.jesterparkec.com
Guided trail rides are offered for ages 8 and up from May through early Nov at this riding facility about a half-hour drive from Des Moines. Horse trails run from the equestrian center through nearby Jester Park, one of the largest county parks near Des Moines, with miles of woods alongside Saylorville Lake. Riding lessons are offered year-round, and boarding is available as well. There are also group wagon and sleigh rides, which can be especially nice in the winter.

ICE SKATING

＊**BRENTON SKATING PLAZA**
520 Robert D. Ray Dr.
(515) 284-1000
www.brentonplaza.com
A true treat downtown: an outdoor skating rink on the east bank of the Des Moines River, just north of City Hall. Public skating is available 7 days a week, throughout the afternoon and evening, for less than $5. Skate rental is under $5 as well, and there's an ample-sized rental shed where you can put on your skates. Parents and kids alike crowd onto the relatively small oval as soon as it opens in mid-Nov. Skating lessons are offered, and the rink also hosts a broomball league that plays regularly from Dec to Feb.

Sledding

For great sledding in Des Moines, check out **Waveland Golf Course** (4908 University Ave.; 515-248-6302), which has numerous hills, many of which slope down into natural "bowls" that give you the opportunity to try out the many different runs. Nearby **Perkins Elementary School** (4301 College Ave.) does not have nearly as many hills, and the ones it does have are much less steep, but that makes them better for smaller kids, plus it's not nearly as crowded. On the south side, **McRae Park** (2000 SW 9th St.) and **Ewing Park** (5300 Indianola Rd.) are popular sledding spots, while the east side boasts sledding at **Grand View Golf Course** (2400 E. 29th St.; 515-248-6301). For adventurous types, the sledding at **Capital Hill** (1111 E. Court Ave.), just south of the State Capitol, is said to be among the fastest in the city.

Sledding is free at all of the listed sites. Golf courses open for sledding only when enough snow has fallen—check with **Des Moines Parks & Recreation** (515-237-1386; www.dmgov.org) to see if sledding is on tap.

SKIING & SNOWBOARDING

Obviously, Iowa is not a mecca for downhill skiing or snowboarding, but some decent runs are available. Many skiing and snowboarding hills are located a bit of a drive outside the city—check out snow conditions before you head out!

SEVEN OAKS RECREATION
1086 22nd Dr., Boone
(515) 432-9457
www.sevenoaksrec.com
This hill roughly an hour's drive from Des Moines has several runs of varying degrees of difficulty for skiers and snowboarders. Free ski and snowboard lessons are offered throughout the day, and additional instruction is available at cost. There are also "snow tubing" shoots with special lifts to bring tubers up the hill. There's equipment rental, chairlifts that go to the top of the hill, and an on-site restaurant and lounge. In the warmer months, the facility is used as a base for canoeing, kayaking, and tubing on the nearby Des Moines River.

✳SLEEPY HOLLOW SPORTS PARK
4051 Dean Ave.
(515) 262-4100
www.sleepyhollow-sportspark.com
Skiing, snowboarding, and snow tubing are all on offer at this hill conveniently located on the east side of Des Moines, near the Iowa State Fairgrounds. The 1,000-foot run down a 15-story hill can actually go pretty fast—helmets are required for snow tubers ages 4 to 6 (the facility provides the tubes). An efficient lift system carries riders back up, including tubers. Free beginner runs and ski lessons are available. Adult lift tickets range from about $20 to $30 and equipment rental ranges from about $10 to $20 depending on the day. The hill stays open a little later on Fri and Sat nights.

SWIMMING

A large number of public outdoor swimming pools dot residential neighborhoods throughout the city of Des Moines and suburbs, providing nice spots to cool off on hot summer days. Pool facilities vary widely, with some having multiple pools as well as play areas and snack bars. Admission fees vary as well. While the pools can be fun, they can also get very crowded, especially in the early afternoon hours, when school groups and camps may descend en masse. You may want to time your visit to avoid the crowds.

Outdoor Pools

Des Moines outdoor pools generally open in early June and close in mid-August, before schools begin fall classes, with the exception of Nahas, which closes Labor Day weekend. Details on pools can be found at www.dmgov.org/departments/parks/pages/poolseasonrentalinfo.aspx.

ASHWORTH POOL
101 SW 45th St. (in Ashworth Park, off Grand Avenue)

BIRDLAND AQUATIC CENTER
300 Holcomb Ave.

NAHAS AQUATIC CENTER
1101 Porter Ave.

NORTHWEST AQUATIC CENTER
4915 Madison Ave.

TEACHOUT AQUATIC CENTER
2601 Hubbell Ave.

Suburbs

CLIVE AQUATIC CENTER
1801 NW 114th St., Clive
(515) 440-0599
www.cityofclive.com/departments
/parks-recreation/aquatics-center

HOLIDAY AQUATIC CENTER
1701 Railroad Ave., West Des Moines
(515) 273-0700
www.wdm-ia.com

NORWALK AQUATIC CENTER
1112 E. 18th St.
(515) 981-4002

VALLEY VIEW AQUATIC CENTER
255 S. 81st St., West Des Moines
(515) 273-0700
www.wdm-ia.com

TENNIS

Des Moines Parks & Recreation operates numerous tennis courts around the city. The two largest by far are at **Birdland Sports Complex** (500 Holcomb Ave.) and **McCollum-Waveland Tennis Complex** (936 Polk Blvd.). Smaller courts are available throughout the city—for a listing of courts go to www.dmgov.org/Departments/Parks /Pages/DesMoinesTennisCourts.aspx.

KIDSTUFF

With a population that includes many young families, the Des Moines area has a number of attractions that cater to children, from the very young to teenagers, with many appropriate for multiple age levels. In addition to the many kid-oriented activities, opportunities for the young ones to have fun can also be found at some of the better-known attractions in the area, like the city's art museum, which has free admission and specific kid-centered activities, and the science museum in downtown Des Moines, which is largely oriented toward children with its plethora of hands-on displays and opportunities to build and move things in several of its galleries.

There are also plenty of kid-friendly activities in the rest of this book, especially in the Parks and Recreation chapters—check out some of Des Moines's many outdoor trails for a hike or bike ride, or have a picnic in one of the limitless parks and green spaces that can be found around the metro area. Wading pools are found in more city parks than can be mentioned here, and the city's swimming pools are always packed with youngsters on hot summer days.

Numerous play areas charge for kids to come in and use their equipment, and though this can be fun, you can also find many fine playgrounds in city parks. Just don't limit yourself to one type of activity or narrow section of the city—there's plenty to see and do all over town, and you might as well take advantage of several offerings while you're here.

This chapter is divided into sections based on the type of activity the listings represent, such as outdoor activities, hands-on museums that offer a lot for children to do or see, and more educational offerings. Some ideas could easily fit in more than one section—check out a few different things if you're looking for a variety of experiences.

Price Code

Price codes are based on the cost of admission for one child. Total costs may vary based on activities a child participates in. Check beforehand for details on pricing.

$	Less than $5
$$	$5 to $10
$$$	$10 to $20
$$$$	More than $20

HANDS-ON FUN

ADVENTURELAND $$$$
305 34th Ave. NW, Altoona
(515) 266-2121 or (800) 532-1286
www.adventureland-usa.com
Kids will love this amusement park with its mixture of rides, games, cheesy shows, and, of course, park food, with lots of fried stuff and sweet goodies available. Rides include roller coasters for older kids and lots of smaller rides for the younger ones, as well as log rides that are a relief on a hot day and

old favorites like bumper cars and a Ferris wheel. The centrifuge drops the bottom out of a spinning room and is not for everyone, but lots of kids want to ride it repeatedly! In addition to the traditional amusement park, Adventureland has a waterpark with numerous slides and pools. Ultimately all the action will probably wear the little ones out, but that's the point—right? Open Apr through Sept, 7 days a week May through Aug.

*BLANK PARK ZOO $$
7401 SW 9th St.
(515) 285-4722
www.blankparkzoo.com
Feed llamas, goats, and other animals at this zoo on the south side of the city that features a wide variety of species. Children will also enjoy the train that loops around the zoo, winding past many animal enclosures. The more than 1,000 animal species include exotic creatures from Africa and Australia and perennial favorites like tigers, sea lions, and giraffes. Besides the petting zoo, there's also a parakeet feeding area where, for a small charge, the birds will land on a stick and gobble down some food. Many areas shut down beginning in late fall and remain closed through the winter.

DES MOINES BOTANICAL CENTER $
909 Robert D. Ray Dr.
(515) 323-6290
www.botanicalcenter.com
Kids may get a kick out of the numerous plants that grow up the inside of this domed greenhouse just east of the Des Moines River, with lots of hidden paths winding past tall trees and colorful flowers, as well as a small fish pond and birds flitting through the treetops. There are tours geared toward children and story hours regularly held at the center, as well as self-guided scavenger hunts that challenge kids to find various plants and a pair of backpacks that will teach them all about the plants they see. Open 7 days a week.

*IOWA HALL OF PRIDE $$
330 Park St.
(515) 280-8969
www.iowahallofpride.com
The endless interactive displays at this sports-focused museum right by Wells Fargo Arena will keep kids of all ages preoccupied for quite a while. Older ones may get into the basketball and football shoot-out games in the back, while younger ones will find plenty of buttons to push and stuff to watch, with the many video displays showcasing every sport imaginable, and visitors may watch videos showcasing legendary games and athletes in Iowa sports history, including in the museum's panoramic theater. You can even take on historic players in virtual simulators! There's a ton of sports memorabilia on display as well.

ARTS & CULTURE

CIVIC CENTER OF GREATER DES MOINES $$
221 Walnut St.
(515) 246-2300
http://civiccenter.org
The main showcase in the city for live theater and other entertainment, the center also includes a family series of numerous shows that will appeal to a younger audience, including comedies, musicals, and plays based on popular children's books. There are also music and dance performances, including some in which children may be invited to participate on stage. Tickets are reason-

ably priced and available at the Civic Center's box office as well as online.

Shows generally are geared toward a narrow age group, such as elementary school age or middle school age.

CLASS ACT PRODUCTIONS $$
201 1st Ave. S., Altoona
(515) 967-7950
www.captheatre.org
With theater "for children, by children," this suburban playhouse puts on shows that kids of all ages will enjoy. Adaptations of classic children's literature and improvisational skits are just some of the things you'll see on stage here, as well as comedy and musicals. It's a great showcase for children interested in theater, with many kids learning the craft of acting as they participate in shows.

> **i** Not far from the Art Center, along the Ingersoll Avenue commercial strip, Bauder's Pharmacy (515-255-1124) is an old-fashioned drugstore and soda fountain with some of the best ice cream in Des Moines. The homemade peach and strawberry are perennial favorites every summer, but there are plenty of other flavors, as well as delicious sundaes and milk shakes.

DES MOINES ART CENTER FREE
4700 Grand Ave.
(515) 277-4405
www.desmoinesartcenter.org
The big draw here—other than the fact that it's a free museum—are the art backpacks provided to young visitors near the front door, which contain a wealth of activities to keep kids preoccupied, like scavenger hunts that will take them through the museum

and opportunities to create their own art. They may also find the museum's collections of interest—with a large number of modern painting and sculpture, there is lots of artwork that will appear to younger visitors. The galleries wind throughout the building, making this a nice spot to spend a couple hours, and the grounds outside are worth exploring as well. It's also adjacent to Ashworth/Greenwood Park, a sprawling city park that has lots of stuff for kids to see and do, including a lagoon, amphitheater, playground, and city swimming pool. The art museum is closed Mon.

DES MOINES PLAYHOUSE
831 42nd St.
(515) 277-6261
www.dmplayhouse.com
The playhouse's separate children's theater has put on productions that include all sorts of shows, from adaptations of books by beloved children's authors to musicals, and even some versions of classic Broadway hits like *Annie*. Many children's shows are staged in the basement children's theater, which seats about 250, although some are performed on the main stage, which seats about 400 and has some very nice sight lines. Acting classes also are held throughout the year, giving kids the opportunity to learn all about acting and theater. Tickets for many children's shows are around $15, although they may be more for main-stage children's productions.

FAMILY FUN

ALL PLAY DES MOINES
615 3rd St.
(515) 333-5050
www.allplaydm.com

A large video game emporium with plenty of other games and attractions, conveniently located 1 block south of Wells Fargo arena downtown. All sorts of electronic video games are here, including Guitar Hero and Terminator Salvation. You have the opportunity to take out some deer with Big Buck Hunter or speed around the track with a NASCAR game. Game cards can be purchased for unlimited play. For those who like their games more low-tech, pool and darts are here as well. There's also mini-bowling, and for a few bucks you can shimmy up a climbing wall. An on-site sports bar and grill provides food.

TOKENS FAMILY FUN CENTER $$
313 Grand Ave., West Des Moines
(515) 222-5656
www.tokensfamilyfun.com
Indoor miniature golf on a far-out black-light course is the main attraction at this kids' entertainment center near Valley Junction. Trying to get your ball into the hole while surrounded by loud fluorescent colors is a whole new challenge. The black-lit backdrops of prehistoric animals are a little freaky, but nothing too scary. The black-light theme extends to the laser tag arena, where you can zap your opponent with a light gun. Pizza and sodas are available, and this isn't a bad place for a birthday party or just a nice place to spend a cold, rainy afternoon. Minigolf and laser tag each cost about $7. Laser tag players must be at least 4 feet tall. Closed Monday.

DES MOINES PARKS

Many of the city's parks have features and facilities that children will enjoy—especially the parks equipped with wading pools in the summer. See the Parks chapter for more

details. Here are a couple other parks with features that kids may especially like.

A. H. BLANK MINI-GOLF COURSE $$
808 County Line Rd.
(515) 248-6300
www.blankgolfcourse.com/mini-golf.html
A nicely landscaped minigolf course adjacent to a city golf course, this largely "natural" course, decorated with trees and rocks, is a nice change from courses with more garish hazards. A round of golf costs about $7. Open May through Sept.

✳HERITAGE CAROUSEL $
725 Thompson Ave.
(515) 323-8200
www.heritagecarousel.org
Located in Union Park on the north side of Des Moines, this wonderful old-fashioned carousel is great even for younger kids—it moves at a fairly slow pace, and there are lots of animals to choose from. It's a replica wooden carousel that turns to the sounds of a traditional carousel organ. The cost to ride is only 50 cents for a child and $1 for an adult, with no charge for an adult who stands next to a child. The park is also one of the better-equipped in the city, and features a wading pool and a large playground with a huge rocket slide as its centerpiece. The carousel is open from May until around Labor Day, when Des Moines schools open for the fall.

PLAY TIME

BACKYARD ADVENTURES $$
3135 99th St., Urbandale
(515) 270-2433
www.comeonletsplay.com

Open play is available at this suburban showroom of outdoor play equipment. Some impressive climbing, sliding, and swinging equipment is found out on the showroom floor, including large, fortlike structures and big tire swings. A few basketball hoops are in the back of the room. Parents must supervise their children. Food and drinks may be brought in from outside, and utensils and napkins are available. Not open for open play on the weekends due to birthday parties. Cost is $5 per child.

CLIMB IOWA $$$
3605 SE Miehe Dr., Grimes
(515) 986-2565
http://climbiowa.com
Iowa's largest indoor climbing gym offers climbing opportunities to children ages 4 and up, who must climb with an adult if they are under 13. There's over 10,000 square feet of climbing space, with lots of challenging routes and hazards. Climbers 13 and under are restricted in their routes, and every climber under 18 must have a waiver signed by their parent and not any other adult—waivers can be printed out from the gym's website. Orientation is provided to adults who are climbing for the first time. Cost for a day pass is around $15 for adults, a little less for kids. Gear and safety equipment can be rented for modest prices. Open 7 days a week.

THE PLAYGROUND FOR KIDS $$
2401 SE Tones Dr., Suite 7, Ankeny
(515) 965-9899
www.theplaygroundforkids.com
An indoor play area north of Des Moines that gives kids ages 2 to 12 plenty of opportunities to bounce around on inflatables, including large slides, and play on other equipment like climbing units. Open to the public all day Mon through Fri and on Mon, Wed, and Fri evenings as well. It may also be available on Sat—check with the facility. Food is not allowed except for scheduled parties.

SAYLOR SKATE PARK $$
6359 NE 14th St.
(515) 289-0303
www.saylorskatepark.com
An indoor skate park with multiple ramps spread out over 15,000 square feet for boards, blades, and bikes, including some challenging half-pipes, quarter-pipes, and jump ramps. Skate sessions cost $8, with all-day passes available. Helmets are required and available for rent. Bikes are not allowed during some sessions. There's a fully stocked skate shop and snacks and sodas for sale. Lessons are available as well. Closed Monday.

SKATE NORTH INCREDIROLL $$
5621 Meredith Dr.
(515) 251-7655
www.skatenorth.net
This rink accommodates both in-line and roller skaters on a large skate floor. Music from a disc jockey accompanies the skating (of course) and there's a game arcade, snack bar, and pro shop. Parents who don't skate may watch from the seats that surround the rink. Admission is around $5 a night, with dollar night on Wed. Skate rentals are available. Closed Monday and Tuesday.

SCIENCE & TECHNOLOGY

**DRAKE MUNICIPAL
  OBSERVATORY**   FREE
Waveland Golf Course
4908 University Ave.
(515) 248-6302
www.drake.edu/artsci/physics
/observatory.html

The night sky opens up to visitors at this large telescope located on a city golf course a few miles west of the Drake University campus, with free astronomy programs on Fri nights in spring, summer, and fall, including an opportunity to scan the heavens for stars, planets, and other celestial phenomena. Smaller telescopes are also set up outside around the observatory.

✳SCIENCE CENTER OF IOWA $$
401 West M. L. King Jr. Pkwy.
(515) 274-6868
www.sciowa.org
There's lots of stuff for kids to explore and learn at this 2-story downtown museum, including the opportunity to build a paper rocket and launch it across a room, push a button and create your own tornado, and scan the night sky with a telescope. Interactive displays throughout the museum teach kids all about different principles of science. On the first floor there's a play area appropriate for younger children, with things to climb on and tunnel through and different games to play. Science demonstrations take place throughout the day in an open area on the first floor, giving kids the chance to do everything from handle reptiles and amphibians to see all sorts of literally explosive chemical reactions. Other programs take place upstairs in the museum's star theater. The museum's small planetarium and IMAX theater (which has a separate admission charge) have a wide selection of shows to choose from.

DOWN ON THE FARM

As the state perhaps identified more than any other with agriculture, Iowa has more than its share of farms to visit, offering youngsters a chance to see the crops and animals up close. Farm visits are especially popular and enjoyable come harvest season in the fall, when many create corn mazes, complicated pathways through the cornfields that, when viewed from high above, often resemble pictures or intricate designs. There is also usually apple cider, lots of pumpkins to pick out for Halloween jack-o'-lanterns, and a general harvest-time atmosphere.

GEISLER FARMS $$
5251 NE 94th Ave., Bondurant
(515) 964-2640
www.growingfamilyfun.com
One of the best corn mazes around is found at this 8-acre farm a short drive north of Des Moines. Some mazes have celebrated historic anniversaries, like the 40th anniversary of the Apollo moon shot or the 20th anniversary of the World Wide Web. It's not always easy to find your way around—be sure to get a map before you head out into the fields! Hay rides take visitors around the edge of the corn maze. Pedal carts, a low-tech version of go-karts, are available to ride around a small dirt track, and there are some other charming, old-fashioned games that kids may enjoy. The corn maze sometimes opens up at night, and it's a whole different experience navigating it in the dark. The pumpkin patch in the farm's front yard has plenty of the round orange gourds that make great jack-o'-lanterns. Yummy pies and other goodies are for sale. There's an admission fee of under $10 per person. Corn maze and pumpkin patch are open weekends Sept through Oct.

HOWELL'S PUMPKIN PATCH $$
3145 Howell Court, Cumming
(515) 981-0863 or (800) 210-1415
www.howellspumpkins.com

Located about 25 miles south of Des Moines off I-35, this farm has a corn maze and pumpkin patch with tractor rides shuttling visitors around, as well as a barnyard with animals including goats, sheep, pigs, and chickens. Kids may also enjoy petting the rabbits on the bunny farm as well as playing on pedal tractors and a giant slide and climbing on the large haystacks. Open Sept and Oct. Admission is around $6. Food is available.

PATCH'S PUMPKINS AND HONEY FARM $
35588 L Lane, Adel
(515) 834-9092
www.patchspumpkins.com

A large "pumpkin cannon" that hurls pumpkins into the sky differentiates this pumpkin patch from others in the Des Moines area. Located about 20 minutes west of Des Moines, it also has a petting zoo with horses, goats, and pigs, tractor rides, and numerous inflatables for kids to bounce on and inside. There's no corn maze, but there is a hay maze for younger kids. Admission is under $5 and includes all activities. Open weekends from late Sept through Oct.

PUMPKINVILLE & CORN MAZE $$
618 Center Ave. S, Mitchellville
(515) 967-0972
www.pumpkinvillecornmaze.com

This large pumpkin patch has over 10 acres of pumpkins, as well as a large "straw jump" and a play area for smaller children. The corn maze is one of the more challenging ones in the area, and there is also a mini maze that younger ones may enjoy. The corn maze opens in early Aug and the pumpkin patch in mid-Sept. Maze admission is around $5. Campfires are available as well.

LIVING HISTORY FARMS $$
11121 Hickman Rd., Urbandale
(515) 278-5286

The harvest theme continues at one of Des Moines's most popular tourist attractions, which, in addition to being a fun destination for children to learn about several generations of farming and pioneer life, also hosts a Halloween celebration that includes horse-drawn wagon rides, marshmallow roasting, storytellers, and scarecrow and jack-o'-lantern displays. It usually runs the weekend of and before Halloween and costs about $5. Otherwise, Living History Farms is open from late Apr through mid-Aug and is a great opportunity to see firsthand demonstrations of farming techniques and pioneer life. Take a look at the Iowa Indian Farm, where some of Iowa's original people grew beans and blue corn, cooked their meals over an open fire, and tanned deer hides. The 1850 Pioneer Farm has log cabins with displays of pioneer domestic life and arts while the 1900 farm features a strong team of draft horses plowing the fields. It's well worth spending an afternoon here, getting a look at so many different ways people lived, including meeting and talking with the historical interpreters.

WINTER FUN

BRENTON SKATING PLAZA $
520 Robert D. Ray Dr.
(515) 284-1000
www.brentonplaza.com

This is probably one of many parents' favorite spots to take kids in Des Moines for a taste of some good all-American fun: A small outdoor skating rink right by City Hall, it fills up on winter evenings with families, including kids of all ages, swishing around the rink. When the crowd thins a bit, there's more room for kids to practice their skating technique. Public skating is available 7 days a week, usually all day and into the evening. Admission is no more than $5, and season passes are available. Skate rentals are available in one of the two sheds at the south end of the rink. Definitely check this place out if you can—it's a fun experience for both kids and parents. There's free parking evenings and weekends in the City Hall parking lot.

SLEEPY HOLLOW SPORTS PARK
4051 Dean Ave.
(515) 262-4100
www.sleepyhollow-sportspark.com
Both kids and adults can shoot down the 1,000-foot-long modest slope at this skiing and snowboarding facility and family fun center near the Iowa State Fairgrounds. The cost of tubing includes the tube, and ages 4 through 6 must wear a helmet, which may be borrowed from the facility. There are also extensive summer activities, including go-karts, bumper boats, and a 9-hole beginner's golf course, as well as a driving range and baseball and softball batting cages. Each activity has its own fee in both winter and summer, with some combination tickets available. For winter sports they are generally closed Mon and Tues and only open in the evening Wed through Fri, although they are open all day, 7 days a week when school's out for winter break. No price code is listed here because rates vary widely, with different prices in summer and winter, depending upon the activity.

PARKS

Des Moines is positively surrounded by parks—just take a look at a map and note the greenbelts that line the rivers and creeks running across the city, as well as large green splotches in the outlying areas. The city's broad and widely used park system dates to the turn of the 20th century, when Des Moines began opening public parks, an effort that dovetailed with the City Beautiful movement to soften some of the effects of rapid urbanization and bring communities across the country more in harmony with nature.

Today residents use the parks year-round, enjoying a dip in a neighborhood park's pool on a hot summer day or strapping on the cross-country skis in winter. Many parks are also stops on Des Moines's extensive system of trails, which are utilized by both cyclists and walkers and wind through some scenic parts of the city. County parks rival those in the city for open space, accessibility, and activities.

Numerous city parks line the rivers or are tucked away in residential neighborhoods. County parks run the gamut from a 40-acre marsh with a nature walk north of the city to a 7,000-acre recovered greenbelt near the Skunk River that provides refuge to animals being reintroduced into the landscape. Each of the state's 99 counties has its own conservation board, which takes an active role in managing the parks, maintaining recreation facilities, and developing park activities. State parks are fewer in central Iowa than in other parts of the state, but there are some choices that aren't too far a drive away.

OVERVIEW

It's easy to find what you're looking for, park-wise—check out www.dmgov.org/depart ments/parks/pages/default.aspx for more information on city parks, including a nice interactive map that helps you pinpoint a specific park's location, or www.conser vationboard.org for county parks, including a clickable lists of parks with facilities listed. State parks are maintained by the **Iowa Department of Natural Resources**— go to www.iowadnr.gov for more information. **Iowa Outdoor Unlimited,** www .iowaoutdoorunlimited.com, can also provide information and assistance when it comes to backcountry activities.

CITY PARKS

While not an exhaustive list of parks in Des Moines, the following is a good sampling of green spaces in different parts of the city, with various recreational offerings available.

ASHBY PARK
3200 38th St.

BEAVERDALE PARK
3333 Adams St.

A pair of nice, well-landscaped parks located a few blocks from each other in a quiet residential neighborhood. Both parks are very popular with neighborhood residents for summer cookouts and get-togethers, and include grills and picnic areas. Ashby has a fairly new wading pool that lures in local kids all summer.

CRIVARO PARK
1012 E. 14th St. (US 69)

This park offers a nice respite from the busy commercial clutter on adjacent E. 14th Street. There's lots of green space here, as well as a wading pool, softball diamonds, picnic shelters, and one of three disc-golf courses in city parks. The park also serves as the southern terminus for the Neal Smith and John Pat Dorrian cycling trails, so it's a good place for a break before you hop back onto the bike.

EWING PARK
5300 Indianola Rd.

Adjacent to Easter Lake Park, this largest of the city's parks bursts with purple colors and sweet fragrance for about 2 weeks every spring when the flowers bloom in its lilac arboretum. The park also has numerous activities, including playgrounds and a disc-golf course, one of three in city parks.

GRANDVIEW PARK
3230 Easton Blvd.

Next to a city golf course, this park is one of the larger options on the east side of Des Moines. Home to one of the city's three disc golf courses, it also has playgrounds, open and enclosed shelters, a softball field and tennis court, and a wading pool.

✳GRAY'S LAKE PARK
2100 Fleur Dr.

Just a short drive, bike ride, or even walk from downtown, this 167-acre park across the street from Water Works Park offers a full slate of activities. There's a swimming beach on the west side of the lake, which is encircled by a 2-mile path that hooks up with trails running to the north and west across Des Moines and into the countryside. Paddleboats, canoes, kayaks, and sailboats are available for rent, and the pavilion at the south end occasionally hosts outdoor concerts and other events. The park is also a nice spot for a picnic lunch, as well as for kite flying near the pavilion.

✳GREENWOOD/ASHWORTH PARK
4500 Grand Ave.

One of Des Moines's oldest and most popular neighborhood parks, this park is divided up into a children's play area and wading pool on a hill to the east, a city swimming pool to the south, and a fabulous rose garden to the west, behind the city's art museum. Heading into the park, you pass a large amphitheater overlooking a tranquil pond, which is a great spot to stop and rest for a bit and, if you prefer, people-watch (it's listed on the National Register of Historic Places). There's a trailhead for the city's bike trail system by the pool.

RACCOON RIVER PARK
2500 Grand Ave., West Des Moines

Part of the West Des Moines park system, this is the place to go for swimming in Des Moines—the beach fronting Blue Heron Lake stretches for 700 feet along the 232-acre lake.

Lots of green space fronts the lake, as well as a large playground and a popular dog park. Can be a bit tricky to get to—if Grand Avenue is not open all the way to the park, usually due to construction, then visitors must head west on E. P. True Parkway and then south on 35th Street before picking up Grand again and heading north up to the park.

UNION PARK
725 Thompson Ave.
Another older, neighborhood park, set on a small hill with some vintage playground equipment, including a towering slide shaped like a spaceship. The vintage theme extends to the beautiful carousel, which is a bargain at just 50 cents a ride. There's also a nice wading pool and plenty of picnic spots.

✳WATER WORKS PARK
2201 George Flagg Pkwy.
Under the supervision of the Des Moines Water Works (515-283-8700; www.dmww.com), this park, with an entrance on Fleur Drive, stretches all the way from southwest of downtown to the western boundary of Des Moines at 63rd Street. It is one of the largest urban parks in the United States, with popular cycling and walking trails winding their way through vast green spaces. Running west, the path crosses 30th Street before it splits, with one path crossing a bridge over the Raccoon River and running north to Greenwood/Ashworth Park, while another runs west to a wide-open field and picnic area before crossing Park Avenue and hooking up with the Great Western Trail as it shoots out toward the cornfields. The park is also known for the **Arie Den Boer Arboretum,** at the east end of the park by Fleur Drive, which boasts a large collection of crab apple trees.

WAVELAND PARK
4908 University Ave.
Primarily a municipal golf course, Waveland Park is also one of the best spots in the city for winter sledding. Typically, after a big snowfall, the park's gates are thrown open and residents pour in with sleds and snowboards to take a ride down several rolling hills (the park may not open for sledding right after it snows—it's wise to check before heading out). Waveland also hosts outdoor concerts in the warmer months and is the site of an observatory that puts on stargazing programs open to the public.

COUNTY PARKS

BROWN'S WOODS
Brown's Woods Drive west of 63rd Street
Two miles of trails pass through this 500-acre forest just past the western boundary of Des Moines in West Des Moines. The trails form a double loop that moves past numerous oak and hickory trees, which soar overhead as the trail crosses and re-crosses a creek that flows into the nearby Raccoon River. Woodpeckers, including the yellow-bellied sapsucker and the yellow-brown flicker, are at work high in the trees. This area is also part of the Makoke (MAH-koh-kay) birding trail, which encompasses several sites in central Iowa where birders have seen a multitude of species. Noise from the nearby airport occasionally intrudes, but you still may be able to spot deer in the woods.

CARNEY MARSH
SE 54th Street and SE Rio Court, Ankeny
This 40-acre preserve north of Des Moines is a fine example of restored wetland, with a marshy habitat unfolding next to a 1-mile nature trail. The habitat also includes a prairie landscape and woods, all right outside

the fast-growing suburb of Ankeny. Hang around and you might spot heron, black-birds, and several types of waterfowl, as well as the muskrats that move silently through the murky waters. Frogs hop across the path with the distinctive honk of Canada geese in the background as they rise from the pond to fly in formation overhead.

CHICHAQUA BOTTOMS GREENBELT
8600 NE 126th Ave., Maxwell

A bucolic wildlife area that comprises some 10,000 acres of wetlands, savanna, and woodlands northeast of Des Moines and is scored with trails and oxbow lakes. Marshy areas along the trail follow the old chan-nel of the Skunk River, which meanders through the landscape, creating habitats for numerous birds, including sandhill cranes, grasshopper sparrows, and herons. Other species are gradually being reintroduced here as well, including river otters and ornate box turtles. Wild raspberries grow along the paths, as do swamp milkweed and other plants. Algae blooms in the stagnant pools. The terrain gets rugged here, and you should really have a pair of good hiking shoes. The area floods frequently when the waters rise on the nearby Skunk River—it's wise to check to see if any trails are closed after heavy rains. To reach the park, head out of Des Moines on US 65/330 to Bondu-rant, then turn north on Grant Street, which becomes NE 72nd Street before curving to the east, becoming NE 134th Avenue, and reaching the park entrance.

EASTER LAKE PARK
2830 Easter Lake Dr.

Set amid the drab boulevards of southeast Des Moines is this gem of a park, featur-ing a kidney-shaped, 172-acre man-made lake with a swimming beach, boat rentals, and fishing, with anglers casting for bluegill, bullhead, catfish, crappie, bass, and walleye. Trails wind their way through the woods above the lake, and there's a playground as well as picnic areas throughout the park. Polk County's last remaining covered bridge was moved here in 1967 from its original location, and nearby are the mine spoils from the area's last operating coal mine, which operated at this site until 1959 and supplied coal for a local power plant. Easter Lake Park is also located next to Ewing Park, which features a popular lilac arboretum.

FORT DES MOINES PARK
7200 SE 5th St.

Not to be confused with the Fort Des Moines Museum (though that's certainly worth a visit as well), this park on the southern edge of the city centers on a large pond popular for fishing, with bluegill, crappie, and catfish all the targets of local anglers. A trail runs through stands of aspen and oak in the southern part of the park and makes for an easy hike. Just up the park road from the pond is a small arboretum with a nice display of 40-plus native trees. There's a playground and picnic areas, as well as a ball field, too.

✳JESTER PARK
11407 Jester Park Dr., Granger

The showpiece in the Polk County parks sys-tem, this multi-use park covers nearly 2,000 acres near the northern edge of Saylorville Lake, north of Des Moines. To get there, take IA 141 north to NW 121st Street, then drive to NW 118th Avenue and head east, passing the golf course, to the park entrance. It's a birders' paradise, noted for the gathering of thousands of migrating white pelicans in Aug and Sept. There are plenty of other

Suburban Park Districts

Many of the towns surrounding Des Moines have excellent parks of their own, including extensive walking, hiking and cycling trails. Contact their parks departments for details on specific parks, including park and trail maps.

Altoona Parks & Recreation
407 8th St. SE, Altoona
(515) 967-5203
www.altoona-iowa.com

Ankeny Parks & Recreation
210 S. Ankeny Blvd., Ankeny
(515) 963-3570
www.ankenyiowa.gov

Clive Parks & Recreation
1900 NW 114th St., Clive
(515) 223-5246
www.cityofclive.com/departments/parks-recreation

Grimes Parks & Recreation
410 S. Main St., Grimes
(515) 986-2143
www.grimesiowa.gov

Johnston City Parks
6400 NW Beaver Dr., Johnston
(515) 278-0822
www.cityofjohnston.com/departments/parks

Pleasant Hill Parks & Recreation
5050 Doanes Park Rd., Pleasant Hill
(515) 309-0049
www.ci.pleasant-hill.ia.us/parks.html

Urbandale Parks & Recreation
3600 86th St., Urbandale
(515) 278-3963
www.urbandale.org/parksandrec.cfm

West Des Moines Parks & Recreation
P.O. Box 65320
4200 Mills Civic Pkwy., West Des Moines
(515) 222-3444
www.wdm-ia.com

Windsor Heights Parks & Recreation
1133 66th St., Windsor Heights
(515) 279-3662
www.windsorheights.org/parks.html

---

species here, too, as well as hiking trails going through thick forest of cottonwood and hickory, horseback riding, and numerous camping sites, as well as a "natural playscape," located right next to buffalo and elk corrals on the north end of the park.

YELLOW BANKS PARK
6801 SE 32nd Ave.

This park is out past the eastern boundary of Des Moines, on bluffs perched above the Des Moines River. Hiking trails run out to the edge of the bluffs, giving a panoramic view of the river valley below, as well as an ideal perch to spot migrating hawks and bald eagles, which soar through the air above the valley. The park also features a nicely restored oak savanna, along with a good explanation of the development of savanna in Iowa's natural landscape. There are plenty of campsites, ball fields, and a boat launch here, too.

OTHER PARKS

NEAL SMITH NATIONAL WIDLIFE REFUGE
9981 Pacific St., Prairie City

About half an hour's drive east of Des Moines, the refuge is a reconstructed prairie and savanna that supports grassland birds and other wildlife on nearly 9,000 acres near Walnut Creek. There are hundreds of plant and wildlife species here, with both elk and bison reintroduced into the landscape and trails winding all over the refuge, as well as an automobile tour. A nature center provides detailed explanation of Iowa's original landscape and efforts to preserve it.

WINDSOR HEIGHTS DOG PARK

Located along the Walnut Creek hiking and biking trail and to the south of Colby Park at 6900 School St., a mile or so west of the Des Moines city limits, this modest dog run has become a popular spot of dog walkers. It has plenty of room for dogs to run and makes for a nice break from walking along the paved path.

HIKING & CYCLING TRAILS

Thanks to the efforts of local conservation departments in Des Moines and surrounding counties and local trail groups, Des Moines has miles winding along creeks as they move through the city and then passing cornfields as they head out into the countryside. There are plenty of nice trails in city, county, and state parks as well. Some trails are reserved just for hikers, while others are multiuse, with cyclists zipping along in the warmer months and cross-country skiers whooshing by in the winter. It's a good idea to contact the agency in charge of a particular trail if there have been recent heavy rains—many trails, especially those near creeks or rivers, can flood and be shut down for weeks or even months afterward. Also carry plenty of water and other essentials if you are heading out on a long hike in the country—the sun can

get hot in the summer! Contact the supervising agency—either a county conservation board or a city parks department—for maps and details on trail regulations, including whether dogs are allowed on any given trail. Other good resources for trail maps and information is the **Des Moines Bicycle Collective** (617 Grand Ave.; 515-288-8022; www .dsmbikecollective.org) and **Greater Des Moines Recreation Trails** (www.dmgov .org/departments/parks/trails/default.aspx).

County Trails

CHICHAQUA VALLEY TRAIL

Running for over 1 mile from the town of Bondurant, northeast of Des Moines on US 65, to Baxter, this trail follows an old rail bed as it crosses numerous bridges over Santiago Creek, which snakes below as it moves through the bottomlands of the nearby Skunk River. In addition to hikers, this trail is popular with cyclists and cross-country skiers, who make good use of the long, flat stretches.

GREAT WESTERN TRAIL

Stretching for nearly 17 miles into the countryside south of Des Moines, this trail is very popular with cyclists, who can get up to some pretty high speeds on the paved path. Walkers utilize the trail as well, for the nice views it gives of creeks and fields as well as wildlife—it's easy to spot deer along the path, once you have gone past the edge of Des Moines International Airport. The trail begins just south of Water Works Park, by the intersection of Park Avenue and Valley Drive/ George Flagg Parkway. Many cyclists who ride the trail make it a custom of stopping off at one or more of the several watering holes found along the path.

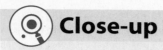

Close-up

RAGBRAI—10,000 Cyclists Rolling Past the Cornfields

An annual weeklong bike ride sponsored by Iowa's flagship newspaper (the name stands for *"Register's* **Annual Great Bike Ride Across Iowa"**), **RAGBRAI** is nothing less than a huge swarm of cyclists riding along Iowa country roads as part of a rolling carnival, party, and cycling event all rolled into one. Still going strong since its inception in 1973, RAGBRAI counts some 10,000 riders per day, who come from all over the world to ride a largely flat route through rural Iowa. Quite a few make the entire ride, which is roughly 450 miles across the state. Near the end of July, towns along the route—it changes every year—brace themselves for the onslaught of cyclists (and the money these hungry and thirsty riders will spend as they pedal across the state).

It starts with a profusion of bike trailers and converted school buses with bike racks on their roofs rolling down to the western border of Iowa. Riders dip their rear tire in the Missouri River, a ritual they'll complete nearly a week later when they arrive at the finish line and dip their front tire into the Mississippi. Anyone can ride and anyone does—the course sees riders in shorts and T-shirts on rusty old bikes as well as serious road racers with high-tech bikes and sleek riding outfits. All ages ride RAGBRAI—in fact, the highest percentage of riders are in their late 40s and early 50s, with the gender breakdown about two-thirds males and one-third females. Many riders ride in teams, and it's not unusual to see a line of anywhere from a few to a few dozen zip by, peddling in sync.

Riders stop off in small towns along the way to take a break, tweak their bikes, and partake of the numerous vendors who dish out everything from burgers and tacos to homemade pasta and pies to appreciative customers. At the end of the day, riders roll into another town for the nightly campout, with tents packed end to end in parks and fields. For many, the nights are the best part of the whole ride—more food vendors set up shop along the main streets, and rock bands and other acts entertain riders well into the night.

HANGING ROCK TRAIL

Located in a small park in the rural community of Redfield, about 30 miles west of Des Moines, this trail is notable for a huge, impressive sandstone bluff jutting out over Middle Raccoon River. After admiring the rock and taking a short stroll through the park's prairie landscape, it's just a short walk or drive to hook up with the Raccoon River Valley Trail (see below). Both trails are managed by the Dallas County Conservation Board.

HEART OF IOWA NATURE TRAIL

One of two trails with a trailhead in the small town of Slater, north of Des Moines, this trail, managed by the Story County Conservation Board, takes hikers and cyclists out into the wide open spaces of Iowa farmland—expect to see some breathtaking vistas over the cornfields, especially if you're out at sunrise or sunset. The scenery isn't the most exciting in the world, but it is somewhat stirring to be able to see so far across the open fields.

HIGH TRESTLE TRAIL

Another trail that begins in the town of Slater, one leg of this paved trail runs west to an impressive bridge over the Des Moines River, while another leg runs south through some picturesque Iowa farming towns and cornfields. There's a good chance you'll spot farmers at work atop tractors or combines, especially during the planting or harvest seasons. There are some small pools of water hidden among the stands of trees along the path, creating homes for frogs, butterflies, grasshoppers, and a variety of birds.

SUMMERSET TRAIL

Beginning in the town of Carlisle, south of Des Moines this trail, overseen by the Warren County Conservation Board, moves past a rural stretch of fields home to numerous species of birds, with a wide variety of flowers and plant life growing along the trail. Once you get past a small residential subdivision by the trailhead, you are largely surrounded by wide-open country. The trail runs 12 miles to Indianola, passing through Summerset State Park and Banner Lakes along the way.

TRESTLE TO TRESTLE TRAIL

This trail, which hooks onto paths running north from downtown, is a nice escape from the bustle and traffic of the city. The trail runs near the Des Moines River, as well as past boggy lowlands and marshy ponds decorated with cattail and lily pads, which are also good places to spot birds and wildlife. Queen Anne's lace, goldenrod, and horsemint bloom alongside the paved path. The rails-to-trail conversion heads past the northern city limits and eventually crosses the Trestle Bridge in Johnston, where it hooks onto the trails in that suburb.

RACCOON RIVER VALLEY TRAIL

Beginning at a picturesque old train depot in Redfield, this stretch of a very long trail popular with cyclists takes a long, winding course past farm fields and Iowa country towns (the entire trail begins on the outskirts of Des Moines and runs 56 miles west-north-west to the rural community of Jefferson in central Iowa). If you can do 9 miles on the trail heading east from Redfield, you'll come to the historic courthouse town of Adel.

City Trails

CLIVE GREENBELT TRAIL

Continuing along Walnut Creek from its starting point northwest of the intersection of 86th Street and University Avenue in Clive, this Clive city trail follows a paved path, which eventually runs by a replanted prairie containing more than 20 varieties of native grasses. Eventually this trail hooks onto the eastern end of the Raccoon River Valley Trail, which runs for many miles into the countryside.

WALNUT CREEK TRAIL

This trail actually splits into two a short distance south of its trailhead by Ashworth Pool in Greenwood/Ashworth Park, with one paved path running east toward Gray's Lake and downtown, and the other taking a more wilderness route along Walnut Creek. Lots of wildlife flit through the woods that hem in the trail, including raccoon, beaver, and deer. The path crosses a few roads in between stretches of woods and also passes an old railroad bridge shortly before it hooks up with the Clive Greenbelt Trail.

ANNUAL EVENTS

Music and food festivals, holiday celebrations, athletic competitions, and everything in between: There's a lot happening at all times of the year in Des Moines, from small neighborhood bashes to citywide events. It all culminates in the Iowa State Fair, where the whole city seems to descend on the fairgrounds on the east side. Residents in particular take as much advantage as possible of the warmer seasons to get outside: The downtown farmers' market is up and running at the very beginning of May, and it seems like a summer weekend doesn't go by without some sort of festival downtown or in an outlying area. Winter doesn't shut down gatherings, just moves them indoors, like the big minigolf tournament that takes place inside the downtown skywalk.

Most events are highly casual—strictly come-as-you-are. Many are free, but some charge admission. Food is an integral part of many events, and you can usually find vendors offering all sorts of comestibles at many of the gatherings listed below.

Take the following calendar with a grain of salt: While some events, particularly athletic contests like the Drake Relays and Hy-Vee Triathlon, happen at the same time year after year, others may change or drop off the calendar completely. It's always a good idea to check before planning a trip out to a particular event.

JANUARY

IOWA SPORTSMAN OUTDOORS SHOW
Iowa State Fairgrounds,
3000 E. Grand Ave.
(877) 424-4594, ext. 149
www.iowasportsmanshow.com
A mecca for fishermen, hunters, and outdoorsmen, this show offers information booths and seminars on all types of gear and services, including the chance to test new products and chat with manufacturers, guides, and conservation experts. Check out everything from turkey calls to bass boats and learn about the newest trends in hunting and fishing. Tickets are only $6 for adults and $4 for kids over age 12.

EVERYTHING BRIDAL SHOW
Hy-Vee Conference Center
5820 Westown Pkwy., West Des Moines
www.hy-vee.com/resources/conference-center/the-everything-bridal-show.aspx
One of central Iowa's largest wedding shows, with a slew of vendors, including photographers, bakers, banquet facilities, catering services, limousine companies, and disc jockeys. Admission is free, and there are numerous prizes and giveaways as well as a fashion show.

IOWA HOME SHOW
Iowa State Fairgrounds
3000 E. Grand Ave.
(800) 756-4788, ext. 47
www.theiowahomeshow.com

Get new ideas to spruce up your home or apartment, with exhibitors of kitchen, bathroom, home electronics, and landscaping items, as well as performances by different entertainers. Tickets are very reasonably priced.

DES MOINES BOAT, SPORT & TRAVEL SHOW
Hy-Vee Hall, 730 3rd St.
(402) 393-3339
www.gototheshows.com
See the latest models of boats and RVs and check out hunting and fishing gear at this show held at Hy-Vee Hall in the Iowa Events Center downtown. Learn tips from professional guides at numerous seminars. You can even watch casting techniques in a 5,000-gallon fish tank.

FEBRUARY

SKYWALK GOLF TOURNAMENT
Downtown Skywalk
(515) 286-4906
www.skywalkgolf.com
Said to be the world's largest indoor golf tournament—the unofficial motto is "Friends don't let friends golf in the snow"—this is a fun way to beat the winter blahs. Up to 4 courses are laid out over the 3 miles of the downtown skywalk, and tee times are assigned. You can play as a single, double, or foursome. Some golfers wear goofy costumes, and everyone has a lot of fun hitting balls down the elevated corridors. Entry fee is around $30 per golfer, and there's usually a free T-shirt or other prize for participating, plus beer and music in the Skywalk food court.

DES MOINES HOME & GARDEN SHOW
Iowa Events Center
730 3rd St.
(952) 933-3850
www.desmoineshomeandgarden show.com
A large show focused on remodeling and decorating, with over 500 exhibitors showing their wares at the Iowa Events Center at the north end of downtown Des Moines. Also features appearances by home remodeling television personalities, full displays of rooms and gardens, and samples from Iowa wineries.

IOWA DEER CLASSIC
Hy-Vee Hall, 730 3rd St. and Polk County Convention Complex, 501 Grand Ave.
(319) 323-0218
www.iowashows.com
Iowa is deer-hunting country, and this is one of the biggest buck shows around, with 100,000 square feet of everything that might possibly be needed for the hunt. There are numerous seminars and speakers each day, as well as archery tournaments and a wall of over 100 mounted trophy whitetail. The biggest bucks taken in Iowa are also on display. Kids' activities and door prizes round out the fun. Admission is only $10, with numerous discounts available.

MARCH

IOWA FLOWER LAWN & GARDEN SHOW
Iowa State Fairgrounds
3000 E. Grand Ave.
(800) 756-4788, ext. 47
www.iowaflowershow.com
Continuous seminars let attendees know all there is to know about gardening just in time for spring planting. Horticulturalists and botanists pass on their tips, and there

are more than 300 varieties of flowers for sale, as well as landscaping, water gardens, trees, and much more. Even a bird show with a variety of winged and feathered friends. There is also a judged flower show and a best landscaping contest.

APRIL

FAMILY EASTER PARTY
Living History Farms
11121 Hickman Rd., Urbandale
(515) 278-5286
www.livinghistoryfarms.org
Lots of family Easter activities at this re-creation of a historic Iowa farm town, including toy hunts, a preschool Bunnyland, live rabbit exhibits, barnyard animal walk, horse and wagon rides, traditional games, and egg decorating. Free sodas and popcorn for everyone. Get there by noon to make sure you can enjoy all the different activities, plus have a look at townspeople's homes. Admission is $5 per person.

DRAKE RELAYS
Drake Stadium
2719 Forest Ave.
(515) 271-3647
www.godrakebulldogs.com
Des Moines's legendary track and field meet, which is famous for showcasing Olympic and world champions, features more than 8,000 athletes competing in numerous events. During the relays, Drake stadium is a flurry of activity as runners race down the track while other events such as shot put and high jump take place on the infield. The opening ceremony is usually midday Friday, and there are events well into the evening, followed by fireworks, before the relays wind down late Saturday afternoon. Tickets can be

purchased online at www.godrakebulldogs.com, or by phone at (515) 271-3647.

MAY

✳DOWNTOWN FARMERS' MARKET BEGINS
Court Avenue Entertainment District, between 1st and 5th Streets
(515) 286-4928
www.desmoinesfarmersmarket.com
One of the city's most popular offerings for residents and visitors alike, the market brings together produce stalls, food vendors, and arts and crafts booths, packed along 4 blocks on the south side of downtown and spilling onto the side streets on Sat mornings. The market officially opens at 7 a.m. and runs until about noon. Bring an extra bag or two—while vendors usually provide bags, you never know what you might find, and it can be easier to carry everything in one sack. There are several restaurants and cafes along the market's streets that make for a nice spot to take a break from shopping—this really is one of the more impressive farmers' markets you'll see, with a veritable bounty of fruits, vegetables, breads, cheeses, meat, and other foods spilling over tables on the sides of the streets. Musical performers often set up along the streets, particularly close to the Polk County Courthouse at the western edge of the market. Park either in a downtown garage or at meters on nearby side streets—it's worth looking for a space south of M. L. King Jr. Parkway, then walking the few blocks to the market.

LAZERFEST MUSIC FESTIVAL
Indianola Balloon Grounds
IA 92 and 150th Avenue, Indianola
www.lazer1033.com

Headbangers rejoice—this all-day festival in a field a half-hour south of Des Moines brings together some of the biggest names in metal and thrash. Alice Cooper, Korn, Kid Rock, Rob Zombie, and Godsmack are just some of the heavyweights who have played the festival, as have numerous lesser-known acts. Sponsored by Des Moines radio station Lazer 103.3, the 2010 festival saw a record 15,000 fans head down to the festival site near the National Balloon Museum. Tickets are around $40 and typically include parking. VIP passes are available as well. No backpacks, coolers, or lawn chairs allowed—you'll have to stand in the dirt and grass with the rest of the crowd.

PRINCIPAL CHARITY CLASSIC
Glen Oaks Country Club
1401 Glen Oaks Dr., West Des Moines
(515) 279-4653
www.principalcharityclassic.com
Played on a course laid out by renowned course designer Tom Fazio, the Principal Charity Classic, which begins in either late May or early June, is Des Moines's preeminent golf event, drawing top golfers and hordes of fans out to an elegant, English-style golf club in West Des Moines. Part of the PGA Champions Tour, the 3-day tournament has hosted notable names such as Fred Couples, Corey Pavin, and Tom Lehman, as well as celebrities playing in the separate Pro-Am event, like *Desperate Housewives* star Teri Hatcher. A record 75,000 fans turned out in 2010 to watch Nick Price take the win. The event raises money for local charities including Blank Children's Hospital and United Way of Central Iowa. Tickets are around $15, with discounts available for multi-day purchases. Children age 15 and under get in free with a paying adult.

JUNE

✳DES MOINES ARTS FESTIVAL
Western Gateway Park
Grand Avenue and 15th Street
(515) 286-4950
www.desmoinesartsfestival.org
For over 40 years, artists have come to Des Moines to showcase their work at this sprawling outdoor festival. Everyone from painters and sculptors to jewelry designers, photographers, and many other types of artists shows up, with widely recognized names alongside new and emerging talents. Artists set up booths along the streets of the Western Gateway section of downtown, with many different items for sale. Stroll among the booths and you might see everything from abstract paintings hanging in one to fine handmade jewelry in another. There's a juried art show as well as a performing arts stage and a Kids' Zone, where children can work on numerous art projects of their own. Food is available from vendors. Admission is free and several parking garages are nearby.

WORLD PORK EXPO
Iowa State Fairgrounds
3000 E. Grand Ave.
(515) 251-8805
www.worldpork.org
Where else but the nation's largest hog producer (some 19 million pigs call Iowa home—compared to 3 million people) would you find a festival dedicated to pork? While the expo, sponsored by the National Pork Producers Council, is largely aimed at pig farmers and the people who buy what they raise, with a trade show and seminars on such topics as pig medicine and marketing pork products, there are a few things for the casual visitor as well, such as pig races and a pig-themed souvenir shop. A musical

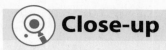 **Close-up**

Summer Music Festivals

As in other cities all over the Midwest, Des Moines residents like to take full advantage of the warmer months to get outside and hear some music. There are numerous outdoor concert series, with everything from jazz to pop to classical. Four of the more popular series, from locations around the city and metro area, are listed here.

FRIDAYS AT THE FOUNTAIN

Fountain Plaza, West Glen Town Center
5465 Mills Civic Pkwy., West Des Moines
(515) 223-7885
www.westglentowncenter.com
An after-work crowd gathers for a happy hour–type event while listening to some live pop or jazz at a new shopping and entertainment center on the southern edge of West Des Moines. It's a great event to relax and listen to music while watching the sun dip below the flat fields in the distance. Admission is $5, and the music usually runs from about 5:30 to about 8:30 p.m.

METRO ARTS ALLIANCE

(515) 280-3222
www.metroarts.org
This family-friendly series of events takes place at locations all over the city, from the golf course at Waveland Park to the State Capitol grounds, Gray's Lake, and various parks and neighborhoods. Tends to be pretty laid-back, with food vendors and families bringing picnics (don't forget the lawn chairs), as well as a good selection of local artists who play all sorts of different styles. There's a street-fair atmosphere at many events, with food and craft vendors setting up shop near the music stage, and kids playing in the available open spaces.

MUSIC IN THE JUNCTION

Historic Valley Junction
217 5th St., West Des Moines
(515) 222-3642
www.valleyjunction.com
Music shows every Thursday night from May through September as part of the popular outdoor farmers' market in a historic downtown just over the border in West Des Moines. All types of bands play here, with shows usually running from about 6 to 8 p.m. The market runs from 4 to 8 p.m. Free admission, and free shuttles available throughout the market to free parking at Hillside Elementary School (713 8th St.).

NITEFALL ON THE RIVER

Simon Estes Amphitheater
75 E. Locust St.
This annual series presents an eclectic assortment of acts, from radio favorites to more alternative bands. Held in a large outdoor downtown amphitheater, where warm breezes blow off the Des Moines River, these concerts have a relaxed, outdoor-festival vibe. Shows start around 7 p.m., and lawn chairs and blankets are allowed. Tickets are reasonably priced at around $15; visit Midwestix.com.

festival during the three-day event usually features classic rock–type acts. And don't forget the rich smell of cooked pork wafting from vendors' grills. Tickets are around $15.

GREEK FOOD FAIR
Greek Orthodox Church of St. George
1110 35th St.
(515) 277-0780
www.stgeorge.ia.goarch.org
For over 30 years, this small church in a quiet residential neighborhood near Drake University has served up Greek delights like souvlaki, Greek salad, and *keftedes,* or Greek meatballs. Don't forget the baklava—this mixture of sweet goodies spread among thin layers of Greek pastry is a favorite item looked forward to by many attendees. Thousands show up for the one-day festival, digging into plates under white tents set up on the church lawn. It's a return event for many families, Greek and otherwise, as well as students and people who come from all over the city and suburbs. Tickets for a "full meal" are around $15 each and can usually be purchased in advance at the church or Dahl's supermarkets throughout Des Moines. A la carte items are also available. In addition to the food, there are Greek dancing demonstrations and a disc jockey playing Greek music. With so many people descending on the church, you may end up parking several blocks away.

CAPITAL CITY GAY PRIDE
CELEBRATION
Grand Avenue/East Village
www.capitalcitypride.org
This event received a major boost following the Iowa Supreme Court's recognizing of gay marriage in April 2009. JUST MARRIED signs joined the multitude of rainbow flags along the streets of the East Village. The

weekend-long festival attracts thousands and showcases the gay, lesbian, bisexual, and transgender community with a parade, street fair, and musical and other performances. It has evolved from a somewhat ribald carnival into a more mainstream event, with plenty of families showing up among the revelers. Numerous vendors and information booths are on hand with all types of merchandise, including gay wedding services. Admission is free.

DAM TO DAM RUNNING RACE
Saylorville Dam to Nollen Plaza
www.damtodam.com
Beginning at Saylorville Dam north of the city and winding from the cornfields to city streets and the finish line at Nollen Plaza in downtown Des Moines, this 20K race has grown from a few hundred runners at its start in 1980 to nearly 10,000 finishers, making it the biggest race of its size in the country (there's a separate 5K race as well). Fans line the route to cheer the runners on, and there's a blowout after-party at the finish line, with music and lots of food. In addition to locals, the race attracts elite athletes from all over the country and the world, including top distance runners from Kenya and Ethiopia. Total purses top $10,000. Registration fees vary for the two races, ranging from about $40 for the 5K to $60 for the 20K.

IOWA STATE BBQ CHAMPIONSHIP
Riverview Park, Marshalltown
(641) 752-3302
www.iabbq.org/marshalltown
That cloud of smoke rising an hour northeast of Des Moines isn't from a fire, but from a whole field of cooks vying to create the best piece of barbecued meat. Contestants arrive from all over for the competition, which

takes over the small burg of Marshalltown for the weekend. Barbecue connoisseurs will enjoy sampling meats from different vendors. It's like the world's largest picnic with some great food.

JULY

80/35 MUSIC FESTIVAL
Western Gateway Park, downtown Des Moines
http://80-35.com
Right around the Fourth of July this multi-day carnivalesque music fest, organized by an almost all-volunteer staff, takes over the Western Gateway, bringing an eclectic list of acts to the outdoor location. The festival has moved in its short life, but it seems settled in Western Gateway Park downtown. Yo La Tengo, Modest Mouse, Spoon, The Roots, Public Enemy, and Flaming Lips have all played the festival, as well as a long lineup of lesser-known bands. Ticket prices vary widely, depending on the number of days attending and standard tickets versus VIP packages. Numerous vendors, food and otherwise, line the festival grounds.

NATIONAL BALLOON CLASSIC
Memorial Balloon Field
15335 Jewel St., Indianola
(515) 961-8415
www.nationalballoonclassic.com
Hot-air balloonists from all over descend on this small town south of Des Moines for a unique festival of flying dirigibles, which runs for about 10 days. Balloon competitions are held throughout the day, and it's quite a sight to see massive numbers of them floating over the surrounding cornfields. Hot-air balloon rides take off early in the morning and around sunset—you'll need to register about an hour or so before the flight. Cost is

around $150. Admission to the festival itself is around $10 per car and may be free up to a certain hour. The festival runs only in the mornings and then from the late afternoon until the early evening. Fireworks shows are scheduled at night. Food is available.

BREWFEST DES MOINES
Principal Park
1 Line Dr.
www.dmcityview.com/events/brewfest
Sample more than 350 varieties of beer at this mother of all keg parties. Since starting at a local bar a few years ago, it has mushroomed in popularity and is now held at the Iowa Cubs' baseball stadium. Admission is $25–$30 and includes unlimited beer—there's a steep discount for designated drivers who want to tag along with their beer-drinkin' buddies. And plenty of drinkers do show up, with large crowds of (mainly) younger people turning out to sample the variety of brews. Advance tickets are available at the ballpark and local Hy-Vee supermarkets.

AUGUST

ITALIAN-AMERICAN HERITAGE FESTIVAL OF IOWA
Court Avenue Bridge, Downtown
www.italianfestivalofiowa.com
Sponsored by the Society of Italian Americans, this festival succeeded Des Moines's long-running Festa Italiana and moved a short distance north, from the city's traditional Italian neighborhood on the south side, to downtown. Food, music, and dancing are on tap, as well as cooking demonstrations, a bocce tournament, and kids' activities, plus, of course, food, with lots of traditional Italian specialties on offer. Free admission.

*IOWA STATE FAIR

Iowa State Fairgrounds
3000 E. Grand Ave.
(515) 262-3111
www.iowastatefair.org

This is the big one, the event that in many ways defines Des Moines (and Iowa). With a million visitors, the fair in effect triples the population of Des Moines. There's plenty to see and do; it just may take a little time to adjust to the sensory overload.

The 400-acre fairground, home to the fair for over a century, is stocked with venerable brick livestock barns where farm kids tend to their animals in hopes of winning a coveted blue ribbon, and exhibit halls showcasing everything from farming techniques to large-animal veterinary science (you may actually see a calf or other farm animal being born during your time at the fair). Butter sculptures are a featured sight, with a new "theme" sculpture every year alongside the fair's venerable butter cow. The midways stretch to the horizon, offering every type of thrill ride imaginable, as well as the main reason many visitors come to the fair: the food. All sorts of items are available from vendors, with most served either on a stick (corn dogs, pork chops, pretzel, pickle, tiramisu) or deep-fried (Twinkies, candy bars . . . the list goes on). Top entertainers have taken the stage in the fairgrounds' grandstand, including Johnny Cash, Sheryl Crow, Charlie Daniels, and Keith Urban (there have been plenty of non-country acts as well).

Allow a full day to really experience the fair (many visitors come back for a second go-round). Admission is around $10 for adults, $4 for kids ages 6 to 11, 5 and under are free. At certain times entry is discounted. Separate tickets are required for grandstand shows, rides, and food, and value packs are available. There's also a separate charge for parking, and golf cart shuttles can bring you to and from the fair from your vehicle. Tickets are usually available for purchase at local supermarkets as well as on the fair website.

SEPTEMBER

IOWA FARM PROGRESS SHOW

US 30 and IA 17, Boone
(309) 586-5888
www.farmprogressshow.com

A biennial event held on a 600-acre plot of land about an hour northwest of Des Moines, this show draws in nearly a quarter million visitors and features hundreds of exhibitors and long rows of tractors, combines, planters, and other farm equipment—if you're fascinated by these massive machines, you'll spend some happy hours here. Farmers pour in from surrounding states and around the country and the world in anticipation of the kickoff for the seed sales year, and giant agribusinesses like Monsanto and Archer Daniels Midland show off their latest strains. Admission is about $10 per adult, less for kids.

HY-VEE TRIATHLON

Raccoon River Park, West Des Moines
www.hy-veetriathlon.com

Since 2007 this competition, the only US race on the International Triathlon Union's World Cup Circuit, has brought world-class athletes to swim, bike, and run on a course laid out in West Des Moines and Des Moines. The 2008 race was the final US qualifier for the Beijing Summer Olympics. In addition to elite competitors, plenty of amateurs take part in the event, and spectators line the streets and cluster at the finish line. There have been some dramatic photo finishes, particularly in 2009, when Canadian Simon Whitfield broke the tape a hair ahead of the next four racers and set an event record time. Registration fees vary depending on whether you are registering as an individual or as part of a team.

AMERICAN QUILTER'S SOCIETY QUILT SHOW & CONTEST
Iowa Events Center
730 3rd St.
(270) 898-7903
www.americanquilter.com
Four days of quilts and quilting classes and events, with 1,000 quilts on display and 300 vendor booths letting you know all that is new in quiltmaking. More than $40,000 in cash prizes is up for grabs in various quilting competitions. Admission is around $10 a day.

OCTOBER

✳WORLD FOOD FESTIVAL
Locust and E. 5th Streets, East Village, Downtown
www.worldfoodfestival.org
A smorgasbord of food and drinks from all over the world that unfolds at the foot of the State Capitol, this festival is one of the last gasps of warm-weather outdoor entertainment in Des Moines before the air begins to turn cool, signaling the forthcoming arrival of winter. Sample treats from local restaurants at food stalls that line the streets, from African to Filipino to Latin American delicacies and everything in between. Several beer and wine tents help slake your thirst. Admission is free.

FULL FRAME DOCUMENTARY FILM FESTIVAL
Des Moines Art Center
4700 Grand Ave.
(515) 277-2205
www.desmoinesartscenter.org

A hodgepodge of films by American and international filmmakers is screened in the museum, everything from topical documentaries to more offbeat and experimental work (these films are intended for adults). The festival is designed to showcase the work of unseen and emerging artists. Admission is free, with different films on each day of the two-day festival.

DES MOINES MARATHON
526 39th St.
(515) 288-2692
www.desmoinesmarathon.com
Over 1,000 runners set off from Nollen Plaza and through the city's residential neighborhoods before returning to the finish line in the Des Moines Marathon, which serves as a qualifying race for the Boston Marathon. Runners expecting a nice, flat midwestern course may be in for a surprise when they hit some of Des Moines's hills, particularly some steeper ones on the west side of the city. In addition to the marathon, several other races are held, including a half-marathon and a 5K. Spectators line the course route cheering on riders and proffering much-appreciated bottles of water. There are also events in the days leading up to the race, including a sports and fitness expo, and a big blowout party following the race—for many runners, it's the best part of the whole event!

OKTOBERFEST DES MOINES
4th Street and Court Avenue
www.oktoberfestdsm.com
Music, German food, and, of course, beer— lots of beer—as this annual favorite spills out onto the street near Hessen Haus bar and restaurant just around the corner from the Court Avenue Entertainment District. A

tented beer garden provides a place to suck down some suds while listening to oompah and watching polka dancers. Ten bucks gets you a mug and your first drink ticket. It all kicks off with the "tapping of the golden keg" and continues with musical acts of all kinds performing well into the night.

DIA DE LOS MUERTOS/DAY OF THE DEAD
Des Moines Art Center
4700 Grand Ave.
(515) 277-2205
www.desmoinesartcenter.org
Come to a traditional Mexican Halloween celebration, with music, food, and activities. Traditional altars are on display in the museum's main gallery, with information plaques explaining their historical importance in Mexico. Children will enjoy decorating *calaveras,* or sugar skulls, while a mariachi band entertains in the museum's garden. Warm up with some Mexican hot chocolate and try some *pan de muertos,* or bread of the dead.

FAMILY HALLOWEEN NIGHTS
Living History Farms
11121 Hickman Rd., Urbandale
(515) 278-5286
www.lhf.org
Wagon rides, Halloween stories, and displays of jack-o'-lanterns make this a good Halloween choice for families. There's also trick-or-treating through the historic farming town on-site for kids 12 and under, and free popcorn and sodas for everyone. Admission is about $5 per person. Perfect for that feeling of harvest time in Iowa, with touches of an old-fashioned Halloween celebration. Just be sure to bring warm enough clothes in case the weather turns cold!

NOVEMBER

BEAVERDALE HOLIDAY BOUTIQUE
Holy Trinity Catholic School
2926 Beaver Ave.
(515) 401-4145
www.htschool.org
Get an early jump on Christmas shopping at this long-running holiday bazaar in the Beaverdale neighborhood on the west side of Des Moines. Over 100 vendors offer all sorts of arts and crafts and other unique gift ideas. There are also lots of yummy baked goods for sale. An on-site cafe gives you the chance to fuel up during the frenzy of shopping.

IOWA WINE & FOOD EXPO
Hy-Vee Hall, Iowa Events Center
730 3rd St.
www.wineandfoodexpoiowa.com
Foodies, this is for you: row upon row of exhibition space with a dizzying array of food items, including an endless number of food samples. Countless wine and beer samples are available as well. Cooking demonstrations will show how to whip up some tasty concoctions, and numerous celebrity chefs cook on the event's stage, as do local culinary artistes. Ticket prices vary, with multi-day passes available.

DOWNTOWN WINTER FARMERS' MARKET
Capital Square and Nollen Plaza
400 Locust St.
(515) 286-4928
The perfect opportunity to stock up on meats and goodies for upcoming holiday dinners, this unseasonal holiday market is held in downtown's main outdoor plaza and the adjacent commercial building, which has access to the skywalk. Lots of holiday gift possibilities are here, food items and otherwise. Over 120 vendors proffer jams, jellies,

honey, wine, and yummy baked goods like pies, cakes, and cinnamon rolls. Musicians play festive Christmas tunes while you shop. Admission is free, and there's lots of parking available at nearby garages. While you're there, get a poinsettia to decorate your home.

HOLIDAY LIGHTS DES MOINES
Brenton Skating Plaza
520 Robert D. Ray Dr.
www.downtowndesmoines.com
Usually held right after Thanksgiving at the downtown ice-skating rink, this event features the lighting of the city's Christmas tree, as well as visits with Santa Claus, carriage rides, musical performances, and food vendors. The rink will be open for skating, and there's a fireworks display right after the tree lighting. Admission is free, with free parking in the city lot north of the Armory building at 602 Robert D. Ray Dr., as well as in the lot east of City Hall at 400 Robert D. Ray Dr. Parking is also free at all city meters after 6 p.m. the day of the event.

✳JOLLY HOLIDAY LIGHTS
Water Works Park
2201 George Flagg Pkwy.
www.iowa.wish.org
This is central Iowa's largest holiday lights display, with numerous holiday characters along a 3.5-mile route in a parklike setting. Also features Santa's wish shop, where kids can meet Santa and have cookies and hot chocolate. It runs through the end of Dec and costs about $10 per car.

DECEMBER

PRAIRIE CHRISTMAS
Living History Farms
11121 Hickman Rd., Urbandale
(515) 278-5286
www.lhf.org

The spirit of Christmas as seen from historic Iowa comes to life, with horse-drawn wagon rides, tree trimming, and a visit with Santa Claus. Check out the old-time decorations in the historic Iowa farm village. Children's activities include crafts and taffy pulls, and Santa's workshop will be open for holiday gift shopping. Admission is about $5 per person.

HOLIDAY OPEN HOUSE
Historic Valley Junction, West
Des Moines
(515) 222-3642
www.valleyjunction.com
Running for several weekends in late Nov and early Dec, this is an old-fashioned Christmas event, with caroling, photos with Rudolph, holiday food vendors, and free carriage rides, plus a chance to meet Santa and Mrs. Claus. It's a festive time, with some 150,000 Christmas lights strung above the 6 blocks of shops in the historic downtown area of Valley Junction—it should be easy to find gifts for the Christmas list here. Admission is free.

ZOO TOTS
Blank Park Zoo
7401 SW 9th St.
www.blankparkzoo.com
Kids get a chance to make crafts, hear animal stories, and eat yummy snacks at this popular event held Wed, Thurs, and Fri mornings over the course of a few weeks. Each event has a different theme revolving around an animal who will be the focus of the children's activity for the day. A fee is charged, and it's a good idea to register early.

HOLLY & IVY TOURS
Historic Salisbury House
4025 Tonawanda Dr.
(515) 274-1777
www.salisburyhouse.org
Rooms are dressed up for the holidays at this historic house on the west side of Des Moines, near the city's art museum. There are gingerbread houses on display and live holiday music. The house also features holiday lights and visits with Santa, although these may be later in the month. Tickets for the tour are around $15 for adults and $6 for children.

DAY TRIPS &
WEEKEND GETAWAYS

Central Iowa is a great spot for weekend road trips, with roads fanning out from Des Moines to numerous interesting destinations. While some, like Pella and the Amana Colonies, have multiple attractions as well as attractive restaurants, shops, and lodgings that make for an inviting weekend getaway, others, like the Herbert Hoover Presidential Museum and National Historic Site, are located in remote areas and more suited for a visit of an hour or two.

There are also plenty of spots that promise an experience of wild nature, particularly the many county and state parks located a short drive from the Des Moines area, many of which offer camping or cabins for rent and promise great hiking, swimming, and other outdoor activities. You might even be interested in a getaway by bike—with cycling trails winding for many miles through the countryside, it's possible to spend a whole day or even longer pedaling past farms and fields. Consult the Parks chapter for more information on trails.

For some of the best weekend getaways, just hop in your vehicle and hit the road. Cruise through iconic country towns that look like something out of a Grant Wood painting, with their dusty water towers and weather-beaten farms. Stop by a cafe for an old-fashioned country meal and take a stroll around the courthouse square, then watch the sun set as tractors chug through the cornfields. This is Iowa, after all, where you don't have to go far to find the picture-postcard vision of the American Midwest in all its glory.

PELLA: A DUTCH VILLAGE

For a taste of Holland amid the rolling Iowa cornfields, take a drive down to **Pella** (www .pella.org, www.pellatuliptime.com), a prosperous town of about 10,000 people located less than an hour's drive southeast of Des Moines and settled by Dutch pioneers. A quiet college town that is one of the main tourist destinations in Iowa, Pella is proud of its Dutch heritage. There's a classic small-town square with buildings festooned with Dutch architectural flourishes, including a popular Dutch bakery, and everywhere you look there are **replica windmills,** including the town's flagship model, at 124 feet high the largest working windmill in America, built by Dutch craftsmen. Other reminders of the Netherlands include reconstructed canals and an animatronic clock tower with figures that include a large pair of wooden shoes. Pella is also home to the eponymous **Pella Corporation,** headquartered on the town's main street, which turns out windows and doors for homes all over the world. **Central College,** a small liberal arts college whose sports teams are nicknamed the Dutch, is operated by the Reformed Church in America, formerly known as the Dutch Reformed Church.

Pella was founded in 1847, when Dominie Hendrik Scholte led a group of 800 Dutch religious refugees to central Iowa and purchased large tracts of farming and hunting lands. The settlement was originally known as Strawtown, due to the fact that the new arrivals spent their first winter huddled in straw and sod shelters, wood for building homes being a scarce resource on the vast midwestern prairie. Eventually the town prospered, and residents began celebrating their Dutch roots. Pella later became known as the boyhood home of famed western lawman **Wyatt Earp**—his house in Pella is open to visitors.

The annual **Tulip Time Festival,** held every May, increases Pella's population tenfold, as visitors pour into town to see the hundreds of thousands of blooming tulips and for various Dutch-related activities. There's a Dutch craft market and an impressive parade through town, while locals in Dutch costume and wooden shoes stroll the streets and the tulip queen is crowned alongside her court on the Tulip Toren stage. Come November, **Sinterklaas** is Pella's Dutch-themed Christmas celebration, with a parade featuring Sinterklaas, the Dutch Santa Claus.

i Pella virtually shuts down on Sundays in observation of the Sabbath. Few businesses are open and the streets are all but deserted, so be sure to visit on Saturday or during the week.

Attractions

CALVARY WAYSIDE CHAPEL
E. Oskaloosa Street
(641) 628-9193
East of the center of Pella, this chapel, built in 1965 by followers of the Calvary Christian Reformed Church, is one of the smallest places of worship you'll ever see. The chapel contains 4 two-seat pews, which are actually all that's left of the original structure—it was rebuilt in 1996, following extensive weather damage accrued over many years. The chapel is free and open to all visitors, just remember that it is a place of worship. Guests are asked to close the door when they leave.

KLOKKENSPEL
629 Franklin St.
(641) 628-2626
Built by a Dutch-American industrialist, this giant cuckoo clock stands just east of Pella's town square, down the street from the town's historical village and large Vermeer Windmill. To the sounds of a 147-bell carillon, 4-foot-tall animatronic figures move through a window set high in the redbrick structure, telling the story of the settling of Pella. Look for town founder Dominie Scholte baptizing a baby and his wife, Mareah, crying over her broken dinnerware. There's another figure working at blacksmithing and one making wooden shoes. A woman in traditional Dutch costume sweeps a broom, while a man in Dutch cap heaves two milk pails on his shoulders using a yoke. Two children offer a bouquet of tulips, and even hometown boy Wyatt Earp turns up, holding a rifle. The Klokkenspel show starts promptly at 11 a.m. and 1, 3, 5, and 9 p.m. daily. At Christmas the Klokkenspel's usual figures are replaced by those telling the story of a Dutch Christmas.

KNOXVILLE RACEWAY

1000 N. Lincoln St., Knoxville
(641) 842-5431
www.knoxvilleraceway.com

Every Sat night from Apr through early Oct, souped-up sprint cars go screaming down the "black gumbo" at this self-proclaimed "dirt racin' capital of the world." The cars themselves are something to see—they resemble nothing so much as oversized go-karts with a large "wing" mounted above the driver's cage. Seeing them barrel down the ½-mile track as they fight for the checkered flag is an even more impressive sight. The 25,000-seat grandstands fill to capacity every Aug for the Knoxville Nationals. Camping is available at the track. The on-site **National Sprint Car Hall of Fame** (515-842-6176; http://sprintcarhof.com) has displays on the history of sprint car racing, as well as some actual cars.

LAKE RED ROCK

1105 Hwy. T15, Knoxville
(641) 828-7522
www2.mvr.usace.army.mil/redrock
/default.cfm
www.redrockarea.com

Iowa's largest reservoir occupies nearly 20,000 acres and is located to the west of Pella. It is very popular for recreation: Camping, boating, and fishing are all big here, as are picnics and hiking on the **Volksweg Trail,** which winds around the north end of the lake and runs all the way to Pella. There are also numerous overlooks above the lake. Recreation areas are concentrated at the eastern end of the lake, as is a visitor center with displays on the history and ecology of the area, including both live and stuffed animals. Step out onto the center's observation deck for a look at the lake and **Red Rock**

Dam, which is built across the Des Moines River. The dam stands more than 100 feet tall and stretches a mile across the river. Near the dam is the **Gladys Black Bald Eagle Refuge** (641-281-4815), a 38-acre area of land east of the dam where bald eagles roost. The birds can be observed from **Horn's Ferry Bridge,** adjacent to the refuge.

The lake is managed by the US Army Corps of Engineers and has several campsites: **Howell Station,** with 143 sites, is the largest and has access to a boat ramp and hiking trails. **North Overlook** has 55 sites set in a heavily wooded area and access to a swimming beach. **Wallashuk** is located on the north side of the lake and **Whitebreast** is on the south side, with access to a boat ramp and swimming beach. **Elk Rock State Park** (811 46th Ave., Knoxville; 641-842-6008; www.iowadnr.gov/parks/state_park_list /elk_rock.html), located on the shores of Lake Red Rock, has both tent and RV camping, as well as 13 miles of hiking, biking, and equestrian trails. **Cordova Park** (1378 Hwy. G28, Otley; 641-627-5935) has a 106-foot-tall observation tower looking out over the lake and river, and features the longest continuous fiberglass staircase in the world. The park also has cabins for rent.

MOLENGRACHT

700 Main St.
(641) 628-2246

This dining and retail complex covers some 100,000 square feet and replicates the canals of the Netherlands 1 block from Pella's town square. Canals do indeed flow through the complex, with the water passing under a drawbridge and flowing past redbrick shops, restaurants, and the Royal Amsterdam hotel. Theme nights and outdoor entertainment are held at the Molengracht during the summer months. The Pella Cinemas movie theater is located in the complex as well.

PELLA HISTORICAL VILLAGE
507 Franklin St.
(641) 628-4311
This village of about 20 buildings and extensive flower gardens is arranged around a courtyard and gives visitors a picture of pioneer life in Pella. Included are a country store, grist mill, log cabin, blacksmith's shop, and a shop featuring wooden shoes, as well as the town's famous Vermeer Windmill. The 25,000 tulips that bloom here for the festival each May later make way for annuals and perennials in the gardens along the redbrick walkways. Buildings are furnished in period decor and furnishings, going all the way back to a replica sod house like those that Pella's original settlers constructed to survive their first brutal midwestern winter. The Wyatt Earp house, located within the village, gives visitors a picture of Earp's childhood as the son of a US marshal and future lawman.

In Nov and Dec, Christmas lights wind their way along the village's paths. The village is closed from Jan through mid-Mar. Admission to the village is around $10 for adults and includes a self-guided tour of the village. Combination tickets are available for tours with Scholte House.

PELLA OPERA HOUSE
611 Franklin St.
(641) 628-8625
www.pellaoperahouse.org
Built in 1900 and renovated in 1990, this redbrick structure on Pella's town square regularly presents music and theater shows, with a nice mix of acts. The building is worth a visit itself for its stained-glass windows and ornate tin ceilings. Tickets for shows are

often very reasonably priced—they usually aren't more than $30.

SCHOLTE HOUSE
728 Washington St.
(641) 628-3684
The home of Dominie Scholte and his family, located on Pella's main square, was finished in 1848, a year after Scholte led 800 Dutch colonists seeking religious freedom and established the town. Many of the home's original furnishings are still here, including some fine antiques. Tours are self-guided, with staff available to answer inquiries. Guided tours are also available. The home's gardens contain thousands of tulips and are free of charge to visit. Admission to the house is about $5, and combination tickets are available, which include admission to the historical village and windmill as well.

SUNKEN GARDENS
Located on Main Street a couple blocks north of the town square, this park is dominated by a man-made pond laid out in the shape of a wooden shoe. As with the many other Dutch-themed sights in Pella, it is surrounded by tulip beds—over 10,000 tulips bloom here in the spring—and there's a modest windmill in the park as well. In the winter the pond's frozen surface is popular with ice skaters. Free.

TASSEL RIDGE WINERY
1681 220th St., Leighton
(641) 672-9463
www.tasselridge.com
Located in a small town east of Pella, this vineyard and winery produce a wide variety of wines, including Chardonnay, Riesling, and Syrah, as well as special Iowa varieties. Free tours give visitors an extensive look at

the winemaking process, with a guide leading visitors through the winery. In warmer months a "grapemobile" takes visitors on a tour through the vineyards (there is a small charge for the outdoor tours, which also include a coupon for a wine purchase). All tours allow visitors to enjoy a complimentary wine tasting. Open 7 days a week.

VERMEER MILL

Visible from throughout Pella, this striking 124-foot windmill serves as the interpretive center for Pella's historical village. It is the tallest working windmill in the United States. Built in the Netherlands by windmill designer Lucas Verbij, the mill was reassembled in Pella by Dutch craftsmen. The mill is 100 percent wind powered, and its stones are used to grind corn into flour, which may be purchased in an adjacent gift shop. Guided tours of the windmill, which is included in admission to the historical village, begin every half hour with the last tour at 4 p.m.

Accommodations

Hotels and other accommodations in the Pella area fill up quickly for **Tulip Fest** in May as well as for major races at nearby Knoxville Raceway—reserve well in advance. The town also has a full lineup of franchise accommodations—check the website www.pella.org for more information.

Hotels

DUTCH MILL INN
205 Oskaloosa St., Pella
(641) 628-1060
http://dutchmillinn.com
A standard motel with very reasonable prices. Rooms are clean if basic and include cable television, with microwave and refrigerator available for an additional charge. Rates range

from about $45 to about $65. Complimentary continental breakfast is included.

ROYAL AMSTERDAM HOTEL
705 E. 1st St., Pella
(641) 620-8400
www.royalamsterdam.com
This 38-room hotel at the Molengracht complex, open since 2001, is ideally located for exploring downtown Pella—it's right across the street from the historic village and large windmill. All rooms have refrigerators, as well as desk, chair, and free high-speed wireless Internet. There's an on-site restaurant and a 24-hour fitness center. Standard room rate is around $100. It's an entirely no-smoking hotel. No pets.

Bed-and-Breakfasts

CLOVERLEAF B&B
314 Washington St., Pella
www.cloverleafbandb.net
Just a few blocks from both Pella's downtown square and the town's historic village, this B&B in a historic Victorian home has 4 guest rooms, each with an antique double bed. The rest of the house is festooned with antiques as well. There are 2 common bathrooms, each with a full tub and shower. Television and telephone are available in the house's common areas, but not in the guest rooms. Breakfast includes Dutch treats like *pannekoeken* (pancake), and they also serve the famous Pella bologna. Smoking is permitted on the front porch. This is not the place for kids; no pets, either. Rooms are $69 a night. No credit cards accepted.

DE BOERDERIJ BED & BREAKFAST
420 Idaho St., Pella
(641) 628-1448 or (800) 720-6321
www.cheesemakersinn.com

A "Dutch farm," this craftsman house sits on the site of a former dairy operation on the outskirts of Pella, near the campus of Central College. The 4 guest rooms are comfy and cozy, and each has a unique bed, including one with an iron frame and another with a four-poster model. You'll find a fireplace in one room, too. Each room has a private bath and television. A yummy breakfast is served in the morning, with great coffee and Dutch pastries. Room rates range from $110 to $140. No pets, smoking, or alcohol permitted.

SPRING VALLEY BED AND BREAKFAST
1567 Rutledge St., Knoxville
(641) 828-9021
www.springvalleybb.com

A short drive from the Knoxville Raceway and National Sprint Car Hall of Fame, this rural B&B has 2 guest rooms in the main house that each include a queen bed and television. One bedroom has a private bathroom, while the other shares a bathroom. Also in the main house is a children's play room with games and books. There's a separate game room with ping-pong and air-hockey tables. A cabin and bunkhouse on the 600-acre farm provide more rustic accommodations, with the cabin including a kitchenette and bathroom with shower. A big country breakfast will fill you up in the morning. Fishing is available, or you may prefer to just watch the ducks on the pond. The owners can take you on a tour of the farm and you may have a chance to feed the animals. Rates are $85 for each room. No credit cards accepted.

Shopping

✴JAARSMA BAKERY
727 Franklin St.
(641) 628-2940
www.jaarsmabakery.com

If you've never had a Dutch letter, you're in for a treat, because this modest bakery on Pella's town square is considered *the* place to indulge in the S-shaped flaky pastries filled with an ambrosia-like almond filling. For more than a century, four generations have been faithfully turning out the sweet slices of goodness, baking tens of thousands of Dutch letters during Tulip Time every May. The "S" shape came about because the letters were originally baked for Sinterklaas, the Dutch Christmas celebration. Plenty of other Dutch baked goodies are available here as well, including strudel, spice cookies, almond butter cake, and sinfully delicious Dutch apple bread with brown sugar, nuts, and cinnamon and frosted with maple icing. Hungry yet?

ULRICH'S MEAT MARKET
715 Franklin St.
(641) 628-2771
www.ulrichsmeatmarket.com

A few doors down from Jaarsma Bakery, Ulrich's specializes in Pella bologna, which is heartier and spicier than what you'll find on a supermarket shelf. It's great for grilling or making substantial sandwiches, and has been a favorite since John Ulrich arrived in Pella with the recipe over 150 years ago. Plenty of other high-quality meat products like bratwurst and summer sausage are available as well, as are a good selection of Dutch cheeses like Edam and Gouda.

MADISON COUNTY
www.madisoncounty.com

Famous ever since the 1995 movie starring Clint Eastwood and Meryl Streep made its iconic covered bridges famous, **Madison County** is a nice spot for a day trip from Des Moines. The bridges are not too difficult to find—they lie along country roads radiating out from **Winterset,** the county seat and only town of any size in the sweep of rolling countryside, about 30 minutes southwest of Des Moines via either I-35 or I-80 and then on smaller highways. Winterset is also home to the John Wayne birthplace, which is a must-stop for fans of "The Duke."

Attractions

BIRTHPLACE OF JOHN WAYNE
216 S. 2nd St., Winterset
(515) 462-1044
www.johnwaynebirthplace.org

This modest, 4-room house was the home of the boy named Marion Morrison, who was born here in 1907 and grew up to change his name to John Wayne and become one of the most famous movie stars of all time. Wayne's father, who had attended nearby Simpson College in Indianola, worked as a pharmacist in Winterset before moving the family to California a few years later.

Numerous items of memorabilia from Wayne's life and movies are displayed, including several costume items he wore in various westerns, and there's a large statue of "The Duke" in full cowboy getup as well. Plans are under way to build a much larger museum adjacent to the house. Guided tours of the house are given, with the last tour departing at 4:30 p.m. There's a modest admission fee. Open 7 days a week.

Covered Bridges

Madison County originally had some 20 covered bridges, which were covered by order of the county board of supervisors in order to protect and preserve the flooring timbers, which were more expensive to replace than the lumber covering the sides and roof. The bridges were built largely by farmers in lieu of paying certain taxes, and usually named for the nearest resident.

The remaining six bridges have all been renovated and are well maintained by the county. A map showing the bridge locations is available from the **Madison County Chamber of Commerce** (73 Jefferson St., Winterset; 515-462-1185 or 800-298-6119; www.madisoncounty.com). Tours of the bridges may also be available—contact the chamber for more information.

Every year, on the second full weekend in October, Winterset hosts the **Covered Bridge Festival,** with food, music, numerous craft displays, and guided tours of covered bridges.

Numerous cafes and chain restaurants can be found in Winterset, including the town square diner where Clint Eastwood's character orders coffee in the movie *The Bridges of Madison County* (see below).

CEDAR COVERED BRIDGE

Spanning Cedar Creek just northeast of Winterset, this bridge was originally located farther to the west, over what is now US 169. It can be seen on the cover of some editions of the novel by Robert James Waller that was adapted for the movie. The original bridge was destroyed by arson in 2002, and this replica, constructed according to the plan and materials of the original bridge, was dedicated in 2004.

CUTLER-DONAHOE COVERED BRIDGE

Probably the most accessible of Madison County's covered bridges, this 79-foot-long bridge sits in Winterset's city park, where it was moved from its original location over the North River near the town of Bevington.

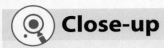

Close-up

The Bridges of Madison County—A Literary and Cinematic Sensation

Robert James Waller's novel *The Bridges of Madison County*, one of the best-selling works of fiction of all time, has resonated with millions of readers and inspired a 1995 movie that was similarly well-received. The story of a four-day affair between a married, lonely Madison County housewife and a visiting photographer who has come to Madison County in 1965 to take photos of the county's iconic bridges, the book sold some 12 million copies. The movie starred Clint Eastwood and Meryl Streep, who received an Academy Award nomination for her performance as Francesca Johnson. The film received numerous critical accolades and grossed nearly $200 million at the box office.

A restored farmhouse in the rolling countryside provided the main set for the movie (the home, unfortunately, was severely damaged by a fire in 2003 and is no longer open to visitors). Several other locations in Winterset and Madison County were also used in the movie, including the **Northside Cafe** (61 E. Jefferson St., Winterset) and the **Pheasant Run** (103 S. John Wayne Dr., Winterset), a bar whose interior was used for a scene that took place inside the "Blue Note Lounge." The stone bridge near the Cutler-Donahoe Covered Bridge in Winterset's City Park turned up in the picnic scene between Robert and Francesca.

Built in 1870, it features a pitched roof and was renovated in 1997.

HOGBACK COVERED BRIDGE

One of the bridges still in its original location, the 97-foot-long Hogback is just north of Winterset, in a valley that sits below a limestone ridge. Built in 1884 by prolific bridge builder Benton Jones, it was restored in 1992.

HOLLIWELL COVERED BRIDGE

This bridge features in the movie *The Bridges of Madison County* and like the famous Roseman bridge (see entry) it spans the Middle River, but southeast of Winterset. It was built by Benton Jones in 1880. It is the longest of the county's covered bridges, at 122 feet, and was renovated in 1995.

IMES COVERED BRIDGE

This is the oldest of the covered bridges still standing in Madison County. Built in 1870, it originally spanned the Middle River near Patterson, then was moved in 1887 to Clanton Creek near Hanley, then moved again in 1977 to its present site near the town of St. Charles, on the eastern edge of the county. It was renovated in 1997 and is 81 feet in length.

ROSEMAN COVERED BRIDGE

Perhaps the best-known of the bridges, this is the bridge that Eastwood's character of Robert Kincaid is looking to photograph when he stops in at the farmhouse of Francesca Johnson (Streep) to ask for directions. Located west of Winterset just off CR G47, the 107-foot-long pedestrian bridge is still in its original location, spanning the Middle

River. It was built in 1883 by Benton Jones and renovated in 1992. The bridge is also said to be haunted by a county jail escapee who disappeared in 1892.

AMANA COLONIES

Comprising seven picturesque villages in the countryside west of Cedar Rapids and Iowa City, the **Amana Colonies** give visitors a fascinating look at a historic pioneer community and its contemporary incarnation. The Amana Colonies are located about 100 miles east of Des Moines, a few miles off I-80.

Founded by a utopian group that traveled from Europe to America and set up a community on the East Coast before seeking out more open space on the Iowa prairies, the Amana Colonies have many interesting things to see. The descendants of the original colonists live in the villages to this day, where they maintain the many historical buildings as well as shops that offer all sorts of handmade housewares as well as hearty food items from the rich agricultural heartland. In fact, shopping is the main reason many visitors come to the Amana Colonies—one can pick up everything from homemade jams and preserves to fine handcrafted furniture and a variety of household items. Large family-style restaurants serving hearty German-style fare are also a draw, filling up with tourists on weekend nights.

Dedicated as a National Historic Landmark in 1965 and placed on the National Register of Historic Places the following year, the Amana Colonies are perhaps the most-visited tourist attraction in Iowa. They are well worth a day trip or weekend visit to soak up the history and culture. To get an idea what there is to see, contact the Visitors Bureau, whose contact information is listed below. While many restaurants and shops are located in the village of **Amana,** which is a good place to start your tour of the area, attractions and other points of interest are scattered among all six Amana villages and the nearby village of **Homestead**—each listing's address includes the village in which it is located.

AMANA COLONIES VISITORS CENTER
622 46th Ave., Amana
(319) 622-7622 or (800) 579-2294
www.amanacolonies.org
Trails through the Amana Colonies give a nice tour of the area, including a rustic walking trail through the countryside. The **Amana Colonies Trail** links the 7 villages in the colonies via US 151, US 6, and IA 220 in a scenic drive that also crosses the Millrace Canal and gives a nice view of surrounding prairie, wetlands, and farm fields. You may also catch a glimpse of hawks, waterfowl, eagles, or other wildlife. The 3-mile **Kolonieweg Recreational Trail** runs between Amana and Middle Amana, navigating around Lily Lake and along the Millrace Canal. This is a nice trail for walking or biking, with more opportunities to see wildlife like geese, ducks, beavers, muskrat, and river otters. You can pick up this trail at the Lily Lake picnic area on IA 220 between Amana and Middle Amana. Finally, the **Amana Colonies Nature Trail** winds through forest and up steep bluffs above the Iowa River Valley. Walking this trail, just over 3 miles, you may get a sense of the landscape as the original settlers saw it. The trail begins at a parking lot just north of Homestead near the intersection of US 151 and US 6. There are also some prehistoric Native American mounds, and other geologic features can be seen on this trail as it winds through forest.

Audio and GPS tours of the Amana Colonies are available—check at the visitor center. There are also specialized tours that give visitors a look at historic barns of the Amana Colonies and modern farming techniques used by the modern-day descendants of the original colonists. Contact the Amana Heritage Museum (see below) for details.

Attractions

Information on each of the Amana heritage sites listed below can be obtained through the Amana Heritage Museum (319-622-3567; www.amanaheritage.org). Several sites charge individual admission, and you may also purchase a package ticket at the museum that gives you admission to all heritage sites (this is a good deal—it's typically just a dollar more than the individual museum admission). Days and hours vary—see each listing for details.

AMANA COMMUNITY CHURCH MUSEUM
4210 V St., Homestead

A circa-1865 church that shows visitors the simple style that defined worship for the residents of the Amana Colonies—churches were typically sparsely furnished and without decorations like religious figures or stained glass. Guides explain the colonists' beliefs and religious practices. Even today services are partly in German and partly in English. Open Mon to Sat mid-June to mid-Aug and Sat only from May to mid-June and mid-Aug to Sept.

✳AMANA HERITAGE MUSEUM
4310 220th Trail, Amana

Three buildings' worth of exhibits give a comprehensive view of the history and communal lifestyle of the Amana Colonies. Artifacts including household items and photos tell the story of the colonies from their founding in the mid-19th century. There is also a library with numerous volumes relating to the Amana Colonies. Admission to the museum is around $7 and is free for children 17 and under, but for just another dollar you gain admission to all the Amana heritage sites, which otherwise each require a separate, additional admission charge. The museum is open 7 days a week Apr. 1 through Oct. 31 and Sat only Nov. 1 through Mar. 31.

COMMUNAL AGRICULTURE MUSEUM
505 P St., South Amana

Housed in one of South Amana's oldest barns, built around 1860, this extensive collection includes agricultural equipment used in the early colonies, as well as historical photographs illustrating the unique practice of communal farming. The barn itself is rather impressive, with rough-hewn beams holding up a large roof—it was originally used to house oxen. Open Sat only Memorial Day through Labor Day, or by appointment.

COMMUNAL KITCHEN AND COOPER SHOP
1003 26th St., Middle Amana

This is the only surviving communal kitchen in the Amana Colonies, and it gives visitors a good idea of what it was like both to prepare meals for large groups of people and to eat all meals as part of that large group. Guides are on hand to talk about the foods made in Amana kitchens and the process of cooking in them, including the kitchen hierarchy, from the head cook on down. They are a wealth of information and are happy to answer questions from visitors. Period cooking and eating implements are on display.

The nearby cooper shop showcases how barrels were made in the colonies. Open Mon through Sat mid-June through mid-Aug, and Sat only May through June, and mid-Aug through Sept.

HOMESTEAD BLACKSMITH SHOP
4119 V St., Homestead
Down the street from the Homestead Store Museum, this shop preserves blacksmithing as practiced by the original colonists, with regular blacksmithing demonstrations. There are also printmaking demonstrations using an old-fashioned linotype and hand-set printing press, and bookbinding demonstrations as well. Open Saturdays from May-September.

HOMESTEAD STORE MUSEUM
4430 V St., Homestead
Unlike the other villages in the Amana Colonies, Homestead was not built by the original settlers but instead was created to link the original villages with the railroad that came later to the Iowa River Valley. Artifacts of early commerce are on display here, demonstrating the Amana Colonies' interaction with the "outside world," as is a display of colony buildings in miniature. Open Mon through Sat from mid-June through mid-Aug and Sat only from May through mid-June and mid-Aug through Sept.

The Arts

IOWA THEATRE ARTISTS COMPANY
4709 220th Trail, Amana
(319) 622-3225
www.iowatheatreartists.org
A fairly new professional theater company that has set up shop in a former restaurant in the village of Amana. The 117-seat theater gives you a more up-close-and-personal performance experience, and the company has presented some fun, all-American shows with musical accompaniment like *Spoon River Anthology* and *Pump Boys and Dinettes.* Tickets are around $25 and can be reserved by calling the box office at (319) 622-3222.

OLD CREAMERY THEATRE
39 38th Ave., Amana
(319) 622-6194 (box office), (319) 622-6034 (main office)
www.oldcreamery.com
Iowa's oldest professional theater company puts on a wide and extensive array of shows, everything from classics like *The Glass Menagerie* and *Who's Afraid of Virginia Woolf?* to more offbeat and unknown shows. They also present several children's productions each year. The main stage, which is also the stage for children's shows, seats 300. A separate studio theater is located nearby in the former Amana Middle School. Tickets for most shows are around $22–$26, while tickets for children's theater are around $8. All tickets are available at the box office, via telephone, or through the theater's website.

Accommodations

Hotels & Motels
AMANA COLONIES GUEST HOUSE MOTEL
4712 220th Trail, Amana
(319) 622-3599 or (877) 331-0828
www.theguesthousemotel.com
Located at one end of Amana's long stretch of shops and attractions, this hotel has 38 rooms divided among 2 buildings: a 125-year-old sandstone house that served as a former communal kitchen houses 12 rooms, while a more modern motel-style building is nearby. Rooms are simple, clean, and comfortable, and include air

conditioning and cable television, with rates around $65. No pets.

HERITAGE INN AMANA COLONIES HOTEL & SUITES
2185 U Ave. (I-80 exit 225)
(319) 668-2700
www.heritageinnamanacolonies.com
A bit more of the traditional motel experience than you'll find at lodgings in the villages, this hotel has a heated indoor pool, as well as breakfast available at the restaurant across the street for a slightly higher rate. The hotel has 61 basic rooms, with either 2 queen beds or 1 king bed. All rooms have a coffeemaker, hair dryer, iron, and ironing board, and some come with microwave and refrigerator. A guest laundry and wireless Internet are available. Rates are around $90.

✳ZUBER'S HOMESTEAD HOTEL
2206 44th Ave., Homestead
(319) 622-3911 or (888) 623-3911
www.zubershomesteadhotel.com
This charming, old-fashioned hotel just a short drive from the main village of Amana has 15 rooms, each decorated in a different theme: The Whitetail Suite has a stag's head over a fireplace, while the Harvester Suite celebrates Amana's (and Iowa's) agricultural heritage with earth tones and a vintage pitchfork in the corner. Other rooms pay tribute to University of Iowa sports and the original Amana Colonies settlers, with period artifacts festooning the room, among other themes. All rooms have period touches such as lace doilies and colorful quilts, as well as modern amenities like flat-screen TVs and wireless Internet. A delicious breakfast is included in the room rate. The solitude of this hotel makes it a nice place to relax and unplug for a weekend. Rates range from $85 to $120.

Bed-and-Breakfasts
ANNIE'S GARDEN GUEST HOUSE
716 46th Ave., Amana
(319) 622-6854 or (866) 622-6854
www.timeandtides.com
Just off the main drag in Amana, the three rooms in this B&B are well-appointed, with antique touches, deep chairs, and comfortable beds, including a canopy bed in one of the rooms. Each room has a private bathroom, and there's free Wi-Fi. Breakfast may include such yummies as baked oatmeal or applesauce pancakes, with plenty of fresh fruit. Take time to unwind in front of the living room fireplace or stroll through the garden. Rooms are $90 a night. No kids under 16, and no pets.

DIE HEIMAT COUNTRY INN
4434 V St., Homestead
(319) 622-3937 or (888) 613-5463
www.dheimat.com
With 18 rooms, it's perhaps a little large for a bed-and-breakfast, but the morning repast is good enough to keep it in this category: Fluffy scrambled eggs, golden-brown French toast, and fresh baked goodies make this a nice place to start the day (it previously served as one of the Amana Colonies' communal kitchens). Rooms have 2 queen beds and private bath. The beds are very comfortable, and rooms are equipped with free Wi-Fi.

ROSE'S PLACE BED & BREAKFAST
1007 26th Ave., Middle Amana
(319) 622-6097 or (877) 767-3233
www.iowacity.com/amanas/rosesbb
A former Sunday school built in 1870, this redbrick B&B has 3 large rooms with queen-size beds and private baths. Two of the rooms have twin beds as well. Breakfast features eggs, meats, pancakes, and fresh baked goods. The location away from the

greater tourist bustle in the main Amana village makes for a somewhat less hectic stay. Rooms are $75 a night. No pets.

VILLAGE GUEST SUITE
4312 F St., Amana
(319) 622-6690 or (866) 624-6690
www.villageguestsuite.com
A bit more upscale B&B experience, yet still with a reasonable cost. There are 3 suites in this former communal residence on a side street in the main village. The large first-floor suite has a fireplace and sleigh bed, as well as a Jacuzzi tub in the bathroom. A spacious 3-room suite on the second floor features an eat-in kitchen and porch for taking in the view. There's a smaller suite on the second floor as well, which is $55, and includes breakfast only if booked with the large second-floor suite. The two larger suites are $95 a night.

All rooms have television with DVD player; two of the televisions are equipped with satellite service.

Restaurants

The Amana Colonies are not the place to look for subtle flavors—big, hearty meals are the rule here, and side dishes are served family style with heaping bowls of mashed potatoes and vegetables. Desserts are delicious and fattening.

COLONY INN RESTAURANT
741 47th Ave., Amana
(319) 622-3030
This restaurant was the first to serve the Amana Colonies' now famous and ubiquitous family dinners, when it began dishing out the platters of meats and bowls of sides in 1935. As at other Amana restaurants, fried chicken and German dishes are the menu mainstays,

with a large selection of sausages, including bratwurst and pork sausage, and other meat dishes like Swiss steak, Wiener schnitzel, and delicious cured ham. This restaurant is also known for its breakfasts: delicious pancakes with homemade jam and some of the best breakfast meats you'll ever eat—big, juicy sausages and thick slabs of bacon. Mmmmm! Dinner entrees are around $15.

OX YOKE INN
4420 220th Trail, Amana
(319) 622-3441 or (800) 233-3441
www.oxyokeinn.com
This pair of restaurants epitomize dining in the Amana Colonies, with big platters of fried chicken, roast beef, and ham, as well as German favorites like sauerbraten, schnitzel, and *Kassler Rippchen* (smoked pork chops). Big slices of pie and cake are offered for dessert. Steaks are broiled to juicy perfection, and there are a few decent seafood options as well. The Amana village location has the charming feel of a country inn, while the interstate location clearly puts less thought into the decor. The food, however, is simple and satisfying at both restaurants. Entrees average around $13–$14. A second location is at 2206 U Ave. (I-80 exit 225, Williamsburg; 319-668-1443 or 877-668-1443).

RONNEBURG RESTAURANT
4408 220th Trail, Amana
(319) 622-3641 or (888) 348-4686
www.ronneburgrestaurant.com
One of a handful of the Amana Colonies' famous family-style restaurants in the original village of Amana, the Ronneburg whips up meals in one of the original village communal kitchens. The menu is meat-and-potatoes, with a German flair, including choices like Bavarian chicken and smoked

pork chops with spiced Fuji apples, as well as more old-country favorites like schnitzel and sauerbraten. Good steak and fish choices, too. They actually serve some smaller plates of some of the dinner choices. Try the Black Forest Brownie for dessert. Entrees average around $16–$17. Nice beer garden, too.

Shopping

Shopping is one of the main reasons people visit the Amana Colonies: There's a long stretch of shops of every variety in the main village of Amana, and the other villages offer shopping opportunities as well. Numerous craftsmen's workshops are scattered throughout the villages, including ironworkers, furniture makers, and quilters. There are several art galleries here, too. Take some time to stroll from shop to shop to see what local artisans have created. Locally made food items are also popular—pick up some jams or jellies or a side of perfectly smoked ham or bacon, and don't miss the chance to sample the beers at Millstream Brewing Company.

AMANA ARTS GUILD CENTER
1210 G St., High Amana
(319) 622-3678
www.amanaartsguild.com
A great spot to pick up traditional Amana folk crafts, created by contemporary Amana artisans from all seven villages. Items like willow baskets, brooms, quilts, rugs, and tinware are all for sale, as well as decorative and household items. The center also runs classes and workshops for adults and children in traditional arts and crafts like basketry, woodworking, and weaving, as well as sponsors seasonal events like art shows and a song and poetry festival.

AMANA MEAT SHOP & SMOKEHOUSE
4513 F St., Amana
(319) 622-7586 or (800) 373-6328
www.amanameatshop.com
Pick up some of the same meats you may have enjoyed at one of the Amana Colonies' family-style restaurants at this smokehouse that dates to 1855. Smoked hams are the main draw here, along with big, Iowa-style pork chops and steaks, sausages, and bacon. If you don't want a whole ham, at least try a sample. Amana-made cheeses, jams, and jellies are also for sale here.

AMANA WOOLEN MILL
800 48th Ave., Amana
(319) 622-3432 or (800) 222-6430
www.amanawoolenmill.com
Get a look at the wool-making process by watching looms in action at Iowa's only operating wool mill, which has been in operation since 1857, and produces Amana's own wool and cotton blankets. Blankets are for sale here in all sorts of colors and patterns, as are sweaters and other items. Poke around their selection to find a bargain or several.

COLLECTIVELY IOWA
4709 220th Trail, Amana
http://ciwines.com
This shop specializes in dry, semisweet, and dessert wines from vineyards across Iowa, which you may sample in the tasting room. The staff can also provide information about Iowa wines and help you pick out a bottle. The shop is right across from the visitor center.

HAHN'S HEARTH OVEN BAKERY
2510 J St., Middle Amana
(319) 622-3439
Pick up some dense German-style breads at this shop, with a stone-hearth oven that

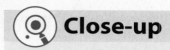

Close-up

Who Were the Amana Colonists?

A group that sought religious freedom and advocated a communal lifestyle of sharing of all property, the settlers who founded the Amana Colonies emerged out of fervent religious and social upheaval in 18th-century Germany, where a movement within Lutheranism known as Pietism, which believed in God communicating through prophecy, led to the formation of a group called the **Community of True Inspiration.** Persecuted in their native lands, they left for America in 1843 and formed a prosperous community near Buffalo, New York, that grew to 1,200 people and eventually adopted the name **Ebenezer Society.** Desire for more land as well as greater isolation in which to live out their Christian ideals led the community to decamp for the Iowa River Valley, where they purchased large tracts of farmland and settled in 1855. The name **Amana,** which comes from a biblical passage and means **"remain true,"** was chosen for the first village. Variations on the name for succeeding villages —Middle Amana, High Amana, and West, East, and South Amana—followed suit.

A commitment to faith, with the Amana Colonies establishing their own Christian church that meets to this day, was, along with economic self-sufficiency and communal living, one of the hallmarks of the colonies. One of the more unique features of the colonies was their communal kitchens: No food was ever prepared or eaten in individual homes. Instead there were numerous communal kitchens in each village, tended to by several women, who prepared meals for large groups and served everyone at the same set times every day (you can visit such a kitchen in the village of Middle Amana).

Residents worked at farming, with land owned by the community, and a variety of other occupations to make the Amana Colonies a functioning community, but were not paid for their services. Rather, they were given credits that could be used to purchase goods in the community's shops. Eventually the community began purchasing more and more goods from outside the colonies, thus challenging the original mission as a completely self-sufficient community.

In 1932, following the Great Depression and a huge fire that destroyed the community's important wool and flour mills, colonists voted to dissolve the utopian community, ending the communal kitchens and other aspects of communal living, and replacing communal ownership of community assets with a joint-stock company that managed some 25,000 acres of farmland and other businesses in the villages. Several years later the company began manufacturing the Amana line of refrigerators and other home appliances, which became the economic mainstay of the community. Some Amana residents still refer to the shift away from communal living, which in effect separated economic life from religious life, as "the Great Change." Today roughly 1,500 people reside in the seven villages of the Amana Colonies, including many descendants of the original colonists. They work at other jobs in addition to running the shops and historic buildings in the villages, which draw close to 800,000 tourists a year.

has been in the building since it was built in 1864—the last such hearth operating in the Amana Colonies, and a throwback to the days when each village had numerous such bakeries. Delicious pastries are available as well. Opens early in the morning, Tues through Sat from Apr through Oct and Wed and Sat in Nov, Dec, and Mar.

HIGH AMANA GENERAL STORE
1308 G St., High Amana
(319) 622-3232
www.amanaheritage.org/highstore.html
Open continuously for over 150 years, this shop still looks like an old-fashioned general store, with a tin ceiling, glass display cases, and barrels stacked along the wooden floor. Vintage-style soaps and other personal items are available, as is a wide selection of toys and Amana food items like pancake mix. Old-fashioned candies stand in glass jars lining the shelves. Open daily Apr. 1 through Oct. 31 and Sat only in Mar, Nov, and Dec.

LEHM BOOKS & GIFTS
4536 220th Trail, Amana
(319) 622-6447 or (800) 840-2387
www.lehmbooksandgifts.com
A mixture of books and collectibles are for sale at this well-stocked shop. There's an impressive collection of dolls and figurines, including lots of angels and teddy bears, and plenty of Iowa memorabilia as well. Books include numerous titles about the Amana Colonies, as well as a nice selection of children's books. Numerous other gift items should give you some ideas, including those for people on your gift list who are impossible to shop for.

✳MILLSTREAM BREWING COMPANY
835 48th Ave., Amana
(319) 622-3672
www.millstreambrewery.com
This modest wooden building on the edge of Amana Village is home to Iowa's oldest microbrewery, which pumps out some excellent varieties, including German pilsner, white ale, and stout. Each beer has a distinctive taste, some with more zip than others— try some free samples in the small tasting room. They also make a delicious root beer, as well as black cherry and cream sodas. The brewery features a small beer garden right outside the tasting room and store, which is a great spot to sample the brew on a warm afternoon or evening.

i Contrary to popular belief, the settlers of the Amana Colonies were not at all related to the Amish or Mennonites, although all three originated in Germany and established presences in Iowa that continue to this day (the similar sound of "Amana" and "Amish" may account somewhat for the confusion).

WEST BRANCH

HERBERT HOOVER PRESIDENTIAL LIBRARY & MUSEUM
210 Parkside Dr., West Branch
(319) 643-5301
http://hoover.archives.gov
Numerous galleries at this museum examine the eventful life and political career of the only president born in Iowa, including two rooms dedicated to the challenges of the Great Depression and related crises. Displays also commemorate Hoover's service leading food relief efforts in Europe during and

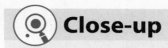

Close-up

Herbert Hoover: Iowa's President

Herbert Hoover gets a bad rap in a lot of history books. The only president born in Iowa, as well as the first president born west of the Mississippi River, Hoover is blamed more than anyone else for the Great Depression and the devastation it caused throughout America. Debate over his policies has long occupied scholars and historians, yet there's no denying he led a life full of activity, including a long career of public service that aided millions of people.

Born in the small hamlet of West Branch, the son of a blacksmith and a seamstress, Hoover enjoyed an idyllic childhood in the countryside. Orphaned by the age of 10, Hoover soon left Iowa and moved to the West Coast to live with relatives. He became a mining engineer who traveled the world to work on different mines, developing new standards for efficiency and eventually amassing a fortune. He entered public life on the eve of World War I, organizing the government's evacuation of Americans in Europe and later spearheading food relief efforts for Belgium. He also oversaw efforts to ensure that American soldiers received sufficient food supplies. After the war he was courted by both political parties and sought the Republican nomination, but eventually became secretary of commerce, a position in which he sought to improve the efficiency of business through more effective regulation and greater cooperation with government.

In the 1928 election Hoover won a landslide victory and stepped up his plans for economic and social reform he had touched on as commerce secretary. After the 1929 stock market crash, Hoover was focused on resuscitating the economy, establishing new government agencies in an attempt to jump-start production, and launching new public works projects. America remained mired in depression, however, with rising unemployment and camps of poor people known as "Hoovervilles" springing up across the land. Hoover was defeated by Franklin Roosevelt in the 1932 election. After leaving the White House, Hoover became a prolific author, writing over 15 books. He also remained active as an elder statesman of the Republican Party and worked again toward food relief efforts following World War II.

Hoover has so far served the longest retirement of any president, living over 30 years past the end of his presidency. He dedicated his presidential library in 1962 and died two years later, in October 1964. Hoover is buried alongside his wife near the library, on the grounds of the **Herbert Hoover National Historic Site.**

after World War I, as well as his pioneering work as a mining engineer before entering public service. There is a re-creation of Hoover's suite at the Waldorf-Astoria Hotel in New York, where he spent much of his time after leaving the presidency, and a life-size diorama of Hoover engaging in his favorite pastime of fishing. Temporary exhibits have examined various aspects of American history and culture.

The museum is open daily except for Thanksgiving, Christmas, and New Year's Day. Admission is $6 for visitors ages 16 through 61 and $3 for ages 62 and over, with ages 16 and under admitted free. It is located less than a mile from exit 254 on I-80 and is part of the **Herbert Hoover National Historic**

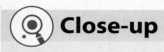 **Close-up**

Khrushchev in Iowa: A Thaw in the Cold War

A rural Iowa farm seems an unlikely spot for a historic détente between the United States and the Soviet Union at a time when both nations were sworn enemies, yet just such a meeting happened when Soviet Premier **Nikita Khrushchev** came to **Roswell Garst**'s corn acreage outside the small Iowa town of Coon Rapids.

Garst, who grew up in the area and began his own farming operation in 1929, developed a highly productive hybrid seed corn and went on to sell it to other midwestern farmers, leading to huge increases in corn output. He would go on to push other new farming techniques on farmers in America and around the world. A legendary salesman with a missionary zeal to improve people's lives through more effective uses of technological and economic development, Garst also believed a more open exchange of ideas between the United States and the Soviet Union could improve relations between the two countries and decrease the possibility of war.

Khrushchev had expressed interest in American agricultural techniques to boost the Soviet Union's dragging agricultural output. In a 1955 speech calling for a large increase in Soviet farm production, he famously called for a midwestern-style corn belt to stretch across the Soviet Union. Responding to this, the *Des Moines Register* published an editorial inviting an exchange of agricultural delegations between the United States and the Soviets. Khrushchev agreed to such an exchange, and when a Soviet delegation arrived in Iowa, Roswell Garst managed to detour its leader to his farm, where he impressed him with his corn operation, details of which were reported to Khrushchev.

Eventually Garst traveled to Moscow and talked farming with Khrushchev. When the Soviet premier began planning a state visit to the United States in 1959, the itinerary included stops in Washington, New York. and Los Angeles for a luncheon with Hollywood stars, yet the only people Khrushchev specifically asked to see were President Dwight Eisenhower and Roswell Garst.

And so on September 23, 1959, a beautiful fall day, tensions between the world's two superpowers eased just a bit as Nikita Khrushchev arrived at the Garst farm to enjoy a picnic lunch—accompanied by a crowd of hundreds that included American and Soviet dignitaries, reporters from the national and international press, and law enforcement officers providing security, all squeezing down the dusty farm roads. As they had on previous meetings, Khrushchev and Garst talked politics as well as farming, with Khrushchev declaring that Iowa corn was superior to Ukraine corn. He also stated that his relationship with Garst had helped ease the way for formal talks with Eisenhower over US–Soviet relations.

Khrushchev continued to pursue improvement of Soviet agriculture even as subsequent events ratcheted up tensions with the United States, including the building of the Berlin Wall in 1961 and the Cuban Missile Crisis in October 1962, before he was deposed from power in 1964. He died in 1971. Roswell Garst died in 1977, and his family later donated land that became Whiterock Conservancy, a nature preserve that includes the Garst farm that was the site of Khrushchev's historic visit. The Garst farm was placed on the National Register of Historic Places in 2009.

Site (www.nps.gov/heho), which contains the modest two-room house where Hoover was born, the one-room school he attended as a child, a working blacksmith shop based on the design of the shop operated by Hoover's father, and the graves of Hoover and his wife, Lou. Walking trails crisscross the surrounding tallgrass prairie.

i Some 25 miles from Coon Rapids in the tiny town of Audubon stands "Albert the Bull" a 35-foot-tall statue of a brown and white Hereford constructed of 45 tons of concrete over a steel rod frame, salvaged from abandoned Iowa windmills. Devised as a promotion for area beef farmers, Albert is a fun backdrop for a vacation photo.

COON RAPIDS

WHITEROCK CONSERVANCY AND RESORT
1390 Hwy. 141, Coon Rapids
(712) 684-2697
www.whiterockconservancy.org
This country getaway consists of over 4,000 acres along the Middle Raccoon River, about an hour and a half's drive from Des Moines. The land for the conservancy was donated by the Garst family, who had a longstanding presence as farmers in the area and sought to create an area dedicated to agricultural research, habitat for rare plants and animals, and outdoor recreation. There are over 30 miles of hiking trails winding through the conservancy, as well as opportunities for canoeing, fishing, mountain biking, and horseback riding. Several accommodations are available on-site, including the **Garst Home Farm Bed & Breakfast,** located in the same farmhouse on the same spot where Iowa farming pioneer Roswell Garst and his wife, Elizabeth, hosted Soviet Premier Nikita Khrushchev in a historic 1959 visit. The house is furnished in period decor and has a small museum of memorabilia, as well as displays throughout the house describing the visit. There are 5 bedrooms for rent, including a deluxe suite and 2 additional suites, all with private bathrooms, and a room and loft that share a bathroom. Rates range from $55 to $105. Also on the conservancy property are 3 guest houses with kitchens that can accommodate 6 to 18 guests and rent from $150 to $300, and a backwoods cabin that accommodates 6 guests and rents for $50. There is no food service in the conservancy, but catering is available—arrangements must be made in advance.

Appendix

LIVING HERE

In this section we feature specific information for residents or those planning to relocate here. Topics include real estate, education, health care, and much more.

RELOCATION

From its humble beginnings as a frontier military outpost on a vast and endless sea of prairie, Des Moines has emerged as an important regional urban center. The area retains some of its rural, homespun charm, as seen every summer at the mammoth and popular state fair, but Des Moines is far from being a square, staid town on the empty plains: It was dubbed "The Hippest City in the USA" in a 2007 article in *Fast Company* magazine. Downtown has not only been reborn as a dining and entertainment mecca, it has also gained several large office buildings and seen numerous commercial and residential development, part of the city's overall economic health that led *Forbes* magazine in 2010 to proclaim Des Moines the number-one city in America for doing business, following on the heels of a similar ranking from the MarketWatch website. The population of Des Moines and surrounding areas has become a reflection of the nation's makeup, with lots of diversity and large numbers of both ambitious young people just starting out and families with children making it their home.

With plenty of charming neighborhoods, good schools, lots of green spaces providing ample recreation opportunities, and an economy that has withstood much of the battering that has been visited on communities across the country, Des Moines is a nice place to live if you can stand the winter—if you move here, plan on getting acquainted with shovels, snow blowers, rock salt, and occasional school closings. When spring comes and the trees begin to bud and flowers begin to shoot up along the bike and hiking trails, it's all worth it.

In this and the following chapters, you will find resources if you are planning on moving to Des Moines or thinking about doing so, including information on neighborhoods, real estate, education, and listings of local media.

NEIGHBORHOODS

With a largely residential layout outside of downtown (and plenty of housing options there as well), Des Moines is full of neighborhoods, with a wide range of housing choices and architectural styles. While the following is not a completely exhaustive list of every neighborhood and suburb in the Des Moines area, it is an extensive and comprehensive sampling from all parts of the city. Neighborhoods on the south side tend to be a little larger and also have bigger lots, while the west side has the old, elegant neighborhoods that cluster south of Grand Avenue, as well as many neighborhoods of older, modest single-family homes, which can be found throughout the east side as well. Suburban development is more concentrated to the east, west, and northwest of the city, while to the south it is still largely rural, and to the north is Saylorville Lake, along with the first

Geography in Des Moines

Des Moines is divided primarily into east, west, and south sides based on the confluence of the Des Moines and Raccoon Rivers, which splits the city into those three areas. Neighborhoods are listed here based on their general geographic location, with east-side neighborhoods lying entirely east of the Des Moines River and south-side neighborhoods lying south of the Raccoon River. West- and north-side neighborhood listings are a little more tricky: West-side neighborhoods are all located west of the Des Moines River, while north-side neighborhoods are on both sides of the Des Moines River.

office buildings and an old hotel converted to condominiums in the core of the downtown business district, lofts in the East Village, charming rehabbed row houses and Victorians in Sherman Hill (see the more detailed listing below), and hip modern constructions in Western Gateway. Living downtown provides great views of the many interesting buildings and access to great restaurants, nightlife and entertainment, and shopping as well as walking, jogging, and cycling trails that head over to nearby Gray's Lake. The Pappajohn Sculpture Park is a popular strolling spot downtown, while the downtown skywalk allows residents to zip from one side of downtown to the other, making it easy to get to shopping and restaurants and providing a buffer from winter weather. Des Moines International Airport is a 10-minute drive away.

Center City

Cheatom Park

Just north of downtown's modest skyline, with easy access to I-235, Cheatom Park is a mixture of older single-family homes, many over 100 years old, as well as duplexes and apartment complexes that are shoehorned among Mercy Medical Center and the urban campus of Des Moines Area Community College. This compact neighborhood is one of the oldest in the city, with the residents a diverse mixture of ages and socioeconomic backgrounds.

Drake

One of the largest neighborhoods in the city, Drake is of course centered around the university and the neighborhood contains a good chunk of student housing, with older houses converted to multi-unit rentals on blocks around the campus. However,

stirrings of residential development. Many suburban communities have been growing steadily for many years now, with lots of new residential development moving into the cornfields that ring the city.

i Remember, West Des Moines is a separate city from Des Moines and must be distinguished from the west side of Des Moines, which is also heavily residential.

Downtown

New residential developments have been creeping into downtown for several years now, with multiple options sprinkled throughout the center of the city, including there are also quite a few rehabbed older homes, occupied by families who have converted divided houses back to multi-family dwellings.

The neighborhood has one of the most active neighborhood associations in Des Moines, which is focused on historic preservation, revitalization of existing housing stock, and future residential and commercial development. A funky slew of businesses and restaurants clusters around the main part of the campus at University Avenue and 25th Street, including a popular farmers' market from spring through fall. Drake Stadium and the Knapp Center basketball arena are to the north of campus, along Forest Avenue—this area gets jammed with parked cars during games. The collegiate atmosphere fades in the western part of the neighborhood, which resembles other westside neighborhoods with its well-tended mixture of newer and older single-family homes. The neighborhoods of Carpenter and Drake Park lie within the Drake neighborhood, in the southeast section.

King Irving

Residents have rolled up their sleeves to remove blight and revitalize this neighborhood, located northwest of downtown and east of Drake University. Improvements have included efforts at Evelyn Davis Park, which adjoins the Forest Avenue Branch of the Des Moines Public Library. Older single-family homes predominate here, with quite a few fixer-uppers on the residential blocks squeezed in between traffic on University Avenue, Hickman Road, and Martin Luther King Jr. Parkway. There has been some new residential construction as well. Broadlawns Medical Center is just past the northern boundary of the neighborhood.

Sherman Hill

An elegant, historic neighborhood on the western edge of downtown, with homes climbing the winding streets running up modest bluffs above the bustle on nearby arterial streets, Sherman Hill has some absolutely gorgeous homes—some date back to the mid-19th century. After suffering some decline, with many homes carved up into multiple dwellings, the area began something of a comeback in the 1980s, after being listed on the National Register of Historic Places. Many young professionals have moved into rehabbed homes as well as new condominium developments, attracted by the easy commute to downtown jobs. In addition to downtown amenities, shopping and dining opportunities are conveniently located on nearby Ingersoll Avenue.

East Side

ACCENT

A triangular neighborhood bracketed by the Iowa State Fairgrounds and the city's large Grand View Park and Golf Course, ACCENT, or A Community of Central East Neighbors in Transformation, is an older residential district located near the busy intersection of University and Hubbell Avenues. The neighborhood is dominated by modest single-family homes, which are conveniently located near shopping options and Teachout Aquatic Center, one of the city's popular outdoor pools, with a zero-depth-entry pool and two water slides. The east branch of the Des Moines Public Library is nearby as well.

Capitol East

A mixture of single-family homes, townhouses, and apartments packed into a tight grid of blocks lying in the shadow of the golden-domed State Capitol and bounded by railroad tracks and state and interstate highways, this is one of the city's oldest neighborhoods. In addition to easy access to the East Village and the rest of downtown, the neighborhood is also home to Ashfield Park, which has a basketball court, softball diamond, and wading pool, and Redhead Park, both of which are located on the eastern edge of the neighborhood.

Capitol Park

A view of the State Capitol and a mixture of housing types make this one of the more diverse urban neighborhoods in Des Moines. Sprawling just east of the Des Moines River, Capitol Park has a mixture of older and newer housing, including some nice restored Victorians. There are other interesting sites here, including the Des Moines Botanical Center at the southern edge of the neighborhood and Burke Park, which includes a tennis court. A popular bicycling and walking trail winds along the river on the neighborhood's western edge. Iowa Lutheran Hospital is near the center of the neighborhood, and East High School is in the southeast corner.

Fairground

Named for a large local landmark (guess which one) just to its east that brings some one million visitors to Des Moines every August, the Fairground neighborhood lies just south of a busy commercial strip on University Avenue from where it exits I-235. Houses are mostly smaller single-family homes, including two-story homes and cozy bungalows.

Fairmont Park

A swath of land in the northeast section of Des Moines, with the interstate and railroad tracks running along its western edge, Fairmont Park is a low-key residential neighborhood noted for its many ranch-style homes. Easttown Park, Teachout Aquatic Center, and the east branch of the Des Moines Public Library are all clustered at the southern end, by the intersection of Easton Boulevard and Hubbell Avenue, while the neighborhood's namesake park is at the northern end and Grand View Park and Golf Course is just to the east.

Gray's Woods

Four-Mile Creek winds its way through the center of this neighborhood on the eastern edge of Des Moines, where city streets begin to fade into more open spaces. There's a hiking and biking trail parallel to the creek, as well as Strasser's Woods State Preserve, a 40-acre nature park and wildlife refuge that contains a wide variety of trees and plant life. The neighborhood has a variety of housing, single-family homes, and duplexes.

Laurel Hill

Older homes stand alongside newer ones in this neighborhood just south of the Iowa State Fairgrounds and west of Four-Mile Creek and the Sleepy Hollow sports park and ski hill. The neighborhood association has worked to develop Laurel Hill Park, a modest park just outside the fairgrounds that features a playground, picnic shelter, and recreation trail and has become the site of numerous neighborhood gatherings.

Martin Luther King Jr. Park

This neighborhood just south of Grand View University is home to many families who have been here for generations, with single-family homes along tree-lined streets. Residents range from young children to senior citizens. There's a row of parks running from east to west across the south end of the neighborhood, including Crowley Park and

King Park, which underwent a $1 million renovation in 2009 and features a heated, fully enclosed park shelter that has numerous activity rooms, including some used for programs for local seniors. There's also a wading pool, tennis and basketball courts, and a softball diamond.

Union Park

One of the city's more storied neighborhoods, Union Park curves along the east bank of the Des Moines River and has two of the best-equipped parks in the city: Birdland Park, which includes a boat ramp and city swimming pool, and Union Park, which has a fabulous retro-style carousel and ample playground equipment, including a large slide shaped like a rocket ship, as well as a popular wading pool. Single-family homes predominate, and people take pride in their homes, staging an annual home tour and presenting a lawn-of-the-week award. The campus of Grand View University is located in the northeastern part of the neighborhood. Major medical facilities are nearby, as is access to I-235 and walking and bicycling trails.

Valley High Manor

This pocket of a neighborhood is right on the eastern border of Des Moines and is seeing an influx of residents due to increased development in the adjoining community of Pleasant Hill. There's still some feeling of countryside here, with residential blocks interspersed with wooded areas that are home to a variety of wildlife.

North Side

Beaverdale

One of the best-known neighborhoods in the city, known both for its small, charming commercial district of restaurants and shops

along Beaver Avenue, which is contiguous with 41st Street, near Hickman Road and Urbandale Avenue, and for its iconic "Beaverdale Brick" homes: Several parts of Des Moines feature brick houses, but this is the mother lode, with some entire blocks lined with redbrick dwellings. Many have immaculately tended hedges and flower gardens, and the streets are tree-lined. A good number of homes are well over 50 years old and have some nice exterior details. There are a ton of families with children in Beaverdale, which stretches from the main arteries of Franklin Avenue in the south to Douglas Avenue in the north, and between 30th Street and 48th Place, and lots of block parties and neighborhood celebrations, culminating with the Beaverdale Fall Festival every September. Beaverdale and Ashby Parks are nice-sized swaths of green space, with grills and picnic tables as well as a wading pool in Ashby.

Chautauqua Park

A small sliver of a neighborhood just west of the Des Moines River, Chautauqua Park was an original "gated community," built as a model automobile suburb in the 1920s. You can see the remains of the gates at 13th Street and Chautauqua Parkway, in the midst of the hilltop neighborhood's smattering of homes, many of which have garages that are either attached or located under the home. The largely brick homes line streets studded with impressive oak trees.

Highland Park

Occupying the second-highest spot in Des Moines, with only the State Capitol standing on higher ground, Highland Park was one of Des Moines's original suburbs, built along a streetcar line. Today it's a fair-sized grid of streets that lies east of the Des Moines River and stretches to the city's northern border, with North High School and Grand View University both just beyond its southern boundary of Hull Avenue. Locally owned businesses line major streets, with the commercial center of the neighborhood the intersection of 6th Avenue and Euclid Avenue (US 6). Nearby is the north branch of the Des Moines Public Library.

Kirkwood Glen

A small corner of homes that march along a narrow wooded ravine just north of the Drake campus, Kirkwood Glen is a scenic area that seems removed from the bustling college town to the south. Families, including newcomers to the city, have settled in the small cluster of older homes, which extends north to Hickman Road.

Lower Beaver

A growing neighborhood on the northern edge of Des Moines, just south of a largely wilderness stretch of the Raccoon River that features the Trestle to Trestle Trail, a nice spot for cycling and nature walks. There are older, nicely tended single-family homes, as well as some new construction. It's a large neighborhood, running from Douglas Avenue in the south to the Des Moines city limits on the north, as well as some large undeveloped patches covered with woods. Merle Hay Mall and shopping along Merle Hay Road are a short drive to the west.

Meredith

An L-shaped neighborhood that includes Meredith Middle School, Hoover High School, and the Northwest Aquatic Center, Meredith has a large number of older and smaller homes, many of which are owned by young families. There is significant commercial activity in the neighborhood as well, with shops and other businesses on Beaver and Douglas Avenues, which make up the eastern part of the southern boundaries. Meredith also has a fairly active neighborhood association that plans lots of activities.

Merle Hay

A long north–south strip that runs all the way from Aurora to University Avenue, the Merle Hay neighborhood is easy to pinpoint due to its proximity to Des Moines's oldest shopping mall, built in 1959, and extensive commercial activity along Merle Hay Road. It is one of the largest neighborhoods in Des Moines and somewhat densely populated. Many homes are older, more modest one-story constructions, but there are some bigger designs as well, with many built in the years following World War II, when Des Moines underwent a building boom mirrored throughout the United States. There is a large selection of restaurants and shopping, but not as many parks as one might hope to find in such a large area on the edge of the city. Waveland Golf Course is nearby.

Oak Park

Adjacent to the Highland Park neighborhood, Oak Park is likewise an older area with a mix of modest homes and locally owned businesses. It is looped to the south and west by the Des Moines River and extends to the city's northern limits. McHenry Park has a playground, tennis court, and wading pool, as well as a picnic area, and is adjacent to a small lake. The namesake elementary school is located along Sixth Avenue, the eastern boundary of the neighborhood.

River Bend

Leaning into a curve along the Des Moines River, River Bend is a narrow neighborhood of homes and apartments a short drive north of downtown. Along the nearby river, Mercy Medical Center is just south of the neighborhood's southern boundary at University Avenue, as is the urban campus of Des Moines Area Community College.

South Side

Easter Lake

Nearly a 5-mile drive from downtown, Easter Lake is a sprawling area with plenty of rural, undeveloped patches gradually filling in with new residential development. The namesake park, overseen by Polk County Conservation, sits at the center of the neighborhood and offers a wealth of activities including swimming, boating, fishing, and hiking through the surrounding woods. The neighborhood association works to balance the area's rural heritage with the advantages of new development.

Gray's Lake

Not just the name of the much-loved lake and recreation area south of downtown, Gray's Lake in 2008 became a recognized neighborhood. The lake is at the north end of the neighborhood, which is also home to Lincoln High. A mixture of older and newer housing is available here, and there is a long stretch of shopping centers and chain stores on Fleur Drive, the neighborhood's western boundary.

Indianola Hills

Homes are a little more spread out in this largely residential neighborhood, composed of wider blocks stretched out between SW 9th and SE 14th Streets. Union Street cuts through the center of the neighborhood and Indianola Avenue cuts diagonally. Downtown is an easy drive over the Raccoon River, where a hiking and cycling trail runs along the south bank and heads west to Gray's Lake, while Principal Park sits at the nearby confluence with the Des Moines River. It's not far to Southridge Mall either, along SE 14th Street (US 69). The adjoining **McKinley/ Columbus Park** neighborhood is an older neighborhood with narrower streets and more modest homes that faces the river confluence and whose northern boundary runs along the larger combined river.

Somerset

Tucked away just north of Fort Des Moines County Park and shoehorned between Southridge Mall and Fort Des Moines, Somerset sits just south of the bustle along Army Post Road. In addition to outdoor opportunities at the park, Blank Park Zoo is nearby, as is A. H. Blank Golf Course. It's just a short drive to Easter Lake Park, the south branch of the Des Moines Public Library and the airport.

South Park

A long, narrow neighborhood of low-key homes, South Park extends along SE 14th Street (US 69) all the way from Park Avenue to Army Post Road, where it meets Southridge Mall. Along the way, Yeader Creek crosses the neighborhood from east to west, while Jordan Park, a modest green space with sports facilities, sits near the southern edge.

Southwestern Hills

This huge neighborhood stretches across the western third of the south side and is adjacent to Des Moines International Airport, with plenty of large homes and commercial development along Fleur Drive on the neighborhood's eastern edge. Park Avenue cuts east–west across the northern edge, making for a quick hop over to Brown's Woods Forest Preserve or Valley Junction in West Des Moines, as well as a turnoff on George Flagg Parkway that then runs to the heart of Water Works Park, an urban gem with vast tracts of green space and extensive walking and cycling trails. The majority of housing is in the northeastern part of the neighborhood, near an elementary and middle school, as well as AIB College of Business. There's a wide variety of homes and apartments, including several contemporary, good-size homes sprinkled throughout the neighborhood. Fleur Drive has long stretches of shopping centers and chain stores, and some nice restaurants are in the area as well.

Watrous South

Another relatively large south-side neighborhood, Watrous South, located a little east of Des Moines International Airport, only officially became a neighborhood in 2008 but has many strong assets, including the south branch of the Des Moines Public Library and the Nahas city pool. There are both homes and apartments here, and many of the houses were part of the post–World War II building boom. Many residential blocks are tree-lined and quiet.

West Side

Arbor Peaks

Only recently designated as its own neighborhood, Arbor Peaks encompasses the old Owl's Head neighborhood and includes Terrace Hill, the Iowa governor's mansion. A pocket of older, elegant homes, it sits on a hilltop above the bustle of the Ingersoll Avenue commercial strip and is just a short drive from Water Works Park, a very pleasant spot with miles of cycling and walking trails and green spaces along the Raccoon River.

Greenwood Historic

This is one of the more charming and desirable neighborhoods in the city, with handsome homes sitting on good-size lots. The streets are festooned with century-old oak trees winding over small hills. Centered on Greenwood Elementary School, this area, including the adjacent neighborhoods listed below, is sometimes referred to as South of Grand, due to Grand Avenue, which cuts across the northern edge of the neighborhood and runs past the campus of Des Moines University. Some blocks have outstanding views of the downtown skyline and Raccoon River below. There are many fine redbrick homes here, and houses come in numerous styles, with quite a few over 100 years old. Many young families with children live here, as do retirees and some students—there are apartment buildings along Grand Avenue. Water Works Park, with its trails and green spaces, is just to the south.

Linden Heights

Similar to Greenwood Historic, this thin slice of a neighborhood is also bordered on the north by Grand Avenue and also features larger, well-appointed homes on winding, hilly streets. In addition to Water Works Park to the south, it is conveniently located next to Greenwood and Ashworth Parks to the west, which are popular for cycling and strolling around their pond and amphitheater and swimming in the park's pool. The park is also adjacent to the city's art museum. Many homes were built as Des Moines grew in population in the early 20th century. Lots tend to be on the large side, with lush landscaping and plenty of tree cover.

North of Grand

This largely residential section of the west side also has the bustle of Ingersoll Avenue cutting through its center, giving residents easy access to a multitude of dining and shopping options. All types of people live here, including young singles, families, and retirees in apartments and high-rises. The side streets consist largely of single-family homes, many over 50 years old and representing a variety of architectural styles. The city's art museum and Greenwood and Ashworth Parks, with their city swimming pool, are just a few blocks to the west on Grand Avenue, which forms the neighborhood's southern boundary. Easy access to I-235 is afforded just north along 42nd Street, although parts of downtown are an even shorter shot down Ingersoll, which has specially designated bike lanes.

Salisbury Oaks

Wedged in between the neighborhoods of Greenwood Historic and Linden Heights, Salisbury Oaks also lies south of Grand Avenue and has huge swaths of oak trees along the quiet, winding streets. Single-family homes go from smaller models to very large homes on impressive lots. Home construction spans from the postwar boom to much newer dwellings. As with the surrounding neighborhoods, there is easy access to both Greenwood and Ashworth Parks and dining and shopping along Ingersoll Avenue.

Waterbury

Another neighborhood in the South of Grand area with a well-regarded elementary school, Waterbury extends to the western border of Des Moines at 63rd Street, placing it a short distance from shopping and dining on both Ingersoll Avenue and in Valley Junction in West Des Moines. Waveland Golf Course is just across I-235 at the north end of the neighborhood, while Grand Avenue forms the southern boundary, running east to Polk Boulevard and the Des Moines Art Center. Some very nice homes are found here in a variety of sizes and styles. Trees line the quiet residential blocks that run over the rolling hills.

Waveland Park/Waveland Woods

Bracketing Waveland Park Golf Course, which also has a large tennis complex, these two neighborhoods extend across the far western side of Des Moines, north of I-235 and between the highway exits at 42nd and 63rd Streets, on the border with the suburb of Windsor Heights. A few newer dwellings are mixed with older homes featuring nice lawns. Roosevelt High School is in the southeastern corner of Waveland Park. There is some shopping along University Avenue, and the nearby Franklin Avenue branch of the Des Moines Public Library.

Westwood

Another sylvan residential district south of Grand Avenue, Westwood has some nice-size homes along tree-lined streets. The triangular neighborhood is bounded on the south and west by Walnut Creek as it flows alongside a popular walking and cycling trail through thick woods, with a trailhead at Greenwood/Ashworth Park by the Des Moines Art Center (the trail runs on to Gray's Lake and the center of Des Moines, and is used by some to commute to office jobs downtown). Several different architectural styles are found here, including the ubiquitous redbrick constructions of Des Moines.

Woodland Heights

Right across Martin Luther King Jr. Parkway from Western Gateway, and thus a short drive or walk from downtown, as well as nearby Gray's Lake, this urban neighborhood has new construction alongside homes from the early 20th century. Its proximity to downtown means many faces along the streets are young professionals, but there are also plenty of longtime residents here, including families with children. Chamberlain Park, a modest patch of green space, is at the southern end of the neighborhood, a couple blocks north of Ingersoll Avenue and adjacent to historic Woodland Cemetery.

SUBURBS & OUTLYING COMMUNITIES

Altoona, Bondurant, Pleasant Hill & Mitchellville

This quartet of towns east of Des Moines are seeing an influx of new housing as they transform from rural communities to fast-growing suburbs. **Altoona,** home to both Adventureland Amusement Park and Prairie Meadows Racetrack and Casino, is perhaps the most prominent of the four, due to being closest to Des Moines on I-80, with rapid commercial and residential development, including everything from luxury homes to more moderately priced offerings. However, like the others it still largely maintains the feel of a quiet, rural community, with open countryside just minutes away. **Mitchellville** is closest to its rural roots, although that may soon change. **Pleasant Hill,** south of I-80 on US 65 and just east of the Iowa State Fairgrounds, has easy access to Yellow Banks County Park, perched high above the Des Moines River valley, while **Bondurant** is not far from Chichaqua Bottoms Greenbelt,

a 10-square-mile nature preserve with numerous recreation and wildlife-watching opportunities. Many students in these communities attend schools in the Southeast Polk Community School District, which opened a new high school in 2009. A new high school opened in 2010 in Bondurant, which is one of the fastest-growing districts in the state. Numerous new recreation facilities have been built or will be built as well throughout the area.

Ankeny

Placing on several lists by national magazines of best places to live, **Ankeny** lies barely 15 miles from downtown Des Moines along I-35. Located along a railroad line that ran through the cornfields between Des Moines and Ames, it has seen its population surge in the past several decades, jumping nearly 50 percent between 2000 and 2010 to some 45,000 residents, with projections for 55,000 by 2020. All that growth is driven largely by families seeking affordable housing and good schools with a reasonable commute to jobs in both Des Moines and at Iowa State University in Ames, about a half-hour drive along I-35, as well as locally—there are significant employers in Ankeny, including a longstanding John Deere works and the headquarters of Casey's General Stores. The school district, of course, is also one of the fastest-growing in the state, with plans to open a second high school by 2013. There's plenty of commercial development just off the interstate, including numerous big-box and chain stores.

Grimes & Johnston

A pair or semi-rural suburbs out past the I-80/35 beltway on the northwestern edge of Des Moines, each town has its own character, with Grimes a bit more low-key and Johnston, the larger of the two, with more commercial activity. Both, however, offer something of a small-town feel a short drive from more urban amenities. In addition to a wide selection of new housing, **Grimes** boasts a 44-acre sports complex with tennis, softball, baseball, and basketball facilities as well as more general outdoor recreation. It is part of the Dallas Center–Grimes School District, with the high school in Grimes and the middle school in the nearby community of Dallas Center. **Johnston,** which incorporated in 1969 and has been one of the state's fastest-growing towns, with its population nearly doubling to roughly 16,000 from 2000 to 2010, is home to Pioneer Hi-Bred International Inc., a large agriculture company, and has a large selection of single-family homes, townhouses, condominiums, and apartments in numerous new developments. There is abundant commercial activity along Merle Hay Road and other major arteries. The Johnston Community School District has numerous elementary schools as well as two middle schools and Johnston High School. Jester Park, one of the largest and best-appointed of Polk County's parks, with ample fishing and boating access to Saylorville Lake, is a short drive to the north.

Clive & Windsor Heights

Sandwiched between the much larger communities of Urbandale and West Des Moines, these two older suburbs offer both convenient access to downtown jobs and amenities as well as a somewhat less urban lifestyle. **Windsor Heights,** with a population of under 5,000 tucked just west of the western border of Des Moines at 63rd Street and south of Hickman Road, in many

places does feel like an extension of the city, including the fact that students on the east side of the town attend Des Moines schools, with students on the west side going to school in the West Des Moines district. There's shopping around University Avenue and it's just a short drive from commercial strips on Hickman and Merle Hay Roads, including Merle Hay Mall. **Clive,** one of the more affluent communities in Iowa, with the 2000 US Census reporting a median family income near $100,000, runs in a narrow east–west strip north of I-235 to the I-35/80 beltway, thus making for easy access to just about anywhere in the metro area. It has a mixture of older housing and newer developments, with many residential areas providing easy access to the Clive Greenbelt, a stretch of woods and a hiking and cycling trail along Walnut Creek. There's also a very well-appointed aquatic center just down the road from the public library. Clive has grown to a population of about 15,000, with most students attending schools in the West Des Moines district, although students who live in the westernmost part of Clive, across the Dallas County line and around Clive Lake, attend school in the Waukee district.

Urbandale

The site of Living History Farms and one of the largest suburbs of Des Moines, **Urbandale** provides a large number of parks and green spaces mixed in with extensive residential development, which skyrocketed in 1998 after the city annexed land to the west in adjoining Dallas County. Average home size is 1,680 feet spread over two stories and with three bedrooms. There are more than 900 acres of parkland and 36 miles of trails in the city, including the lengthy Walnut Creek Trail. There are extensive recreation facilities, including numerous sports fields, tennis courts, a year-round city pool, and winter sports facilities for sledding and ice skating. Merle Hay Mall sits on the Urbandale–Des Moines boundary, and there's lots of shopping along nearby Douglas Avenue. The Urbandale Community School District serves a diverse population of nearly 4,000 students in its six elementary schools, one middle school, and one high school.

Waukee

Ringed by cornfields, **Waukee** offers homes that look out over wide, flat vistas that are the epitome of the Iowa landscape. Population has exploded, more than doubling since 2000 to about 12,000 residents. This is one of the fastest-growing school districts in Iowa, with close to 7,000 students in the Waukee Community School District, and two new elementary schools and a new middle school opening in the last years of the 2000s, as well as additions to the high school, in order to someday accommodate close to 2,000 students. Growth has been mirrored in an expanding parks and recreation department as well, with numerous parks and sports facilities. There's also a large YMCA near the center of town. There's easy access to hiking and cycling trails that head out into the nearby countryside.

West Des Moines

By far the largest suburb of Des Moines—the population approached 55,000 in 2010—with a huge amount of residential and commercial development that includes Jordan Creek Town Center, the newest, largest mall in the Des Moines area, as well as in the state, and one of the largest malls in the Midwest, with more than one million square feet

of shopping space. The Valley West Mall, a decent-sized mall in its own right, is in **West Des Moines** as well. The West Glen area, in the southwest part of West Des Moines off I-35, has numerous restaurant and nightlife options—some say more than are offered downtown! A surfeit of recreational opportunities includes two nicely appointed city aquatic centers with multiple pools, water slides, and other amenities. There's also Raccoon River Park, with a beach, playground, and other facilities. All types of housing are found here, including plenty of new condominiums and rental apartments. Valley Junction, the older part of the city that was once an important railroad center, is now a charming shopping district that also has many blocks of older single-family homes.

Indianola, Cumming & Norwalk

While the area south of Des Moines is still largely wide-open farmland, there are some housing options in **Indianola,** home to Simpson College and about 20 miles from downtown Des Moines. It remains a small-town atmosphere as county seat of Warren County and has its own school district. **Norwalk** and **Cumming** are also largely rural communities located much closer to Des Moines, just past the southern city limits, with the popular Great Western cycling and hiking trail running past both towns.

REAL ESTATE

With a strong local economy and a large population of homeowners—some 70 percent of homes in the Des Moines area are owner-occupied—Des Moines has a generally solid housing market. The median sale price for a single-family home is about $150,000 and has remained relatively steady, without the hyperinflation and subsequent bust in more freewheeling locales—in late 2010 Des Moines–West Des Moines was ranked 112th in percentage change in house prices compared to 298 other metro areas by the Federal Housing Finance Agency.

A mixture of new and older housing can be found throughout the city and suburbs. The most popular Des Moines neighborhoods tend to be on the west side, with areas south of Grand having some of the most elegant and historic homes in the city. Beaverdale is another well-regarded area west of the Des Moines River and farther to the north. The south side also has quite a few large, well-appointed homes.

Homebuyers in a number of Des Moines neighborhoods may qualify for funding from **Neighborhood Finance Corporation (www.neighborhoodfinance.org)** to purchase and make improvements on a home—contact NFC for more details. First-time homebuyers may qualify for the Homestead Tax Credit—contact your county treasurer's office for more information.

The **Des Moines Area Association of Realtors** website, **www.dmaar.com,** has a feature that allows you to search real estate listings by price, size, and location. The website **www.seeiowahomes.com /des_moines_ia_real_estate.aspx** lets you narrow listings by criteria, and the site **www .mls.com/search/iowa.mvc** lets you search cities across central Iowa.

Apartment Finder (4524 E. P. True Pkwy., #105, West Des Moines; 515-327-0606), **www .apartmentfinder.com/iowa/des-moines-apartments,** is a good resource if you're looking for an apartment, with lots of listings in Des Moines, surrounding suburbs, and outlying communities. Apartment rents average around $500 for an efficiency to close to $1,000 for a three-bedroom unit.

Local Real Estate Firms

BURNETT REALTY
10200 Hickman Rd., Suite 100, Clive
(515) 334-4900
www.burnettrealty.net

CENTURY 21 SIGNATURE REAL ESTATE
2641 86th St., Urbandale
(515) 224-4002
www.c21sre.com

COUNTRY ESTATES REALTY
317 S. Ankeny Blvd., Ankeny
(515) 964-2814
www.countryestatesrealty.com

IOWA REALTY
3501 Westown Pkwy., West Des Moines
(515) 453-6222
www.iowarealty.com

NEXT GENERATION REALTY
3220 100th St.
(515) 224-9900
http://dsm.nextgenerationrealty.com

PEOPLE'S COMPANY
1300 50th St., West Des Moines
(515) 222-1347
www.peoplescompany.com

PRUDENTIAL FIRST REALTY
5500 Westown Pkwy., West Des Moines
(515) 453-7200
www.firstrealtyhomes.com

RE/MAX REAL ESTATE GROUP
6600 University Ave.
(515) 279-6700
932 N. Shadyview Blvd., Pleasant Hill
(515) 265-7200
www.dsmhomes.com

SERVICES FOR NEWCOMERS

Driver's License

Written and driving tests are administered only at the Ankeny location. Renewals may be obtained at the Des Moines location. They do not accept credit or debit cards. For more information on licenses, see the Iowa Department of Transportation's Office of Driver Services website at www.iowadot.gov/mvd/ods/index.htm.

IOWA MOTOR VEHICLE DIVISION BUILDING
6310 SE Convenience Blvd., Ankeny (I-35 exit 89)
(515) 244-9124

POLK COUNTY RIVER PLACE
2339 Euclid Ave.
(515) 244-8725

Libraries

Des Moines has an excellent public library system, **www.desmoineslibrary.com,** with a large main library downtown and branch libraries located throughout the city. Books, music CDs, videotapes, and DVDs are all available for checkout by Des Moines residents, as are back issues of magazines. Each library has computers with Internet access available for use as well. Numerous story times and other children's activities are offered throughout the system. The library's selection of books includes a large number of new releases and best sellers, and an online reservation system allows patrons to request that books from other library locations be sent to their local library, as well as place holds on new titles that have not yet arrived. The central library has a non-circulating section of local and Iowa historical materials that are invaluable to anyone doing research on the area. Branch libraries are closed on Sunday, and the central library is open Sunday from September through May only. All libraries are usually closed the days before and after major holidays—check the website for details. All libraries can be reached by calling the main telephone line at (515) 283-4152.

Locations

CENTRAL LIBRARY
1000 Grand Ave.

EAST SIDE LIBRARY
2559 Hubbell Ave.

FOREST AVENUE LIBRARY
1326 Forest Ave.

FRANKLIN AVENUE LIBRARY
3800 Merle Hay Rd., Suite 210 (Merle Hay Mall) (temporary location)

NORTH SIDE LIBRARY
3516 Fifth Ave.

SOUTH SIDE LIBRARY
1111 Porter Ave.

Voter Registration

To register to vote in Iowa, you must be a US citizen and at least 18 years old by Election Day (you may register if you are at least 17½). Registration must be completed at least 10 or 11 days, depending on the type of election, before you intend to vote. A voter registration form is available at **www.sos.state.ia.us/pdfs/elections/voteapp.pdf,** as well as at public libraries. The completed form must be returned to the county auditor's office in the county where you live. You may also register to vote at other locations, including driver's license facilities. You may also register to vote on Election Day if you were unable to do so prior, and you must provide identification as proof of identity and residence, usually an Iowa driver's license. Re-registration is required if you fail to vote in elections for four years, and you must update your voter registration if you change your name, address, or political party affiliation. For more details on voter registration, including locations where you may register and acceptable forms of identification, go to the voter registration section of the Iowa Secretary of State website, **www.sos.state .ia.us/elections/voterinformation/voter registration.html#1.**

WORSHIP

A wide variety of religious and faith-based groups can be found in Des Moines. Several Christian denominations predominate, especially Catholic, Lutheran, and Methodist, but there is every other type of congregation imaginable, including local Hindu and Buddhist groups, and ranging in size from just a few worshippers to megachurches with multiple community facilities. For a general source of information on area religious groups, see the **Des Moines Area Religious Council** (515-277-6969; www.dmreligious .org).

The Catholic Church is part of the **Diocese of Des Moines,** which celebrates its 100th year in 2011 and stretches across 23 counties covering the southwest quadrant of Iowa. The diocese has been actively involved with resettling refugees from Bosnia, Sudan, Vietnam, and other parts of Asia and Africa, and also works with the area's growing Latino community. The historic **Basilica of St. John,** located at 1915 University Ave., in the Drake neighborhood, is a limestone basilica built in the Romanesque

revival style, with marble and gold detail. Its campanile is 115 feet tall and holds a 600-pound bell.

There are several synagogues in the Des Moines area, including Orthodox, Conservative, and Reform congregations. Contact the **Jewish Federation of Greater Des Moines** (515-277-6321; http://desmoines.ujcfedweb .org). Among its projects is a supplementary Jewish school for students ranging from pre-kindergarten through high school age. Muslim groups include the **Islamic Center of Des Moines** (515-255-0212; www.goicdm .org).

MEDIA

Newspapers & Magazines

Many publications, free and otherwise, line the entryways of supermarkets and fitness centers throughout the Des Moines area, including:

DES MOINES REGISTER
www.desmoinesregister.com
The city's daily newspaper has separate zoned editions for Des Moines and other parts of Iowa. Part of the Gannett Company's news empire, it traces its history back to 1855 and the founding of the *Iowa Citizen*; it adopted the *Register* name in 1915. For many years the paper was owned by the Cowles family, and at the time it was sold to Gannett in 1985, only the *New York Times* had won more Pulitzer Prizes for national reporting.

JUICE
http://dmjuice.desmoinesregister.com
A free weekly paper published as an arm of the *Register*, this paper has a youthful staff that focuses on local nightlife, entertainment, and fashion, with extensive pages

of event listings. Some of the same stories appear on different days in the *Register* and *Juice,* including restaurant and movie listings. Multiple pages of photos show locals out and about at various nightspots. Pick up a copy at locations all over the city.

CITYVIEW
www.dmcityview.com
Another free weekly, this tabloid sheet takes a somewhat more serious and aggressive tone, with columnists and cover stories pointing out the peccadilloes of local politicians and others. They also have lengthy listings of area entertainment and nightlife, including restaurant and movie reviews and all sorts of photos. Like *Juice, CityView* is available for free on stands all over Des Moines. The publisher also publishes a thick portfolio of **Iowa Living** magazines (www.iowaliving magazines.com) showcasing news in communities throughout the Des Moines metro area.

DES MOINES BUSINESS RECORD
www.businessrecord.com
There's lots of news for and about the local business community in this weekly publication, with items organized by industry and some well-written stories and features about business trends and local companies. Part of a line of publications that includes other specialty publications for the Des Moines market, including directories and visitor guides.

DSM
www.dsmmagazine.com
A thick, glossy lifestyle book that has some interesting content about local history and culture as well as extensive lists of local favorites. The beautiful photo layouts take in interior spaces as well as local landmarks like the State Capitol.

THE IOWAN
www.iowan.com
A somewhat thinner, locally published culture and lifestyle magazine that covers the entire state, not just Des Moines, with a mixture of articles looking at everything from favorite foods to outdoor activities to area music scenes. The writing can be top-notch and there are some good photos, too. This is a good resource to find destinations for weekend trips and exploring the state's back roads.

MIDWEST LIVING
www.midwestliving.com
Not a Des Moines– or even Iowa-focused magazine but published by locally based publishing giant Meredith, and worth a mention for the stories and smaller items it does publish about Iowa and the rest of the Midwest—they are superbly written and expertly photographed. Use it to plot a weeklong road trip across the Midwest or just to find a great hotel or restaurant in an area you'll be visiting.

WELCOME HOME DES MOINES
www.welcomehomedesmoines.com
Cooking, home and garden, and health matters are the focus of this glossy, bimonthly subscription-based publication, with several recipes included. It also has a front section in each issue of goings-on in central Iowa.

Television Stations

KCCI-CHANNEL 8 (CBS)

KDIN-CHANNEL 11 (PBS)

KDSM- CHANNEL 17 (FOX)

RELOCATION

KFPX-CHANNEL 39 (PAX)

KPWB-CHANNEL 23 (WB)

WHO-TV CHANNEL 13 (NBC)

WOI-TV CHANNEL 5 (ABC)

MEDIACOM
http://mediacomcable.com
This is the cable television provider for the Des Moines area, including digital cable. They also offer Internet and telephone service.

Radio Stations

KASI 1430 AM
News/Talk

KBGG 1700 AM
Sports

KPSZ 940 AM
Contemporary Christian

KRNT 1350 AM
News/Sports/Adult Contemporary

KWKY 1150 AM
Religious

KXNO 1460 AM
Sports

WHO 1040 AM
News/Talk

KAZR 103.3 FM
Active Rock

KCCQN 105.1 FM
Modern Rock

KDFR 91.3 FM
Family radio/Christian Gospel

KDMR 88.9 FM
National Public Radio/News

KDRB 100.3 FM
Adult Hits

KFMG 99.1 FM
Community radio

KGGO 94.9 FM
Classic rock

KHKI 97.3 FM
Country

KIOA 93.3 FM
Oldies

KJJY 92.5 FM
Country

KJMC 89.3 FM
Urban Contemporary

KKDM 107.5 FM
Contemporary hits

KLTI 104.1 FM
Soft Adult Contemporary

KNWI 107.1 FM
Religious

KPTL 106.3 FM
Adult Album Alternative

KPUL 99.5 FM
Religious

KSTZ 102.5 FM
Adult Contemporary Hits

KWQW 98.3 FM
Talk

WOI 90.1 FM
National Public Radio/Classical

EDUCATION & CHILD CARE

The Des Moines area has some top-notch schools in both the city and suburbs, with excellent academic opportunities as well as extensive extracurricular programs and facilities at schools in the city and suburbs. Under state law, a student may apply to enroll in a public school outside the district in which he or she lives. Contact individual school districts for details on open enrollment in their schools.

Preschool programs are generally available at schools throughout the city and suburbs. Private schools include quite a few religious-based schools, including a well-regarded Catholic high school, as well as a few independent options.

Higher education includes one large university, Drake, as well as small liberal arts colleges in outlying areas and an extensive community college system with several campuses. More and more institutions are utilizing distance and online learning, making for easier access to college classes and degrees.

The listings of private schools and higher education options is by no means a complete selection, but rather a cross-section of some of the education choices in the Des Moines area.

PUBLIC SCHOOLS

DES MOINES PUBLIC SCHOOLS
901 Walnut St.
(515) 242-7911
www.dmpsk12.ia.us

The district has 32,000 students from Des Moines and surrounding communities who attend 40 elementary schools, 10 middle schools, and 5 high schools, as well as 1 alternative school apiece for middle school and high school students. The racial mix of the district is 50 percent Caucasian, 21 percent Hispanic, 17 percent African-American, 5.5 percent Asian, and 6.5 percent other. More than 10 percent of students speak a native language other than English, totaling over 40 languages, and the school offers English as a Second Language classes (ESL). About 55 percent of students receive free or reduced-price lunch. The citywide average high school graduation rate is around 80 percent. The district's average ACT score has been slightly lower than the state average, and every high school student is required to take the ACT. High school students have the opportunity to attend classes at the district's Central Academy, located downtown, which offers advanced placement classes for college credit as well as the international baccalaureate curriculum, a mode of learning that teaches students to ask challenging questions and understand other countries and cultures. Students from outside the Des Moines district are eligible to attend classes at Central Academy, and come from nearly 40 districts throughout the metro area and central Iowa. The district also operates

Central Campus, which offers classes in numerous career and technical programs, including college prep areas, and is also open to students from outside the district. The international baccalaureate curriculum is also utilized in a few elementary and middle schools, and there are other unique programs at the elementary level, including Cowles Montessori, a public Montessori school located in Windsor Heights, and the downtown school, which has combined grade levels and a year-round class schedule (there are a few other year-round elementary schools in the district). Beginning with the 2011–12 school year it will move to Central Campus, on the western edge of downtown. Both these elementary schools draw students from throughout the city and metro area. Preschool programs are offered at locations throughout the city.

ANKENY COMMUNITY SCHOOL DISTRICT
306 SW School St., Ankeny
(515) 965-9600
www.ankeny.k12.ia.us
One of the fastest-growing districts in the state, Ankeny serves more than 8,500 students at eight elementary schools, two middle schools, and a high school. The district is in transition to two systems, divided between north and south, with four middle schools feeding into two high schools that will be virtually identical in both floor plans and curriculum. Students will be able to move between the two high schools for certain technical classes. The 95 percent–plus high school graduation rate is one of the highest in the state, while the average ACT composite score is above the state average. The district, which has just over 5 percent minority students, has programs in

special education, gifted and talented, and English as a second language, and for at-risk students.

DALLAS CENTER–GRIMES COMMUNITY SCHOOL DISTRICT
1414 Walnut St., Suite 200, Dallas Center
(515) 992-3866
http://dcgschools.com
There are around 2,000 students in this district out near the edge of Des Moines's northern suburbs, who attend three elementary schools, one middle school, and one high school. An alternative school is available as well. The district is in the process of constructing a new school for grades 8 and 9. Average class size is around 20 students at the elementary level, 25 in middle school, and 27 in the high school. The ACT composite score is above the state average.

JOHNSTON COMMUNITY SCHOOL DISTRICT
5608 Merle Hay Rd., Johnston
(515) 278-0470
www.johnston.k12.ia.us
This rapidly growing suburban district also has students from parts of Des Moines and Urbandale as well as rural areas around Grimes and Granger. Enrollment is over 6,000 students at five elementary schools, two middle schools, and a high school, which itself has close to 1,300 students. There is also an alternative high school and special education, as well as English as a second language classes and a gifted and talented program. ACT scores are consistently above the state average. Minority student population is around 15 percent, as are students receiving free and reduced-price lunches. The high school graduation rate is close to

95 percent, with about 90 percent going on to some form of higher education.

SOUTHEAST POLK COMMUNITY SCHOOL DISTRICT

8379 NE University Ave., Pleasant Hill
(515) 967-4294
www.se-polk.k12.ia.us
Another rapidly growing suburban and rural district, this one is east of Des Moines. Students come from Altoona, Runnells, and Mitchellville as well as Pleasant Hill and Des Moines, with many attending classes at a central campus in Pleasant Hill that includes the senior high school, junior high school, and a sixth-grade building. There are 8 elementary schools located throughout the district. A new high school opened in 2009. There is also an alternative school. The ACT score is above the state average, and the high school graduation rate is close to 100 percent.

URBANDALE COMMUNITY SCHOOL DISTRICT

6200 Aurora Ave., Urbandale
(515) 457-5000
www.urbandaleschools.com
This is a large suburban district north of Des Moines with nearly 4,000 students at six elementary schools, a middle school, and a high school. All students come from Urbandale, with over 40 languages spoken. Class sizes range from the high teens in the elementary grades to around 25 students at the middle and high schools. There is an English as a second language program, as well as a gifted and talented program and an alternative program. The high school graduation rate is above 95 percent.

WEST DES MOINES COMMUNITY SCHOOLS

3550 Mills Civic Pkwy., West Des Moines
(515) 633-5000
www.wdm.k12.ia.us
The district draws nearly 9,000 students from parts of Clive, Urbandale, and Windsor Heights as well as West Des Moines. There are 8 elementary schools plus an early childhood center for students in kindergarten through third grade, 3 junior high schools, and 3 high schools: one for freshmen, one for grades 10 through 12, and an alternative school. Minority enrollment is about 15 percent. The student–teacher ratio is 24:1 for elementary school, 19:1 for junior high, and 15:1 for high school. Classes are capped at 26 students for kindergarten through third grade and 28 for grades 4 through 6. More than 80 percent of high school graduates go on to some form of higher education.

PRIVATE SCHOOLS

BERGMAN ACADEMY

100 45th St.
(515) 274-0453
www.theacademydesmoines.org
A private, K–8 school with about 150 students and located in Greenwood/Ashworth Park on the city's west side. The school utilizes both Montessori and traditional teaching, and also offers full- and half-day preschool options. Class sizes are small, with a 15:1 student–teacher ratio in grades K–8 and 9:1 in preschool. There are numerous student clubs and extracurricular activities.

CHRIST THE KING SCHOOL

701 Wall Ave.
(515) 285-3349
www.cksdesmoines.com

Both Catholic and non-Catholic students attend classes from preschool through eighth grade at this parish school on the south side of the city. Enrollment is just over 200, with a curriculum that includes reading, math, science, and social studies, as well as art and music.

DOWLING CATHOLIC HIGH SCHOOL
1400 Buffalo Rd., West Des Moines
(515) 225-3000
www.dowlingcatholic.org
A coed school with about 1,200 students in grades 9 through 12, located just off I-235 and west of 73rd Street just across the border from Des Moines, Dowling offers a full curriculum of classes in English, math, science, social studies, and fine arts, as well as other subjects. A low student–teacher ratio makes for more in-depth instruction. Numerous extracurricular activities include band and choir as well as a number of student clubs, and a full slate of athletic teams, including football, basketball, baseball, swimming, golf, volleyball, soccer, wrestling, track, and tennis. The school's campus features well-tended athletic fields.

GRANDVIEW PARK BAPTIST SCHOOL
1701 East 33rd St.
(515) 265-7579
Affiliated with the adjacent church, Grandview Park has about 330 students in preschool through twelfth grade. Education at the school is based on biblical principles, with a curriculum that includes reading and math in the lower grades and offers advanced placement courses as part of the college prep instruction at the high school level. There are also technology and fine arts classes. Activities include student clubs and a full slate of athletic teams.

HOLY TRINITY SCHOOL
2926 Beaver Ave.
(515) 255-3162
www.htschool.org
This Catholic school located by the church of the same name has just over 500 students from preschool through eighth grade. Class size averages about 23 students, with teacher assistants helping out in the lower grades. The curriculum includes accelerated reading classes as well as writing, math, science, and other subjects. Numerous extracurricular activities are available, including academic groups and athletics. There is a weekly Catholic liturgy.

IOWA CHRISTIAN ACADEMY
2501 Vine St., West Des Moines
(515) 221-3999
www.icblazers.org
About 250 students from preschool through twelfth grade attend this independent, nondenominational school, which opened in 1999 and stresses Christian values and a biblical worldview. In addition to the academic curriculum, there is instruction in art and music. More than 80 percent of graduates go on to higher education. There are several athletic and extracurricular activities to choose from.

SACRED HEART SCHOOL
1601 Grand Ave., West Des Moines
(515) 223-1284
www.edline.net/pages/SHES
With about 500 students in kindergarten through fifth grade, this Catholic school has a curriculum that includes reading and literature, writing, math, science, and social studies, as well as opportunities in art, music, and other extracurricular activities. The school

offers all-day kindergarten, and there is a preschool program as well.

HIGHER EDUCATION

CENTRAL COLLEGE
812 University, Pella
(877) 462-3687
www.central.edu

Nestled by the picturesque, Dutch-influenced village of Pella (the school's athletic teams are nicknamed the Dutch), Central is a liberal arts college with an enrollment of about 1,600, affiliated with the Reformed Church in America. Bachelor's degrees are offered across the humanities, sciences, fine arts, and business disciplines. Average class size is 20 students, with a student–faculty ratio of 16:1. Close to 90 percent of faculty have earned the highest degree in their field. Some 50 percent of the student body participates in study abroad, attending school-sponsored programs in Europe, Asia, Mexico, and Africa. Close to three-quarters participate in internships, working with Iowa-based companies or in other states. The college has an active Greek life, as well as a full slate of musical and athletic programs. The 130-acre campus, where students live the entire four years, dates to 1853 and has many unique architectural features.

GRAND VIEW UNIVERSITY
1200 Grandview Ave.
(515) 263-2800 or (800) 444-6083
www.grandview.edu

A four-year liberal arts college on a residential campus on the north side of Des Moines, Grand View offers liberal arts degrees in close to 40 majors, including programs in business, communication, education, fine arts, and nursing as well as humanities and sciences. The school is affiliated with the Evangelical Lutheran Church in America and has about 2,000 students. There is an active campus life, with numerous residence halls and apartments and a full slate of student clubs. The Grand View Vikings compete in NAIA athletics and participate in the Midwest Collegiate Conference.

DES MOINES AREA COMMUNITY COLLEGE
(515) 964-6200
www.dmacc.edu

This large community college system has an enrollment of over 20,000 in classes in more than 100 fields of study, with a focus on computer and nursing programs, as well as programs in business, agriculture, and automotive technologies. Associate's degree programs are offered, and there are also several certificate programs. DMACC has campuses in Ankeny, Boone, Carroll, Des Moines, Newton, and West Des Moines as well as additional learning centers in Des Moines and other communities and online classes. On-campus housing is available.

DRAKE UNIVERSITY
2507 University Ave.
(515) 271-2011 or (800) 44-DRAKE
www.drake.edu

With more than 75 academic majors in arts and sciences, education, business and public administration, and journalism and mass communication, Drake is by far Des Moines's largest four-year university, with numerous campus and community resources. In addition to bachelor's degrees, there are professional degree programs in law and pharmacy. Undergraduate enrollment is more than 3,000, with students coming from all over the United States and many foreign countries. There are over 1,000 graduate students as well. The student–faculty ratio of 14:1 allows for smaller classes, and Drake has consistently ranked high in *U.S. News & World Report*'s "Great Schools, Great Prices" category. Drake has a 150-acre urban campus just a few miles west of downtown Des Moines, including a large football stadium, which also hosts the annual Drake Relays, and a basketball arena. Many students live off-campus in nearby apartments and homes, including several Greek houses just off University Avenue, the main street past campus. There are a number of student-oriented businesses around the campus as well. Athletic teams compete in NCAA Division I, with the football team a member of the Pioneer League and other athletic teams part of the Missouri Valley Conference.

SIMPSON COLLEGE
701 North C St., Indianola
(515) 961-6251 or (800) 362-2454
www.simpson.edu

A liberal arts college affiliated with the United Methodist church and with an enrollment of about 2,000, including 1,500 full-time students on its main campus, Simpson awards bachelor's degrees in the humanities and sciences, as well as in business, education, computer science, fine arts, and other disciplines, including preprofessional programs for various health careers. There are also graduate programs in education and criminal justice. The academic schedule includes a unique feature called May term, in which students spend three weeks taking a single course focused on one specific topic. Many May term courses involve domestic and foreign travel, as well as internships and other experiential learning. There is also a separate study abroad program with several countries to choose from. The college

occupies a tree-lined campus in Indianola, a small town a half-hour's drive from Des Moines. It has a very active Greek life, with several houses located just off campus, and a large number of athletic programs for such a small school: There are close to 20 men's and women's teams, including baseball, basketball, football, golf, soccer, softball, swimming, tennis, track and field, volleyball and wrestling. Simpson competes in NCAA Division III and is a member of the Iowa Intercollegiate Athletic Conference. Simpson is also home to the Des Moines Metro Opera, which features singers who come from around the world every summer to perform at the Blank Performing Arts Center on campus. In addition to the main campus, there are also satellite facilities in Ankeny and West Des Moines that offer evening and weekend classes. These are especially popular with adult students in the business and criminal justice programs.

Other Higher Education

AIB COLLEGE OF BUSINESS
2500 Fleur Dr.
(515) 246-5358 or (800) 444-1921
www.aib.edu

This business school about halfway between downtown and Des Moines International Airport offers bachelor's degrees in accounting, business administration, and court reporting, as well as associate's degrees in numerous disciplines. It's possible to earn a bachelor's degree in three years, and night and online classes are available. Enrollment is between 500 and 600 students. There's a library on campus with books, multimedia materials, and access to the Internet and electronic databases, and a 26,000-square-foot activities center that is utilized by the school's athletic teams, which include men's and women's basketball and golf and women's volleyball, who compete in NAIA athletics. Apartment housing is available.

DES MOINES UNIVERSITY
3200 Grand Ave.
(515) 271-1400 or (800) 240-2767
www.dmu.edu
This health sciences university offers graduate degrees in osteopathic medicine, physical therapy, health care administration, public health, anatomy, biomedical sciences, podiatry, and physician assistant studies. Enrollment is around 1,750, with classes meeting on a campus on the west side of Des Moines that includes a simulation laboratory and surgery skills center.

ITT TECHNICAL INSTITUTE
1860 NW 118th St., Suite 110, Clive
(515) 327-5500 or (877) 526-7312
www.itt-tech.edu
This Des Moines–area location of the national technical school offers associate's and bachelor's degrees in drafting, electronics, information technology, and criminal justice. Operating out of an office building in Clive, it also offers online courses.

KAPLAN UNIVERSITY
4655 121st St., Urbandale
(515) 727-2100 or (800) 987-7734
www.kaplan.edu
The Des Moines–area campus of this largely distance learning college has programs that include business administration, criminal justice, health and medical studies, and information technology with several bachelor's and associate's degrees available. It's a good choice for adults who are working full-time and need flexible class schedules.

VATTEROTT COLLEGE
7000 Fleur Dr.
(515) 309-9000 or (877) 281-4803
http://vatterott-college.edu
The Iowa branch of a tech school with locations in several states, the school offers programs in a wide variety of disciplines and careers, including computer systems and network technology, dental and medical assistants, HVAC, and diesel mechanics, with hands-on facilities for most programs.

CHILD CARE

A wide variety of child care options are available in Des Moines and surrounding areas. Private and church-based day care centers, Montessori schools, and in-home day care are just some of the options. Contact school districts in Des Moines and individual suburbs for more information on what child care or preschool options are available in public schools. Many programs have waiting lists that in some cases can be quite long, so be sure to contact your preferred choices as soon as possible.

It's always a good idea to check out a child care facility before enrolling your child. Telephone the provider to get some basic information, and schedule a time when you can visit. Inspect the facility and make note of the amount of indoor and outdoor play space available for the children. Check out cooking and dining facilities if your child will be eating while attending child care. Have questions ready for the facility's director and staff: How many children are in the facility? What is the adult to child ratio? How long has the facility been in operation and at its current location? How long have staff members been working in child care, and what sort of training and experience do they have? Be sure to ask about staff training and certification in CPR and pediatric first aid. Some child care providers offer classes as well as play time—find out exactly what will be taught to children at the facility. The visit is really an opportunity for you to talk with the staff and see how comfortable you are with them, so make sure your questions are answered to your satisfaction. You may also want to ask the provider for references of parents whose children currently attend the facility so you may speak to them.

Find out what sort of accreditation and/or certification a provider has as well. The **Iowa Department of Human Services** regulates child care providers, with requirements varying depending on the size and type of center, and covering such matters as space requirements, fire exits and extinguishers, and age and background of staff members. For more information, check out the department's website at **www.dhs .state.ia.us,** which also allows you to search for child care providers throughout central Iowa based on the county, city, and type of provider. Another helpful resource is **Iowa Child Care Resource & Referral** (**www .centraliowachildcare.org),** which has lots of information on what to look for when choosing a provider, as well as its own search feature.

The periodical *Moms Like Me,* published by the *Des Moines Register* is available for free at numerous locations in Des Moines and surrounding locations, and also has a website, **http://desmoines.momslikeme.com,** with a wealth of resources, including numerous active online discussions addressing every conceivable issue relating to parenting and child care. Websites of local parenting groups can be useful as well for information on child care and other issues. Listed below is a small sampling of groups, with additional ones available online—check out a group to see if it is right for you.

MOMS CLUB OF DES MOINES
http://momsclubdm.tripod.com

MOMS CLUB OF WEST DES MOINES
www.momsclubdmwest.com

DES MOINES STAY AT HOME MOMS GROUP
www.meetup.com/desmoines-SAHM

NO DRAMA MAMAS
http://groups.yahoo.com/group /NDMIOWA

HEALTH CARE

Des Moines is the major medical center for central Iowa, with hospitals and other facilities clustered in and around downtown, including Lutheran Hospital, Methodist Hospital, and Blank Children's Hospital, which are all operated by Iowa Health, as is Methodist West Hospital in West Des Moines. Mercy Health Network has also added a hospital in West Des Moines to complement its large downtown facility. Des Moines University has an on-campus clinic with specialties including ophthalmology, osteopathic medicine, and physical therapy in addition to general family medicine.

HOSPITALS & MEDICAL CENTERS

BLANK CHILDREN'S HOSPITAL
1200 Pleasant St.
(515) 241-5437
www.iowahealth.org/blank-childrens-hospital.aspx
Established in 1944, this is the only hospital in Iowa to focus solely on children, with spacious rooms to comfortably accommodate overnight stays by parents and family members. There are also play areas for siblings and other young visitors. The 85-bed hospital has undergone renovation and expansion and features a level-one pediatric trauma center and a level-three neonatal intensive care nursery, one of the first such facilities anywhere to offer private rooms that offer specialists to work more closely with newborns. There is also pediatric cancer diagnosis and treatment. The staff has more than 60 pediatric subspecialists.

BROADLAWNS MEDICAL CENTER
1801 Hickman Rd.
(515) 282-2200
www.broadlawns.org

Located a short drive north of downtown, this community hospital has general medical and mental health care, including surgery and pain management. There are more than 300 physicians on staff as well as nurse practitioners and physician's assistants. Additional specialty clinics provide treatment in family health, pediatrics, podiatry, internal medicine, dentistry, mental health, and women's care.

IOWA CLINIC
5950 University Ave., Suite 321, West Des Moines
(515) 875-9100
www.iowaclinic.com
More than 130 physicians practice in a multitude of specialties, including cardiology, physical therapy, surgery, trauma care, obstetrics/gynecology, orthopedics, and many others. Treatment is available at the main location as well as at others throughout the Des Moines metro area and outlying communities.

IOWA LUTHERAN HOSPITAL
700 E. University Ave.
(515) 263-5612
www.iowahealth.org/iowa-lutheran-hospital.aspx

Established in 1914, this 224-bed hospital has one of Iowa's largest private hospital-based mental health facilities, with advanced treatment of mental illness and emotional and behavioral problems. It also has a leading chemical dependency center that has been treating individuals for more than 25 years. Other services include orthopedics, child and adolescent psychiatry, women's services, general and outpatient surgery, and cardiovascular care, as well as cardiac rehab, emergency care, maternity care, and other services.

IOWA METHODIST MEDICAL CENTER
1200 Pleasant St.
(515) 241-6212
www.iowahealth.org/iowa-methodist-medical-center.aspx

From its beginnings in a single building in 1901, Iowa Methodist has grown to become a leading teaching hospital and medical center for central Iowa. With 370 beds on a 42-acre downtown campus adjacent to Blank Children's Hospital, it also has one of the state's only level-one trauma centers, including an air ambulance program. The **John Stoddard Cancer Center** offers surgery, radiation, oncology, and ancillary services. Other areas of specialty include cardiology and vascular care (the hospital was second only to the Mayo Clinic in performing open-heart surgery, in 1956), as well as diagnosis and treatment of other heart problems. There is an extensive physical therapy center and a large maternity center, as well as orthopedic treatment and other services.

MERCY MEDICAL CENTER
1111 Sixth Ave.
(515) 247-3121
www.mercydesmoines.org

Founded in 1893, this Catholic hospital is Des Moines's oldest continually operating hospital. With 802 beds, it offers treatment in numerous medical areas including cancer and oncology, cardiology and vascular services, surgery, women's services, and neuroscience—it is central Iowa's leading provider of neurological care, including treatment of strokes, Alzheimer's, and Parkinson's, as well as other treatments. Behavioral health and rehabilitation services also are available, as well as a number of specialty clinics throughout the Des Moines area.

MERCY MEDICAL CENTER WEST LAKES
1601 60th St., West Des Moines
(515) 358-8000
www.mercywestlakes.org

Part of the Mercy Health Network, this hospital opened to serve the growing population in Des Moines's western communities. The 146-bed hospital offers a number of services including cardiac care, surgery, emergency medicine, and birthing services.

METHODIST WEST HOSPITAL
1660 60th St., West Des Moines
(515) 343-1000
www.iowahealth.org/methodist-west-hospital.aspx

Since opening in 2009 to serve the rapidly growing western suburbs of Des Moines, Methodist West has joined the other hospitals of Iowa West in providing care in areas including cardiovascular and pulmonary treatment, radiology, orthopedics, and emergency medicine. The 95-bed facility has round-the-clock neonatal staff who work in partnership with Blank Children's Hospital, while a 12-bed maternity center allows mothers to stay in one room for their entire stay. Surgery is performed in a number of new operating rooms.

CLINICS & URGENT-CARE FACILITIES

In addition to the listings below, which include free and low-cost clinics, several of the major health care providers listed above provide urgent-care clinics throughout the Des Moines metro area.

DOCTORSNOW WALK-IN CARE
5731 Greendale Rd., Suite 100, Johnston
(515) 270-1000
640 S. 50th St., Suite 1100, West Des Moines
www.doctorsnow.com

FREE CLINICS OF IOWA
3200 Grand Ave.
(515) 271-1642
www.freeclinicsofiowa.org

ENGEBRETSEN MEDICAL CLINIC
2353 SE 14th St.
(515) 248-1400
www.phcinc.net

EAST SIDE MEDICAL
3509 E. 29th St.
(515) 248-1600
www.phcinc.net

CONCENTRA URGENT CARE—DES MOINES EAST
2100 Dixon St.
(515) 265-1020
11144 Aurora Ave., Urbandale
(515) 278-6868
www.concentraurgentcare.com

RETIREMENT

Des Moines and central Iowa have a growing number of opportunities for retirees. Numerous senior communities are growing up around the metro area, and many activities and programs are available for retirees. The weather limits the population of retirees somewhat, especially in the winter, when some older residents depart for warmer climes, but Des Moines's wide array of cultural and recreational activities keeps some in the area year-round.

Many seniors take advantage of Des Moines's superb cultural offerings, including the symphony, theater companies, and opera in nearby Indianola, as well as the area's wealth of outdoor recreation opportunities, notably the many miles of walking and cycling trails that wind through the city, suburbs, and surrounding towns. The city's compact size and relatively short travel times to shopping and other amenities also make Des Moines an attractive option for seniors.

SERVICES

AGING RESOURCES OF CENTRAL IOWA
5835 Grand Ave., Suite 106
(515) 255-1310 or (800) 747-5362
www.agingresources.com
A good place to start for retirees is Aging Resources of Central Iowa, a nonprofit clearinghouse of information of interest to seniors, including links to government agencies and organizations like AARP, as well as adult day care and other providers of health, nutrition (including home-delivered meals), recreation, transportation, and other services. They also have information on community activities and can provide confidential assessments to retirees who are interested in exploring their options for independent living, including referrals to home-based and community services for seniors.

SENIOR CENTERS

SENIOR SERVICES OF POLK COUNTY
1914 Carpenter Ave.
(515) 286-3679
www.polkcountyiowa.gov/CFYS/pages
/seniorAboutUs.aspx
Senior Services of Polk County operates roughly 16 senior centers and meal sites throughout Des Moines and its outlying towns. A complete listing of centers is available at **www.polkcountyiowa.gov/CFYS /pages/seniorMealSites.aspx.**

Senior centers are open Mon through Fri from 8 a.m. to 5 p.m., while meal sites are open Mon through Fri from 9 a.m. to 1 p.m. There is also a center for deaf seniors open Wed only. Both centers and sites serve meals on days they are open. Seniors who are attending meals for the first time should contact the closest center at least a day in advance. Special meals are available for seniors who require them. Transportation is available to senior centers and meal sites, which can also arrange transportation for grocery shopping and other errands.

Each senior center offers its own selection of activities, which may include craft and art classes, book and discussion groups, games like cards, dominoes, and electronic games, and dances and exercise classes. There are also health services available, including blood pressure checks and foot clinics. Meal sites offer some of the same services as senior centers, although their offerings are more limited—check with individual centers and sites for details on their offerings. Donations are suggested for materials for some classes.

i The *Senior Bulletin* is a newsletter that offers a full list of activities and classes at centers and sites, as well as meal menus and information on Senior College and leisure time travel for seniors. Subscribe to the bulletin by contacting Senior Services. Archived issues of the bulletin can be found online at www.polkcountyiowa.gov /CFYS/pages/news.aspx.

POLK COUNTY LEISURE TIME TRAVEL
1914 Carpenter Ave.
(515) 286-3526
www.polkcountyiowa.gov/CFYS/pages /leisureTime.aspx
This group organizes travel to numerous destinations, with both single-day and extended trips. Past trips have gone for at least a week to destinations including Pennsylvania Dutch country, Niagara Falls, Branson, Mackinac Island, and the Great Smoky Mountains. There have also been shorter trips of two or three days to closer destinations in surrounding states like Minnesota

and Missouri. Day trips have gone all over Iowa, including to historic sites like the Herbert Hoover Presidential Museum as well as antiquing and theater excursions and visits to working farms and wineries.

Travel is usually by bus, although some extended trips include air travel. Rates are very reasonable and a deposit is required. Accommodations and some meals are included in trip fees. Trips are open to anyone age 21 and over but are marketed more to seniors. Trips are listed in the *Senior Bulletin* and through the Senior Services of Polk County website.

SENIOR COLLEGE
1200 Grand Ave., Suite 315
(515) 244-0361
www.myseniorcollege.com
A cooperative effort involving local businesses and several area colleges and universities, Senior College offers a long list of short-term courses throughout the year. Classes cover a wide variety of subjects, including history, science, religion, foreign language, and art. Classes generally meet for a few hours one day a week for a few weeks and take place at locations around Des Moines, including college classrooms, churches, and senior living centers. Some classes are held at locations central to the class topic, such as the Des Moines Playhouse and Des Moines Botanical Center, and there are also one-day excursions to museums and other sites in Des Moines. Fees are charged for tuition and class materials.

HOUSING

Numerous senior housing options are available in the Des Moines area, including both independent and assisted-living and nursing home care. Listed below is a small sampling of senior housing choices, several of which are continuum-of-care communities, allowing residents to move from one level of housing and assistance to another. Memory units are designated for residents with Alzheimer's disease or dementia. Facilities vary in their housing arrangements, amenities, and medical care available for residents—contact individual facilities for more information.

CALVIN COMMUNITY
4520 Hickman Rd., Des Moines
(515) 277-6141
www.calvincommunity.org
Calvin Community offers several levels of senior living in the residential neighborhood of Beaverdale, on the west side of Des Moines. Independent-living units include housekeeping service and kitchens, as well as meals available in a separate dining room. Assisted-living units, which make up the largest part of the facility, include numerous sizes of apartments and include housekeeping, laundry, and meals as well as 24-hour nursing services available. There is also a health center, which provides nursing home care, and a memory unit. Each level of care has its own separate dining area, and there are also banking services available for residents and a beauty shop and barber, as well as a computer room, library, and flower and vegetable garden. A social staff organizes activities for residents, including games, music, and other on-site entertainment. There are numerous recreational opportunities, including fitness classes and other wellness programs, as well as outdoor walking trails.

DEERFIELD
13731 Hickman Rd., Urbandale
(877) 336-9478
www.deerfieldrc.com

Located in a woodsy, suburban setting on nearly 50 acres north of Des Moines, Deerfield has independent- and assisted-living options and nursing home care. Independent living, which includes some seniors who are still working, is in apartments or townhouses with kitchens and laundry, as well as home health care available. Assisted living also includes apartments with kitchens, but also with all meals prepared and weekly housekeeping service. Nursing care offers both private and semi-private rooms with housekeeping and all meals prepared. Residents can move from one level of care to another without significant changes in monthly service fees.

The facility has both formal and casual dining facilities on-site, as well as a library, computer room, beauty and barber shop, and banking services for residents. There is a wide range of activities for residents, including games, arts and crafts classes, and music performances as well as day trips and excursions around town for entertainment and shopping. Many residents are very involved with committees and clubs that meet regularly to plan activities. The grounds connect with walking trails that move through nearby undeveloped stretches of greenbelt through the surrounding town.

EDGEWATER
9225 Cascade Ave., West Des Moines
(515) 978-2400
www.wesleylife.org/edgewater-west-des-moines.cfm
Just a few minutes from Jordan Creek Mall in a fast-growing part of the Des Moines metro area, this large facility is operated by WesleyLife and offers several types of senior housing. Independent-living units are apartments or villas, which are separate from

the main facility and have kitchen, laundry, and housekeeping. Assisted-living units have smaller kitchens with microwave and refrigerator, as well as housekeeping and laundry service and assistance with medication and daily living. There are several dining options. The facility also offers nursing home care and a memory unit with private rooms, as well as short-term stays for residents who need skilled therapy. Home health services are available to residents as well.

The facility has an extensive wellness program, including 2 gyms, fitness trainers, exercise classes, and a swimming pool. Walking paths are nearby and bicycles are available for residents to use. There are 2 spas, 6 libraries, a performing arts center that features music, lectures, and other entertainment, an art studio that offers classes, and 3 restaurants, ranging from casual cuisine to fine dining.

SCOTTISH RITE PARK
2909 Woodland Ave., Des Moines
(515) 274-4614
http://scottishritepark.org
Scottish Rite Park is a 12-story tower housing about 250 residents just off the bustling Ingersoll Avenue shopping district and a short distance from downtown Des Moines. Independent-living units, which include the possibility of owning a unit, include laundry and kitchen, as well as the option of dining in the facility's restaurant or having prepared meals brought in to the residence. Residential living units are all-inclusive, providing meals, housekeeping, laundry service, medication assistance, and some nursing services. Nursing home care is also available. Amenities include a wellness center with walking track, exercise room, and staff trainers available for residents, indoor and outdoor walking trails, a full-size lap pool, craft room,

game room, garden plots, library, and movie theater. Residents can get involved with numerous clubs and committees that work on planning excursions and entertainment.

VALLEY VIEW VILLAGE
2571 Guthrie Ave., Des Moines
(515) 265-2571
http://elimcare.org/facilities/valley-view
This 16-acre landscaped campus has several buildings and is located on the east side of Des Moines, just off I-235 and near Grand View Park and Golf Course. A wide range of housing options are offered, including independent living, which has apartments with kitchen and laundry provided and housekeeping available, and catered care, which is similar to independent living, but with meals and housekeeping included. Both independent and catered living also provide access to home health care services. Assisted living has meals and housekeeping provided along with 24-hour nursing care, while long-term care is a nursing home option. There is also a memory care unit.

The facility has staff in occupational, physical, and speech therapy. There are several dining areas, as well as a recreation room, beauty and barber shop, and library. Residents are involved in many clubs and take part in excursions around Des Moines and surrounding areas. Valley View Village is part of Elim Care, which operates senior living facilities in Iowa and surrounding states.

WESLEY ACRES
3520 Grand Ave., Des Moines
(515) 271-6500
www.wesleylife.org/wesley-acres-des-moines.cfm
Though the front of this facility faces a busy stretch of Grand Avenue, the back

looks out over a wooded area in the sylvan South of Grand area on the city's west side, with a walking trail weaving into the trees. Independent-living units come in several sizes, with kitchen and laundry available. Assisted-living apartments have kitchenettes and include meals and laundry service. Both independent- and assisted-living options include housekeeping, residential care, or "helpful living," which has a level of service between assisted living and nursing home care, features an open floor plan, as do nursing home and memory care. Every level of care has at least one dining room, and the facility is a complex of several connected buildings. There are about 300 residents.

There is a wellness center with daily fitness classes, swimming pool, movie theater, library, and computer lab. Excursions have taken residents to the opera and symphony, and the facility has numerous lectures, performances, and other on-site entertainment. Residents also have the opportunity to take classes through continuing education programs offered by area colleges and universities.

INDEX

Getaway ideas for the local traveler

Need a day away to relax, refresh, renew?
Just get in your car and go!

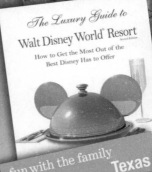

INSIDERS' GUIDE ®

The acclaimed travel series that has sold more than 2 million copies!

Discover: Your Travel Destination.
Your Home. Your Home-to-Be.

Albuquerque

Anchorage &
  Southcentral
  Alaska

Atlanta

Austin

Baltimore

Baton Rouge

Boulder & Rocky Mountain
  National Park

Branson & the Ozark
  Mountains

California's Wine Country

Cape Cod & the Islands

Charleston

Charlotte

Chicago

Cincinnati

Civil War Sites in
  the Eastern Theater

Civil War Sites in the South

Colorado's Mountains

Dallas & Fort Worth

Denver

El Paso

Florida Keys & Key West

Gettysburg

Glacier National Park

Great Smoky Mountains

Greater Fort Lauderdale

Greater Tampa Bay Area

Hampton Roads

Houston

Hudson River Valley

Indianapolis

Jacksonville

Kansas City

Long Island

Louisville

Madison

Maine Coast

Memphis

Myrtle Beach &
  the Grand Strand

Nashville

New Orleans

New York City

North Carolina's
  Mountains

North Carolina's
  Outer Banks

North Carolina's
  Piedmont Triad

Oklahoma City

Orange County, CA

Oregon Coast

Palm Beach County

Palm Springs

Philadelphia &
  Pennsylvania Dutch
  Country

Phoenix

Portland, Maine

Portland, Oregon

Raleigh, Durham &
  Chapel Hill

Richmond, VA

Reno and Lake Tahoe

St. Louis

San Antonio

Santa Fe

Savannah & Hilton Head

Seattle

Shreveport

South Dakota's
  Black Hills Badlands

Southwest Florida

Tucson

Tulsa

Twin Cities

Washington, D.C.

Williamsburg & Virginia's
  Historic Triangle

Yellowstone
  & Grand Teton

Yosemite

**To order call 800-243-0495
or visit www.Insiders.com**